MICROSOFT FLIGHT SIMULATOR MANUAL

Expert Tips and Tricks to Mastering Microsoft Flight Simulator

WisdomBytes Solutions

TABLE OF CONTENTS

MICROSOFT FLIGHT SIMULATOR MANUAL

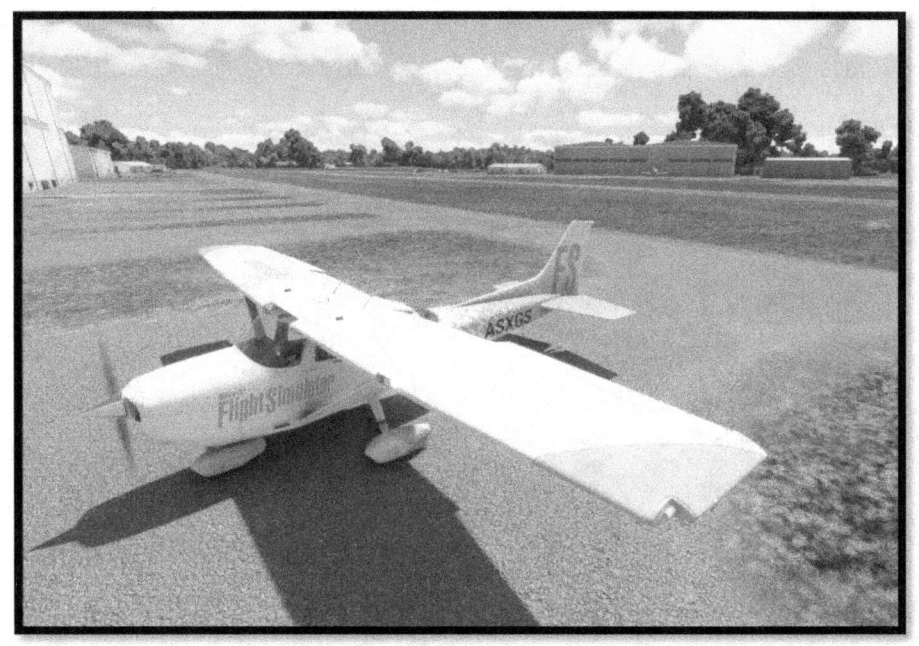

Enjoy the ultimate virtual flying adventure

INTRODUCTION

Microsoft just made a surprise announcement on the future of Microsoft Flight Simulator - Microsoft Flight Simulator 2024. This game is amazing, making the already great flight simulation experience even better.

If you thought the old versions were good, just wait until you see this one. Firstly, the graphics are awesome. The developers have done an incredible job, making the landscapes look just like real life, the airplanes look super detailed, and the weather effects are mind-blowing. You'll feel like you're really in the cockpit when you see the clear skies, fluffy clouds, and thunderstorms.

But it's not just the pretty pictures that make this game so special. Everything is designed to feel authentic and realistic - from the instruments in the cockpit that respond to your controls, to the air traffic control chatter that keeps you on your toes. And the game world is massive, with the entire planet faithfully recreated for you to explore, from the tall mountains to the busy cities.

Now, I know what you might be thinking - "Isn't flight simulation all about boring, complicated stuff?" Not this time. The developers have made the game easy to use, with lots of tutorials and help options to guide you, whether you're a pro pilot or a complete beginner. And the best part? You can play with your friends. You can team up to fly together, compete in fun challenges, or just watch each other fly around. It's the perfect way to hang out and explore the virtual skies.

This book will equip you with the basics to get the most out of the new Microsoft Flight Simulator 2024 game. From the illustrations to the realistic flying controls, you'll be amazed at how real it all feels and you'll be flying high in no time.

Are you ready to take to the skies like a pro? Let's get started.

OVERVIEW

This book takes you on a complete journey through the world of flight simulation.

In Chapter 1, the book shows you how to get started with flight simulation. It leads you through the process of buying, installing, and setting up the simulator. You'll learn about the initial setup, the home screen, and how to choose the best version for your needs.

Chapter 2, talks about the rich history of this game. It traces the development of the series from the early versions to the latest release, highlighting the key improvements and innovations along the way.

The book then explores the basic principles of flight in Chapter 3. Here, you'll learn about the basic controls, forces, and dynamics that affect how aircraft work.

Chapters 4 and 5 focus on the practical side of flying. You'll discover how to prepare your aircraft, start the engines, and master the basic flight controls. You'll also learn how to efficiently manage your aircraft and navigate the various systems and interfaces.

Chapter 6 shows you how to customize your viewing experience and capture stunning footage of your flights.

Chapter 7 takes a close look at the intricate layouts and functions of airliner cockpits, helping you better understand and operate these complex machines.

The book then explores the electrical and hydraulic systems of aircraft in Chapter 8, providing a comprehensive overview of these critical components.

Chapters 9 and 10 introduce you to the different categories of aircraft available in the simulator and the fundamental flight operations, so you can confidently fly a wide range of planes.

Chapter 11 teaches you how to plan and execute successful flights, including the use of GPS and instrument landing systems.

The book then tackles the dynamic world of weather in Chapter 12, showing you how to customize and control the environmental conditions to enhance your simulation experience.

Chapter 13 looks into the collaborative aspect of Microsoft Flight Simulator 2024, guiding you through the setup and navigation of multiplayer sessions and how to fly with others.

Chapters 14 and 15 provide troubleshooting advice and tips for making your flight simulation experience more realistic, respectively, ensuring that you can optimize your setup and get the most out of the simulator.

Finally, the book concludes with two chapters, 16 and 17, dedicated to tips and tricks for both beginners and experienced users, covering a wide range of topics from tutorials and challenges to advanced techniques and pro tips.

Overall, this is a comprehensive and engaging guide that will equip you with the knowledge and skills to master the art of virtual aviation, whether you are new to the hobby or a seasoned flight simulation enthusiast.

CHAPTER 1
GETTING STARTED

In this chapter, we're going to show you how to set up Microsoft Flight Simulator on your PC.

What is a Flight Simulator?

A simulator is used to teach pilots how to fly. They learn how to take off, how to land, and how to react in case of emergencies, because, it wouldn't make much sense to set fire to a real plane just to teach a pilot how to respond.

With a simulator, a pilot can learn to respond to all kinds of emergencies like an engine fire and it's all done in a completely virtual world so there's absolutely no danger.

Normally, in an airplane, you have room for about 300 passengers but with the simulator, there's no room for 300 people. On the inside, it is exactly like being inside the cockpit of a real airplane.

For some, we have the legs called Hydraulic jacks and they let the simulator move in every direction just like a real plane does. The pilots inside the simulator experience the real sensation of taking off, turning, and landing an airplane but these hydraulic jacks can be pretty strong.

We also have a computer system. These are all the computers that drive the simulator.

In the simulator, we have the throttle, the runway, the cockpit, and the instructor station (which is where the instructor sits, where he sets up the weather and does other things).

Here, everything feels real but the good thing to know is that this is a completely virtual world so everything we do here is safe and this is the exact type of exercise that a pilot would do when he or she trains on a flight simulator.

Purchasing Flight Sim

The first thing you need to do is purchase Microsoft Flight Simulator. Simply go to **flightsimulator.com**, click on Store, scroll down to the bottom and you'll see three different packages (we'll show you those in just a second) and then you get to the page that has the three different options. You have Standard, Deluxe, and Premium Deluxe.

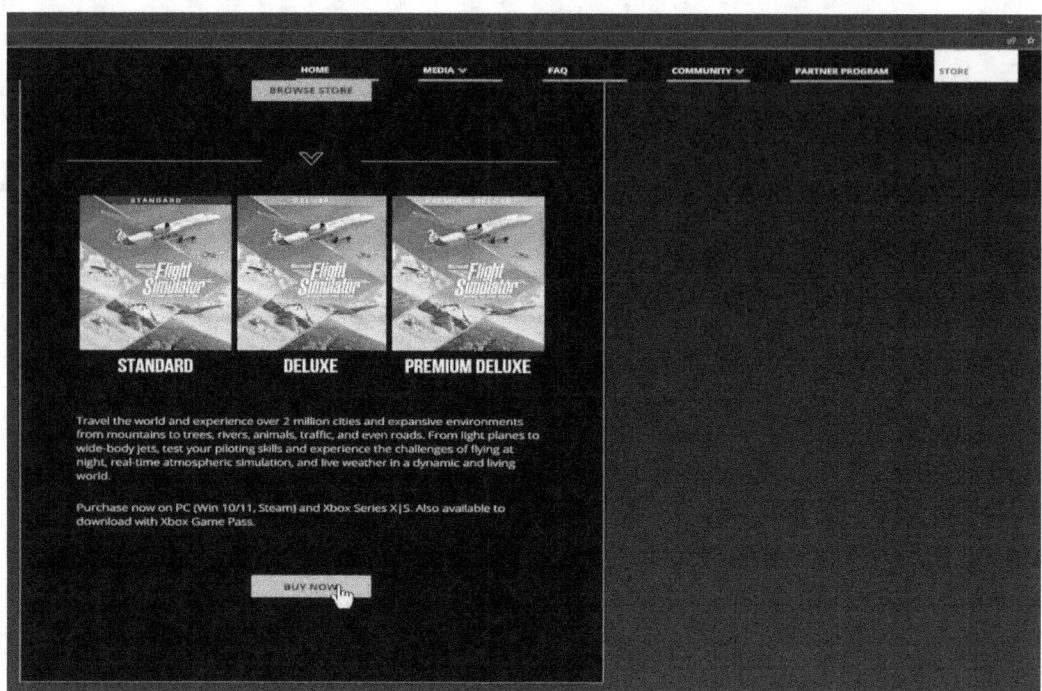

What's the difference? The difference is essentially how many aircraft you get and how many handcrafted airports or detailed airports that you get. In the Standard package, you have a 152, a 172, a couple of Diamond aircraft and you have a cub.

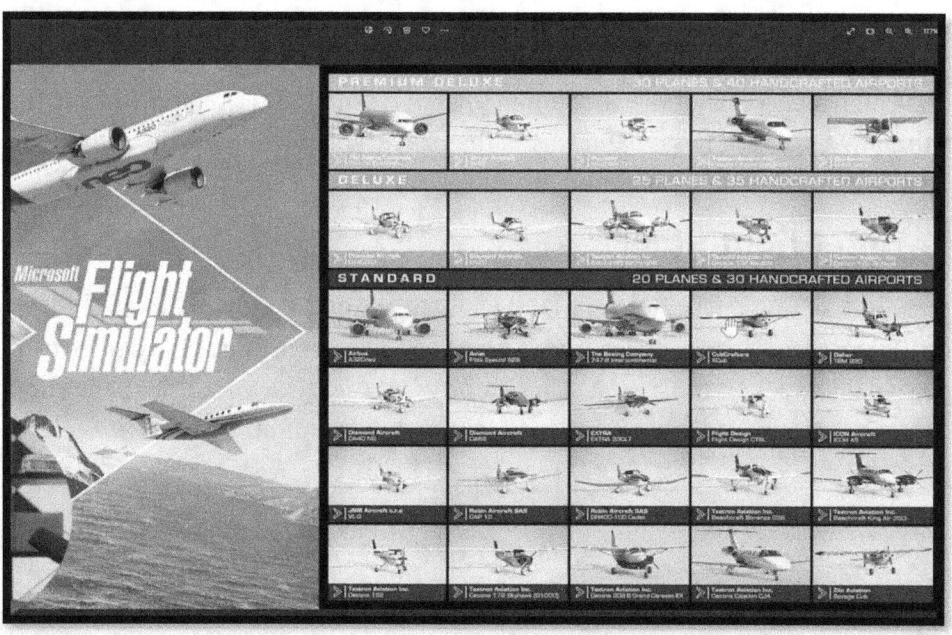

In the Deluxe package, you get five more planes and five more airports. You have another set of 172 that's not the G1000 so if you're used to flying six packs you might want to go with this Deluxe package. You also get a couple of diamonds in a baron.

In the Premium Deluxe, you get the SR22. If you want to go with the Premium Deluxe, scroll down and click on the Premium Deluxe then click on the drop-down, there's PC and Steam. If you already have Steam on your computer you can go through Steam, otherwise, click on PC and go to the Xbox route. You have the option to get it with a Gamepad class and save twenty-four dollars for game passes or ten dollars a month. If that's worth it to you to save 24 dollars, great. Now you're just going to click on "Buy" and then you can sign in or create an account with Microsoft.

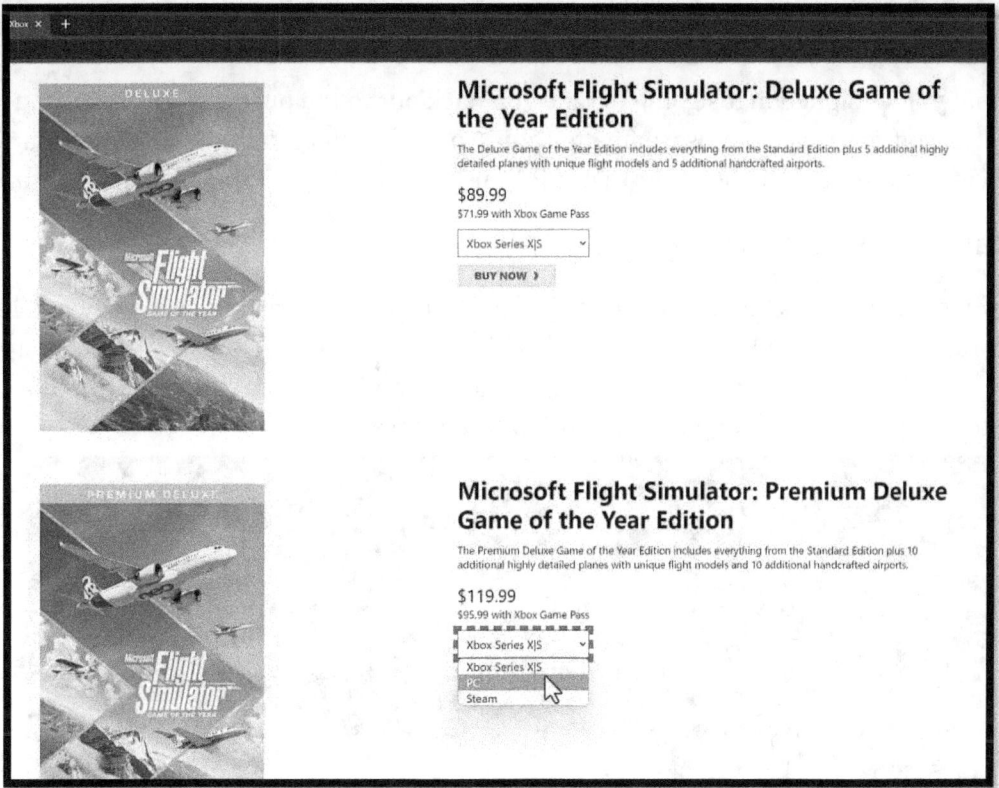

If you already created one right before this you're just going to log in. Now if you don't already have an Xbox profile associated with your Microsoft account it'll ask you to create one. You're not going to click any of those boxes there, just click "I accept."

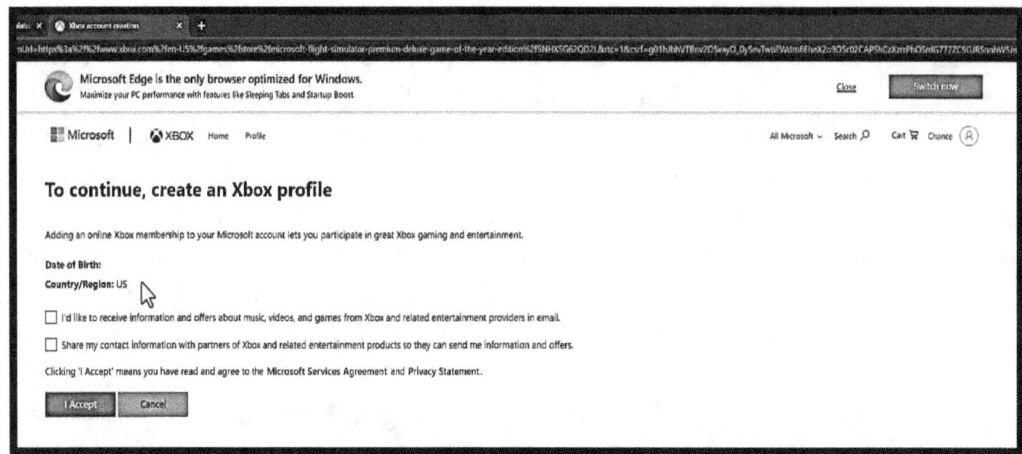

Now that you've signed in it's going to take you back out to the purchase page and you'll see that Microsoft has created a username for you. You can change that to whatever you want; you'll get a one-time code too. After that, click on "Buy," add a payment, and click Close.

Installing your package

Now you own this. Click on Install, choose PC, and launch. Then open the Xbox app and install it. We recommend installing it on the M.2 SSD if you have one. That way, it loads up and performs fast. The next step is to download the installer, after which you'll click on "Play." It's going to load up and go through a couple of different screens.

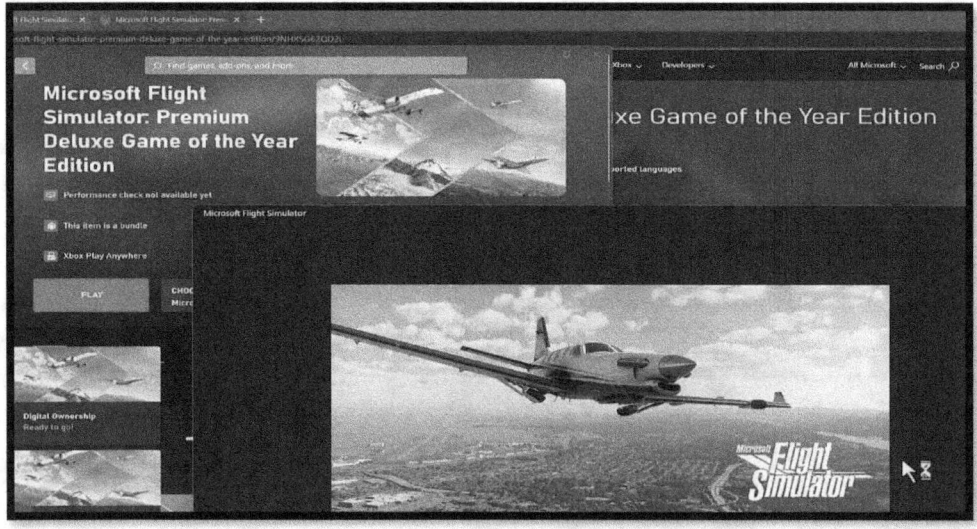

Loading it for the first time

When you initially load up it's going to come to open up a page shown and a robot is going to narrate the entire thing. That'll go away as soon as you click next; you don't have to change anything on this page, keep it the same, then click Next, and then you get to the download page.

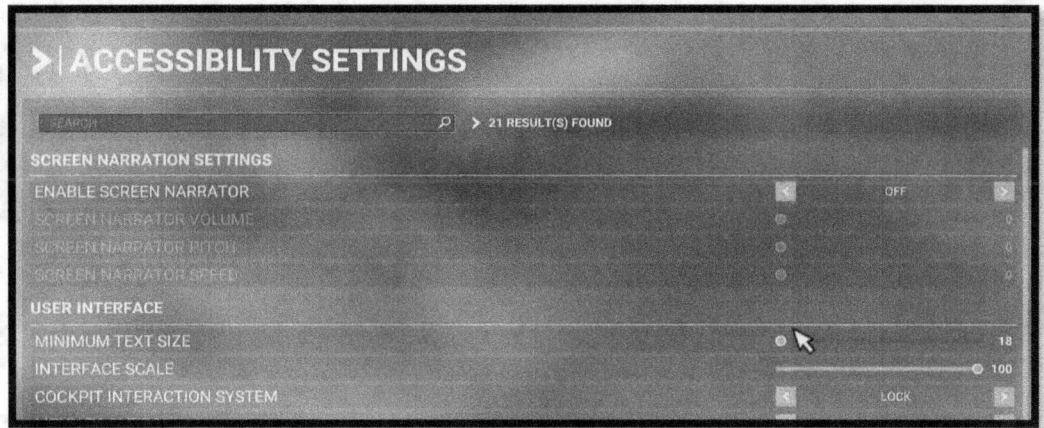

You can see it's 125 gigabytes and then it allows you to change the location where you download the game. We highly recommend that you do this.

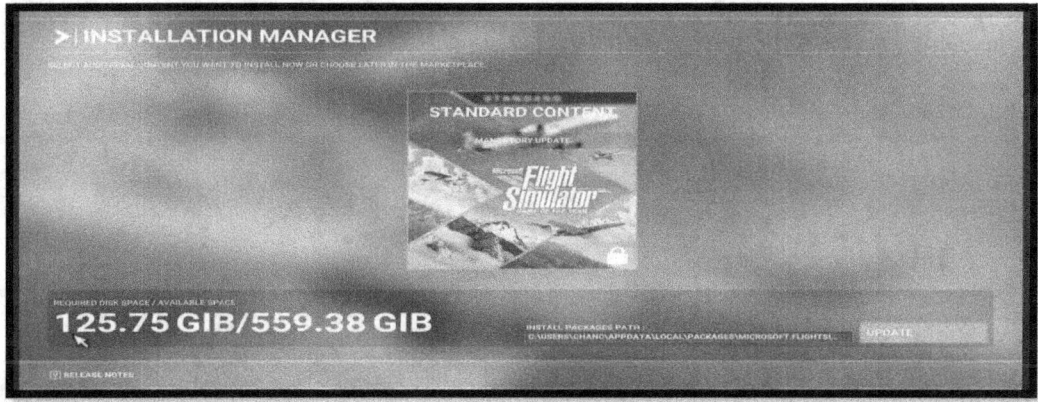

This app data folder is hidden and you don't have all the permissions in it on your PC so you might run into some problems if you were to ever download some third-party software or aircraft try to put it in there as it might not let you. To avoid all that you're going to change the location by clicking on it, going to your local disk C, and making a new folder called Microsoft Flight Sim 2024. Now that that's done, click "Update" and this download is going to take a few hours depending on your internet connection.

Initial set up

When it's done and you are good, it's going to allow you to change your graphic settings. This depends heavily on your PC specs so if you're running something like an i5 or a Ryzen 3 with only a couple gigabytes of VRAM then you're going to want to go in the lower end. They recommend at least 8 gigabytes of VRAM and 32 gigabytes of RAM with an i7 or an i9 since that's going to allow you to push it to ultra.

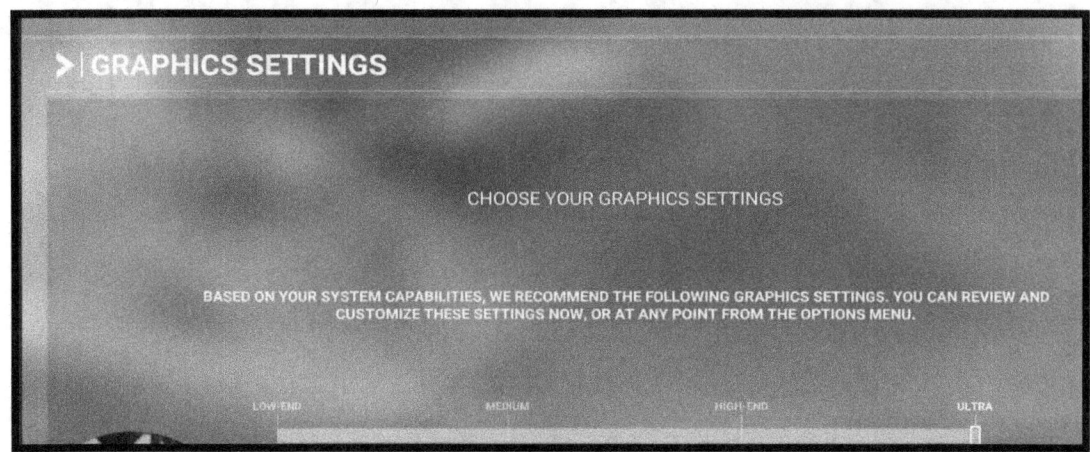

Let's say your PC is running an I9 with 12 gigabytes of VRAM on a 3080 and 32 gigabytes of regular RAM you're going to try Ultra and then if you have a good internet connection you can choose if you want to do Data Streaming or No World streaming. If you have a little internet connection you can go with the No World Streaming then click on Next.

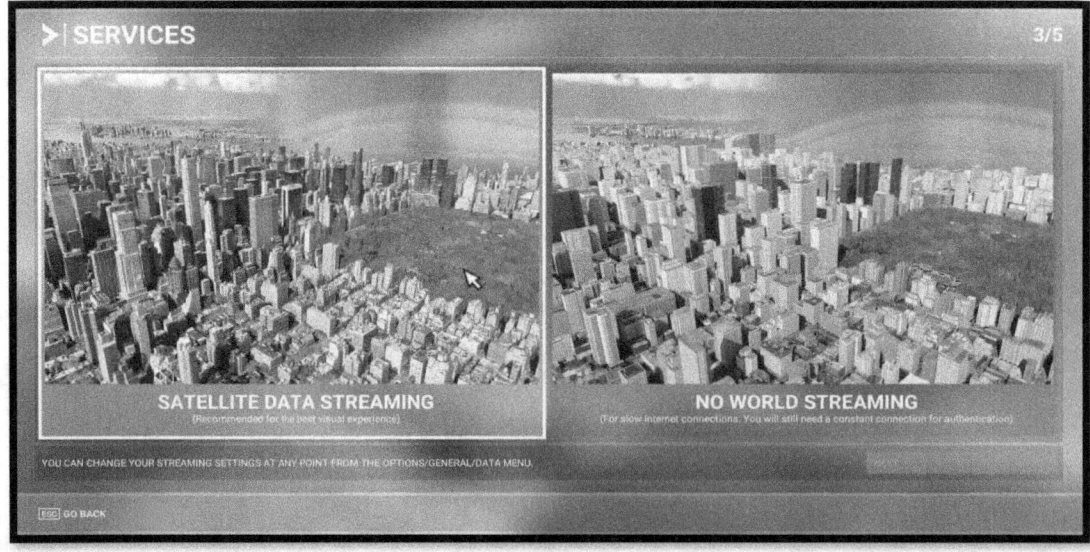

For the Control Settings, if you have a yoke or a throttle installed it's going to allow you to customize the settings. Most of the time it reads it accurately but then you can just make sure it's recognizing it at least then click on Next.

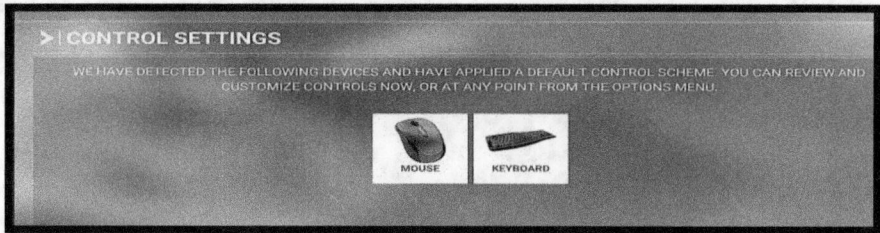

The Assistance window, it's going to allow you to change your assistance so if you are new to Aviation and you've never flown a plane before and you just want to kind of have fun and play the game then keep it on easy. However, if you want to challenge yourself like you're flying a real aircraft then you should select hard. Click Done.

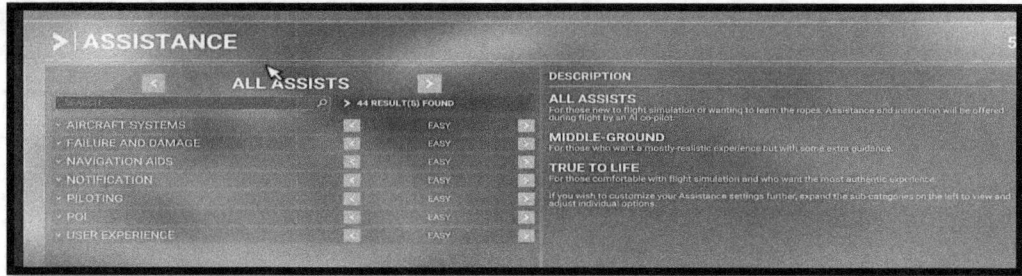

The Home Screen

Now you are officially loaded in, you'll get to the Home screen where it has Discovery flights, a World map, Flight Training activities, and a Marketplace. We'll go through these quickly just so you have an idea of what's in here.

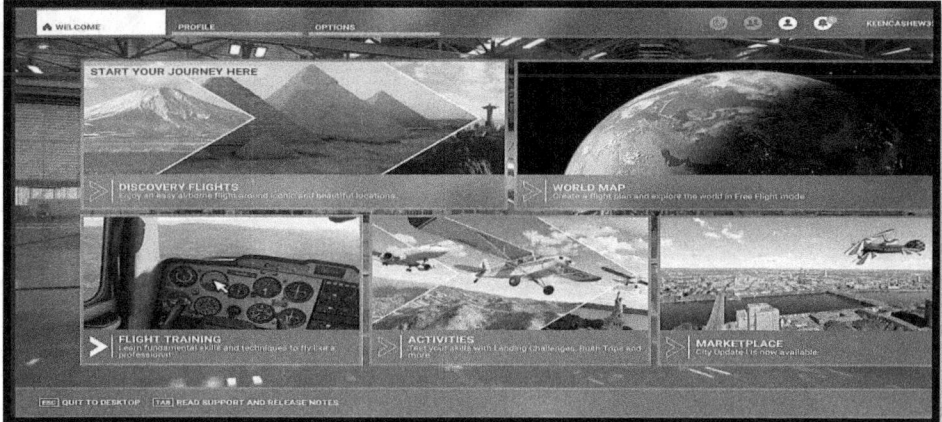

This first section, **Discovery Flights,** shows you places where you can drop into Mount Everest, Egypt, and Bora Bora, and then there are some extra downloads down at the bottom if you want to do some flying in Japan, San Francisco, Yosemite National Park.

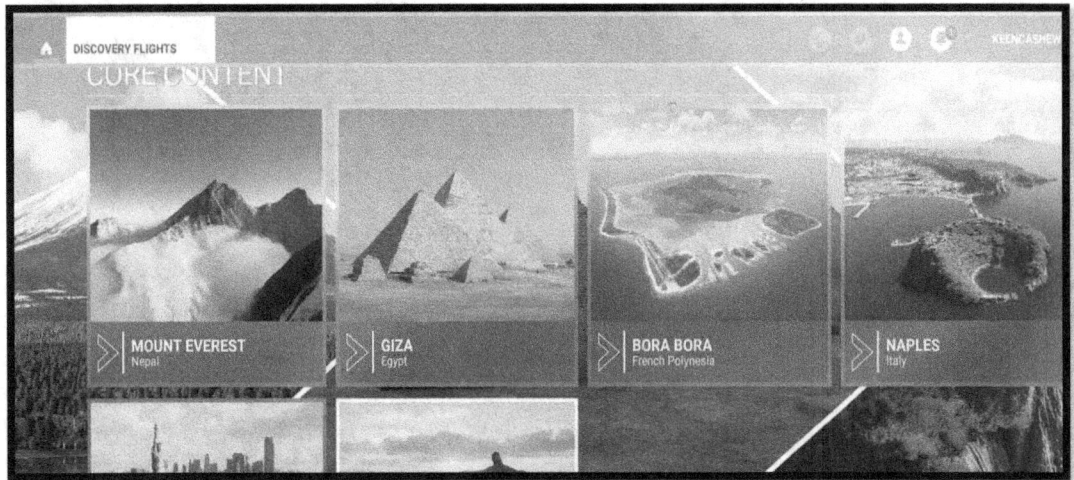

Going down here to the bottom left, click back and now you're back to the main page. Scrolling over to **World Map**, this is where you can create your own flight plans. You can customize your A to B and select your departure airport.

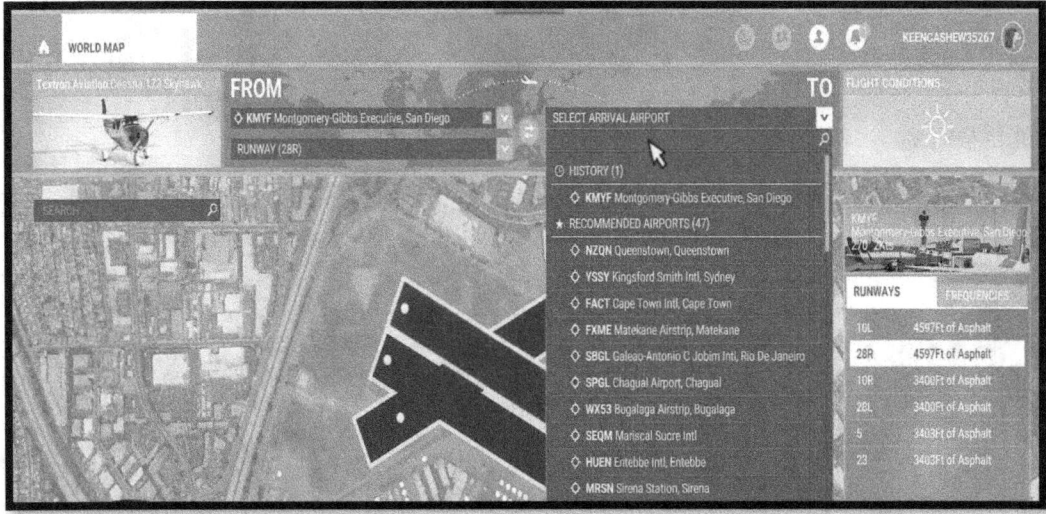

For example, we'll click on the Montgomery field (KMYF), and let's say we want to go to Santa Monica so we'll just click on Santa Monica. You can add more waypoints over here with the search bar and in the NAV LOG section, you can change your altitude, then click on "Fly" when you're ready to fly or click Escape to go back.

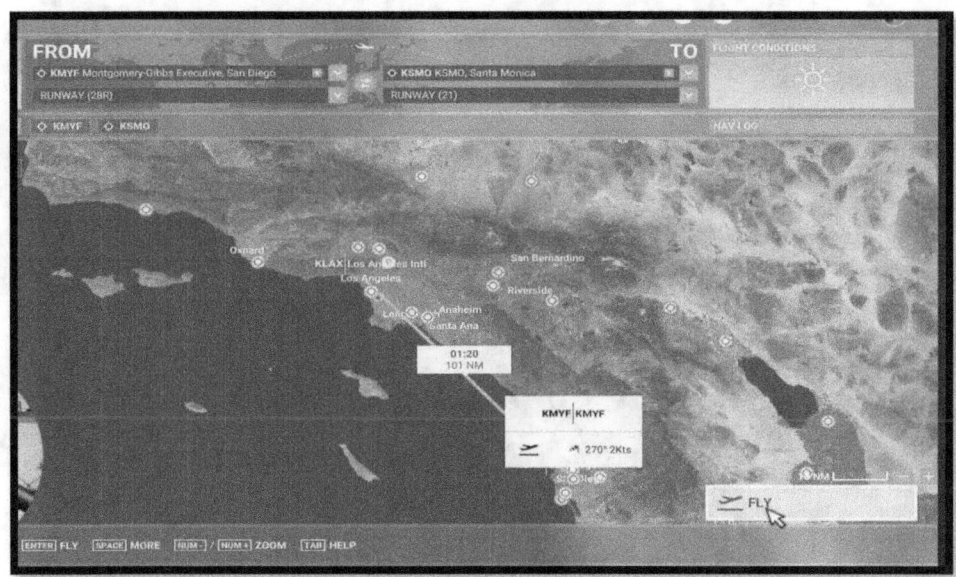

Going over to the **Flight Training** tab is where you can learn some of the basic handling, Takeoff, and Landing VFR Navigation. If you want to do Bush Flight Training they have an Icon for Bush pilots. You also have IFR Navigation at the bottom.

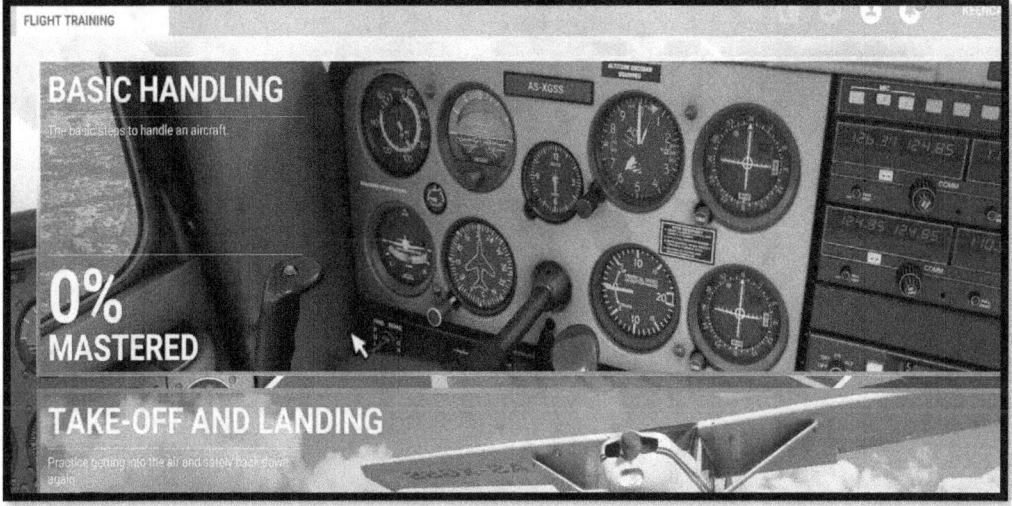

In the **Activities** section, these are premade scenarios that you could go through. There's the Flight Training section, there's Landing challenges, and Bush trips that you have already downloaded into the game and then you can scroll over for some extra downloads. You could purchase that Reno Air Race or you can do the Maverick Activities so download that and check that out. You also have Custom content where you can download some third-party content and do some challenges that way.

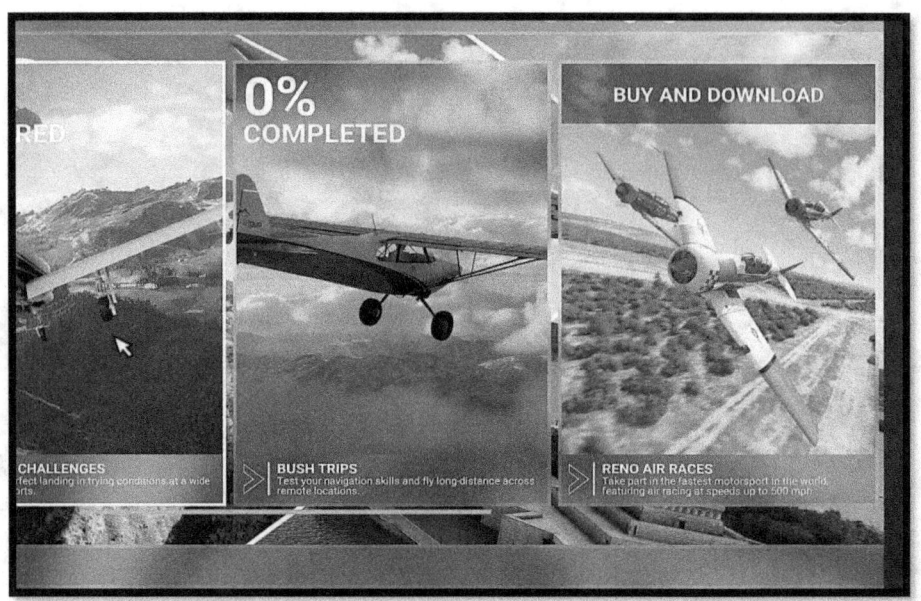

The last tab, which is **Marketplace**, is where you can purchase aircraft, handcrafted airports, or extra activities that you could do. Let's say you want to own a Bonanza, you could purchase this Bonanza right here for about 14.99 and they have all kinds of other things including a PC12, an F/A 18E, a Caravan, so you could spend days searching through this and finding items to play with.

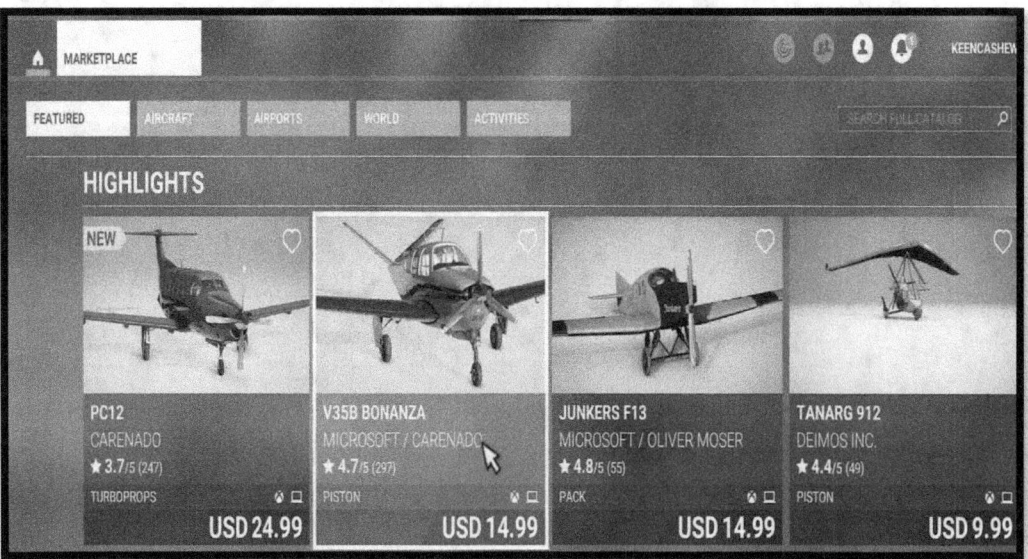

We want to show you two more things on the Home screen: the two tabs up here labeled Profile and Options.

Under **Profile**, you can see how many hours you have or what your pilot level is. You have Content Manager for anything you download, your Logbook to see what type of flight time you've gotten as well as "My Hangar" and this is where you can change the airplane.

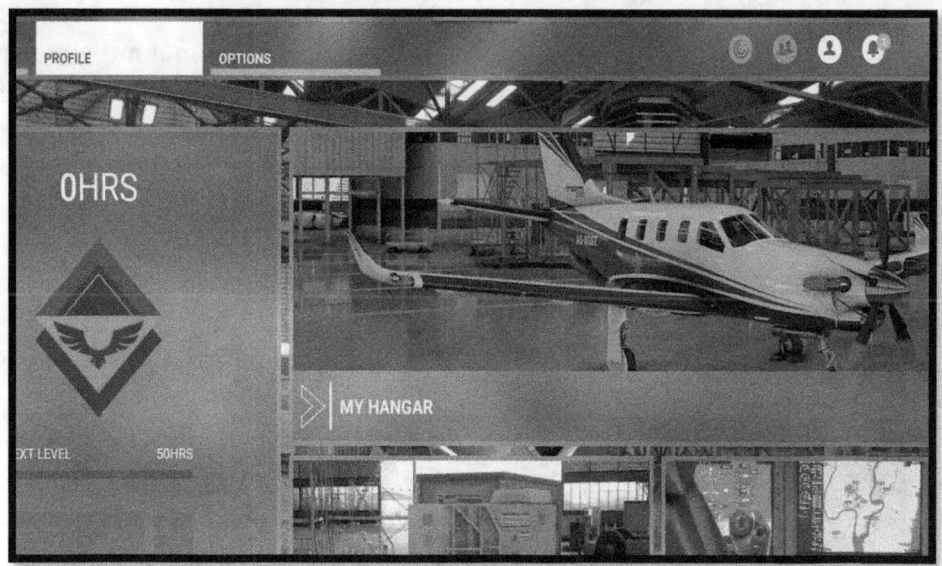

If you click on the **Options** tab you'll see that we have General Options. You can go in there and change whatever you want to change. You also have Assistant Options which we already looked at in the beginning where it was easy, medium, or hard and then you have Control Options.

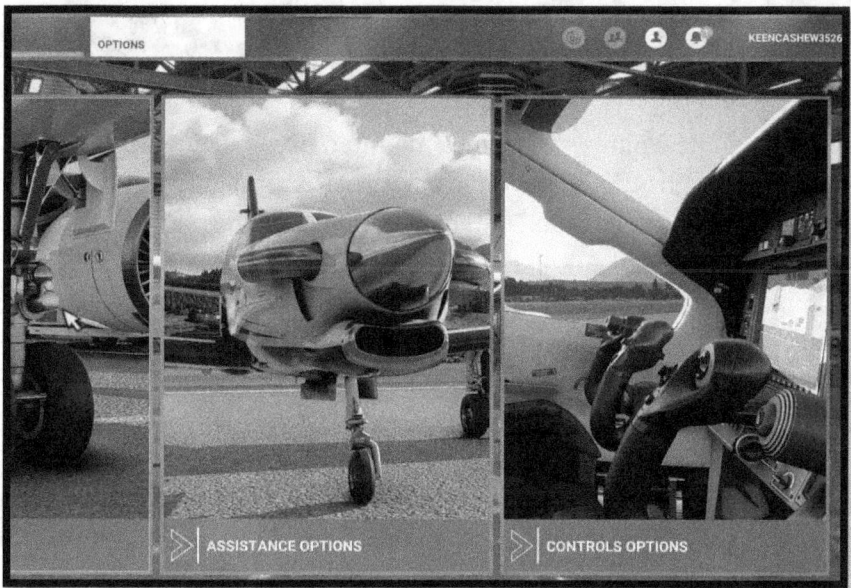

Mounting your Yoke top

For this illustration, we are going to attach our Real Simgear YokeTop Simulator Package with the Yoke and throttle. That way, you can see how to set those up here and customize them if you want. Now what we have right here is a Real Simgear YokeTop mount flight simulator package and this closely resembles what you would normally see in a general aviation training aircraft.

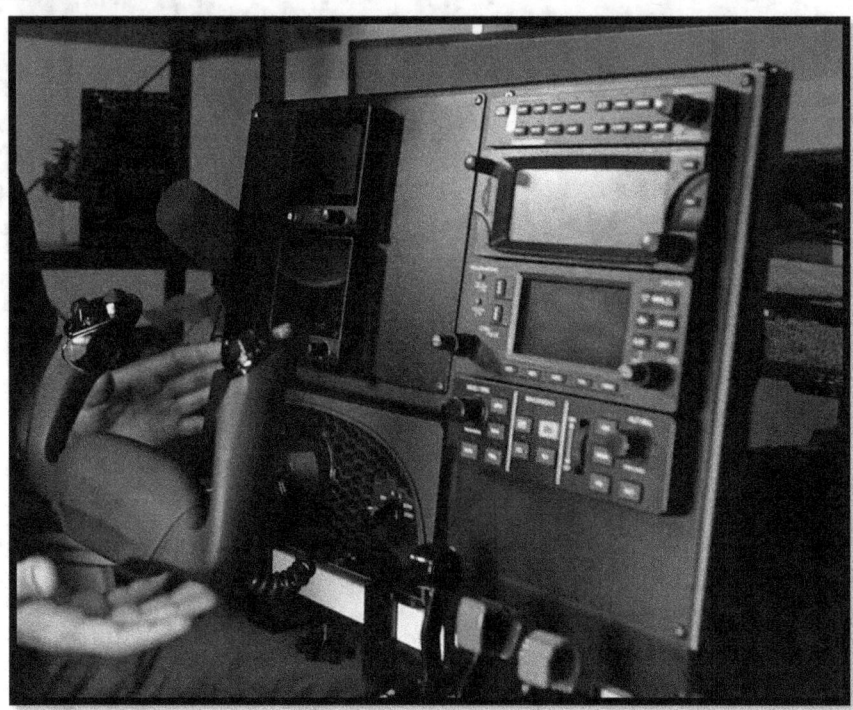

All of this is a bunch of Real Simgear avionics mounted onto our metal plate with a throttle. You can change which throttle that you want there and all of that is mounted onto a honeycomb yoke which you can switch out for a virtual fly if you want.

What we have here are a couple of dual G5s which are very common in GA. We also have a GMA 350 audio panel so we can switch between Com1 and Com2 easily and if you're using Pilotedge that increases the immersion. We have a GTN 650 GPS, a Garmin 430 GPS, the GFC 500 autopilot and then down here we have virtual flight TQ3 single engine throttle. Like we said, we have all that mounted onto a honeycomb yoke so we just barely connected all this to the PC.

Typically, what you're going to see when you connect it is going to say "New Device Detected" and here we have the two pieces of Hardware that we have connected to it, which are the flight controls (the Yoke) and then the virtual flight throttle.

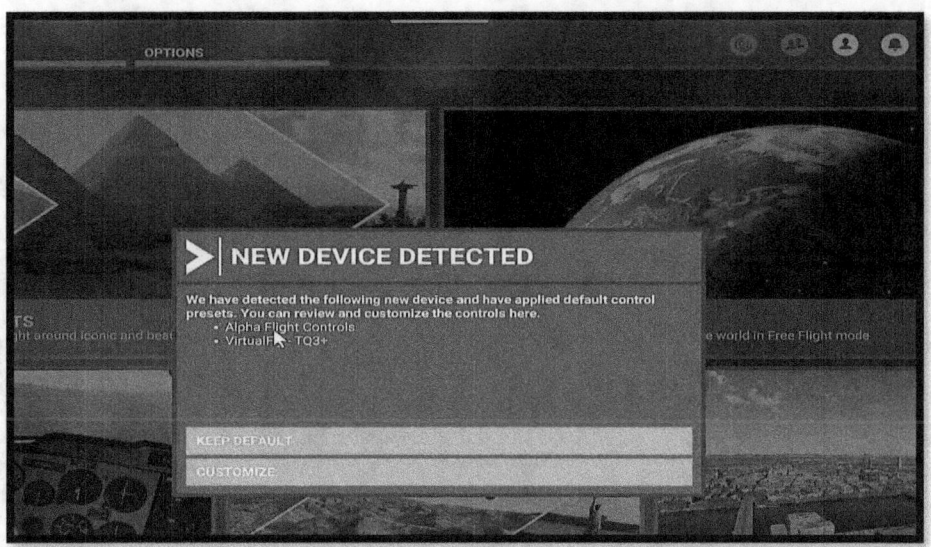

You can customize or keep it the same. We're going to click "Keep Default" but if you want to customize it, simply go back to that Options menu, go over to Control options and now you're going to see the **Alpha Flight Controls** and the **VirtualFly**. You can click on these different pieces of hardware and then it's going to show you all the options for you to map the different buttons to different functions.

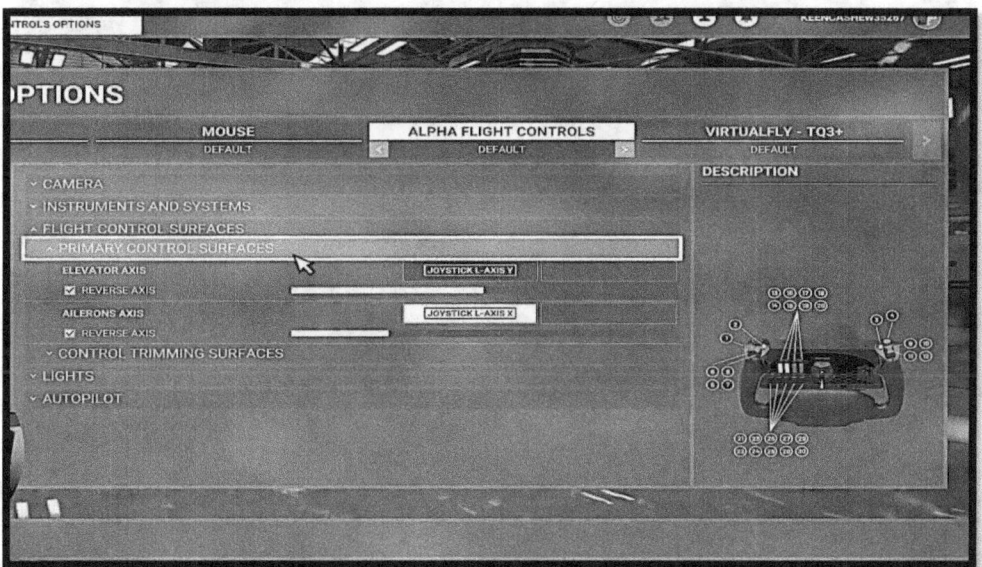

The Yoke itself is probably already going to be calibrated but you can double-check that it is. Click on Flight Controls and then Primary Flight Controls and now when you move the Yoke, move it to the left and the right. You'll see if your ailerons are working just fine if that's going to the left and the right. You'll proceed to do the elevator next. Push forward and pull back to confirm those are working just fine. You can decide not to change anything but it's got all these different buttons that you can customize to it.

You can have your Avionics Master go on and off. You can do the Battery Master on and off. The engine instruments are already mapped to the Magnetos but make sure if you turn that off it shows off. You also have Left Mag, Right Mag, Both Mag, and Start Mag. We're going to leave everything at default.

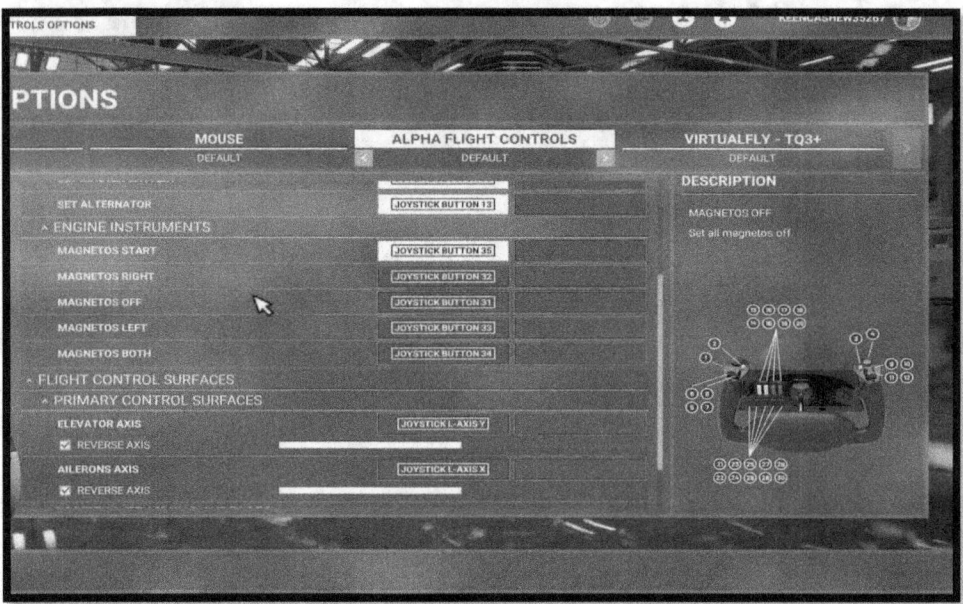

We'll click on the VirtualFly just to triple-check that this is working. All that pulls up is the three options for power management. We have our Throttle, Mixer, and Propeller. We'll click on Throttle and just make sure that that's working. We'll click on Propeller and Mixer to also ensure that's working just fine.

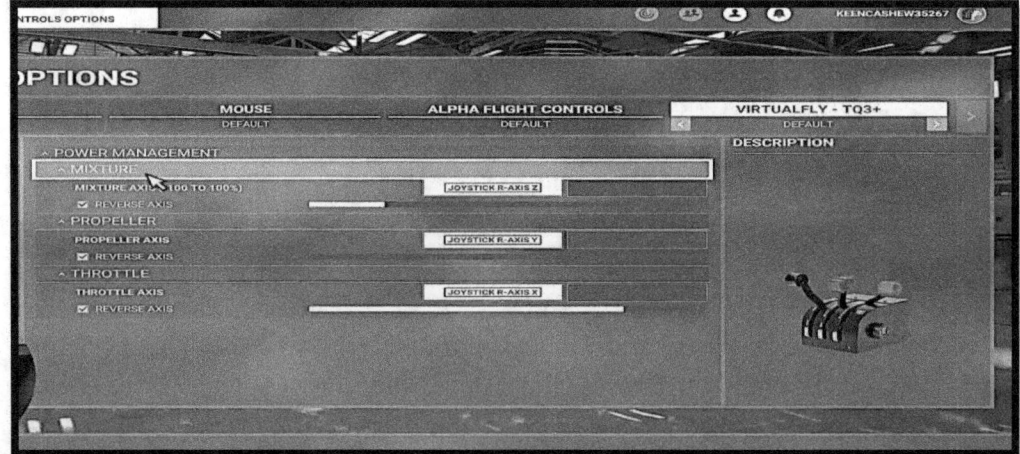

You'll find there that they are the opposite meaning if you go for a full mixture but it's a mixture cut off in the airplane then you can just hit the reverse axis right here. That way, it does the opposite.

Now we'll go into our World map and start our flight plan. We'll go ahead and click "Ready to fly" and we can see the yoke is moving accordingly, our throttle is moving accordingly, we have our mixture, we can go idle cutoff but the engine's running so we'll keep that there and then we could just go take off right now.

Deciding the best version for you

In this section, we're going to be talking about the different versions of Microsoft Flight Simulator and which version is likely to be best for you.

If you've seen all the hype with Microsoft Flight Simulator and you want to explore a little bit but don't know if you like simulators and if your computer can run it, we would recommend getting Microsoft Flight Simulator on game pass or the PC game pass beta which you can do for a pound at the moment and that gets you the full basic version of the game. It's for a month so obviously you can cancel it after a month if you don't want to stay on the game pass and you don't like the game but that would just make sense to do.

The game pass situation will take about 10 hours of playing it, setting up your controls, loading into it, getting it to run nice, and then doing a bit of flying and after 10 hours you'll know if this is the kind of game you want to keep playing or not. This makes sense for those of you who want a good solid demo of it to make up your mind so that's the casual category.

The second category of people would be people that are not hardcore flight simmers but love simulators and so for people like that, the Standard edition is going to be the best version to buy. The only difference between the Standard Edition, the Deluxe, and the Premium Deluxe is that you get additional airplanes and airports with the Premium Deluxe.

For the Deluxe edition, you get five more planes and five more airfields handcrafted airfields and for the Premium Deluxe you get another five on top of that.

Microsoft Flight Simulator has every airport in the world in it. The standard airports in it look fine unless you're like a crazy flight cinema type person, the standard airports in this that haven't been handcrafted are great; you're not going to be landing them thinking this airport looks terrible and at the end of the day even if you bought the the Deluxe edition, well that's another 10 airports so you're still going to be landing at the basic airports anyway.

When it comes to airplanes, the basic version has enough planes in there to cover the range of flying dynamics and characteristics like a passenger jet, a small propeller plane, and a small jet plane icon. This is so that you can experience all the range of physics and handling characteristics and approaches to flight that you can enjoy all of that with the basic version so yes, it just doesn't make sense if you're money-conscious to bother with the Deluxe or the Premium Deluxe version.

Only the Premium Deluxe has Heathrow Airport handcrafted. The non-handcrafted version looks fine anyway but only the Premium Deluxe has Heathrow so if there's a local airport to you or an airport you particularly want to experience you can land there all the time.

The other thing worth saying is if you buy it through the Microsoft Store or the Windows shop you can also use it on the Xbox if you ever get one of the new Xboxes which might be quite appealing to certain people like if your PC is mid-or low-end and you know you're going to be getting a new games console then this will run nicely on the new Xbox so you can steam.

The advantage of the Steam store is typically the whole pre-loading and the download system of Steam. When you download this on Steam you'll then launch the game and it downloads the content in the game itself so even if you've bought it on Steam you still have to download things through the game, it's not like Steam's going to manage that component. It's also worth keeping in mind that you will have about 90 gigabytes down to update and download so be prepared for that.

Review Questions

1. What is a Flight Simulator, and how does it differ from playing a traditional video game?
2. What are the key factors to consider when purchasing a Flight Simulator package?
3. Describe the initial setup process for loading and configuring Microsoft Flight Simulator 2024 for the first time.

CHAPTER 2
THE EVOLUTION OF MICROSOFT FLIGHT SIMULATOR

Since 1982, Microsoft's Flight Simulator has enabled us to take to the skies from the comfort of our own homes. The experience has improved somewhat since the initial version and the continual updates to Flight Simulator 2020, plus its re-release on the latest generation of consoles, as well as for Windows 11 and via Xbox Cloud, make it truly deserving of a closer look.

For those wanting to control airplanes and explore the world from the comfort of their home, there has never been a more exciting time.

How it started

It all started with a pilot named Bruce Artwick, who was interested in computers. Bruce founded a software company named Sublogic in 1977 and, just two years later, published the very first version of the flight simulator we'd soon all come to know and love. At the time, computers couldn't handle much more than a few lines at once.

FS1 Flight Simulator, as it was called then, was released on the Apple II computer and was pretty basic. That's because the Apple II was an 8-bit computer that only had 4 kilobytes of RAM and a processor running at 1 megahertz.

Version 1.0

Microsoft soon expressed an interest and obtained the license from Sublogic to create the original Microsoft Flight Simulator in 1982, also referred to as Flight Simulator 1.0. It featured better graphics, with color this time, variable weather, and the time of the day.

One of the more enjoyable aspects of this inaugural Microsoft Flight Simulator was its "Europe 1917" mode. Similar in premise to the "British Ace" mode found in the Apple II version, it involved the player flying a Sopwith Camel, one of the best-known fighter aircraft of the First World War. The player could navigate a grid-divided area with mountains and declare war by firing at enemy aircraft.

Version 2.0

Version 2.0 was launched in 1984. Minor improvements were made to the graphics as well as the game's precision. With version 2.0, it was also possible to use a joystick or a mouse.

Version 3.0

In 1988, Microsoft released version 3.0. It came in a box with a floppy disk inside to play the game. Version 3.0 added new airports, had higher frame rates, and better graphics, and it was finally possible to use external camera angles.

Version 4.0

In the following year, Flight Simulator 4.0 came out. The box was almost identical to the previous Microsoft Flight Simulator, so it wasn't very clear which version you had since all the newer box said was "New version." Version 4.0 featured upgraded aircraft models, dynamic scenery, random weather, and special modes, including a mode where you could fly a World War 1 airplane to shoot down enemies. It also had some very beautiful, nostalgic music.

Version 5.0

Released at the end of 1993, Flight Simulator version 5.0 ramped up the realism by using textures to create scenery for the first time. Graphics and aircraft models were further enhanced, weather systems upgraded, artificial intelligence was introduced, and users could modify their cockpits for each aircraft. It was also the first game in the series to have sound effects.

Version 5.1

In 1995, Microsoft Flight Simulator 5.1 was the first version to be released on CD-ROM. It featured satellite imagery, and faster performance, and it had many weather effects, like storms. There was also a program to build your own airports and cockpit panels.

After the release of Windows 95, Microsoft developed a Flight Simulator for the newer operating system. It was almost the same as its predecessor, but the simulator had better frame rates and additional aircraft. It also included major airports outside of Europe and the US for the first time.

Flight Simulator 98

The next edition, Flight Simulator 98, came in 1997. The game was a huge success and sold over 1 million copies. It was the first to take advantage of 3D environments with graphic cards through Microsoft's DirectX technology. Flight Simulator 98 had better performance, more modeled airports, and distinct sounds for every type of aircraft, and helicopter.

Flight Simulator 2000

Two years later, Flight Simulator 2000 was released. Many were disappointed that the game demanded a high-end computer to play it, and even on expensive systems, frame-rate stuttering was a problem in denser areas of maps. Flight Simulator 2000 was a major improvement in terms of graphics and details, incorporating rain and snow for the first time while also allowing users to download real-world weather conditions.

New aircraft were introduced, including the Boeing 777, which had recently entered service at the time, and there was the Supersonic Concorde. GPS made its debut, dynamic scenery was updated with more detailed models, and AI was improved to avoid collisions while taxiing. However, the most notable expansion was the 17,000 airports that were added. This brought the total to over 20,000 airports in-game.

In 2001, Microsoft came up against some stiff competition in the Flight Simulator market when Russian software developer 1C released its first installment of the "IL-2 Sturmovik" series. Awards were evenly split between the two games that year, with different critics acknowledging each title as the top simulator in 2001. The "IL-2 Sturmovik" series was named after an aircraft produced by the Soviet Union in large numbers during World War II. The developers continued producing some impressive World War II combat flight simulators but soon lost ground to Microsoft's Flight Simulator.

Flight Simulator 2002

Flight Simulator 2002 was released in 2001, shortly after the 9/11 terrorist attacks. Microsoft found itself at the center of much controversy because reports showed that the terrorists had used Flight Simulator to prepare for the attacks. Due to the terrorist's actions and out of respect for the victims, the Twin Towers were abruptly removed from the game. The 2002 simulator introduced Air Traffic Control to communicate with airports and artificial intelligence aircraft to fly alongside computer-controlled air vehicles. As expected, the visuals once again outshone all previous versions, and the game seemed to run much smoother thanks to some tinkering by Microsoft.

Flight Simulator 2004

Next up was Flight Simulator 2004: A Century of Flight, which celebrated the 100th anniversary of the Wright Brothers' first aerial achievements. It featured several historical aircraft, including the Wright Flyer, that was used by the famous duo. One of the key focuses for the 2004 edition was the weather, which benefited from a revamped system. Players could now see clouds in 3D, and the weather was localized, meaning it varied according to where you were and what the weather was likely to be in that region in real life. Adding to the realism was a more reliable GPS and more detailed air traffic control.

Flight Simulator X

Then came Flight Simulator X in 2006. With its higher resolution textures and a more engaging multiplayer experience, it lived up to its name by offering an X factor that had been missing from the previous titles. Flight Simulator X allowed players to be an Air Traffic Controller and two players to fly in a single airplane. The game included 18 planes, 28 detailed cities, and over 24,000 airports for the Standard version, while the Deluxe version had even more planes and detailed cities. While the game's framerate was at times an issue, it nonetheless received favorable reviews, scoring 80 on Metacritic.

On top of its innovations and multiplayer capability, an expansion pack named "Flight Simulator X: Acceleration" became available a year after the Standard version was released, increasing the game's longevity by adding new missions and several more aircraft.

The soundtrack used in the main menu for Flight Simulator X was composed, orchestrated, and produced by Stan LePard, who is best known for his contributions to the Halo game franchise. Anyone who played Flight Simulator X will likely recognize the default audio track, "Pilot for Hire" or "FSX01," which was brought back as a "Legacy" menu option in 2020.

Microsoft Flight Simulator 2020

That longevity would be sorely needed, as it turns out since people had to wait an agonizing 14 years for the next game in the series. When it did finally arrive, though, on August 18th, 2020, Microsoft Flight Simulator 2020 surpassed all expectations, becoming without a doubt the best flight simulator of all time.

It currently holds an outstanding 91 out of 100 score on Metacritic and has picked up several awards, including "Best Sim/Strategy Game" at the Game Awards in 2020. Why is it so good, though?

- Firstly, the graphics speak for themselves, especially if you're playing on a modern system with the best possible resolution enabled.
- The in-game environment is essentially a virtual recreation of the entire Earth, built using textures and data from Bing satellite imagery in conjunction with Microsoft's Azure system.
- This ground-breaking technology was used to generate photorealistic 3D models of buildings, trees, water, and other geographical features.
- Incredibly, you can fly anywhere on the planet, including above the skyscrapers in New York, the Pyramids in Egypt, and even your own home.
- Famous landmarks everywhere in the world can be seen, and new hand-crafted locations are added all the time.

- What's more, the flying conditions are as close to authentic as possible, with advanced physics and real-time weather updates, meaning if there's a storm outside your real window, you can fly through it and experience it from the sky in-game.

The level of realism, combined with the scale of the environments and seemingly endless features in this game, is breathtaking. However, when the game first came out, there was a sharp intake of breath for another reason. It was suggested that to play the game at its best, a high-end computer was needed. A minimum of 150 gigabytes of storage was required for the PC version, but the game has since become much more accessible now that it has been released on the Xbox Series X/S, and even on the Xbox One via the Xbox Cloud. You can now even fly planes on Microsoft Flight Simulator in virtual reality, making flying more realistic than ever before.

So far, three editions of the game have been released. The Standard edition consists of 37,000 airports, 30 of which are hand-crafted plus 25 flyable aircraft. The Deluxe edition adds 5 aircraft and replaces 5 more airports with hand-crafted versions. Then there's the Premium Deluxe edition which adds another 5 aircraft and replaces 5 more airports with hand-crafted versions.

The game's developers, Asobo Studio, are constantly improving the game in the form of "Sim" updates, which deal with aircraft models, flight controls, flight modeling, physics, weather engine, and user interface. There have been 10 Sim updates in total as of August 2022. There are also regular "World" updates that aim to keep the global terrain in check, ensuring airports, water masks, buildings, roads, and landmarks are all as they should be.

In addition to maintaining an air of realism, attention to detail, and the satisfaction that comes with it, the development team released expansions that add a whole new element of fun and competitive action. The Reno Air Races expansion came out in November 2021 and featured multiplayer races with global leaderboard and single-player time trials. The Full Collection of the Reno Air Races DLC went on sale at $59, for which the buyer would receive 40 unique, officially licensed, and carefully modeled planes that could be flown anywhere in the base sim once purchased. Alternatively, you can buy 4 starter planes for only $19.

The second expansion released for Microsoft Flight Simulator 2020 was "Top Gun: Maverick" in May 2022. Offered as freeware to coincide with the movie, the DLC brings fighter jets, training missions, and a fully functional aircraft carrier to the game.

Microsoft Flight Simulator 2020 was so popular that it led to a shortage of flight sticks in stores. Even on Amazon and in many stores, the best-selling sticks were unavailable to buy new for quite some time during the game's release month.

Flight Simulator 2024

On June 23rd, 2023, Jorg Neumann the head developer of Microsoft's iconic Flight Simulator Series held a presentation at the Flight Sim Expo. Along with Sebastian Wloch, the CEO of

Asobo showcased new gameplay details for the next entry in the franchise Microsoft Flight Simulator 2024. Their presentation went into great detail highlighting some of the biggest and newest features, gameplay mechanics, and graphical improvements.

Up until its release the Microsoft Flight Simulator team attended the FS Expo for the first time this year and during the show's kick-off the Microsoft team gave updates on some new information about the new Sim developments. The team started the presentation by mentioning currently there are over 12 million unique simmers that have been using the Microsoft Flight Simulator 2020. They predicted that there's most likely 3 million core PC users, 3 million core game users and the rest are makeup casual users, and that has led the Microsoft team to grow their numbers up to over 175 staff, growing to make this next Generation Sim which Microsoft said is going to be the biggest undertaking in flight simulation history.

The team focused on the presentation of a few different focuses that they have planned with the new Simulator and the first one they talked about is kicking off with an Aviation career. Microsoft said that they have worked with many Aviator professionals around the globe in all sorts of careers to make this as detailed as possible. They call this the Aviation activity system and it will ensure that it's as close to real-world operations as possible

The team alluded there will be more variety when it comes to careers in the simulation than what has been showcased in the trailer including Airlines have received a bunch of feedback. There weren't any Airlines included. They did allude there were definitely airliners when it comes to this new Aviation activity system as part of the Sim.

When it comes to the new Sims core and Technology the simulator will have a smaller client. All the users will be able to download what they need. The team wants to keep more of their side in the cloud that way, reducing the size of the simulator. With Microsoft Flight Simulator 2020, after 33 updates so far the team understands it's getting quite large so they aimed at reducing the installation and loading times as well as keeping the Sim available to minimum spec users. They are changing the architecture to be backward compatible with current add-ons in the community folders.

The team also mentioned the new symbol has massive performance improvements and the Sim will be multi-threaded when it comes to CPU usage.

One of the other focuses that the team had mentioned when it came to the new simulator was aerodynamics. The Sim would have an improved physics and aerodynamic engine and this will be given to third-party developers who will have more control over the flight dynamics of the aircraft that they develop. The team showcased how this was done compared to the 2024 system and showed how many control points there are available now on different aircraft.

Microsoft had mentioned the new sim will be available to handle a rigid and soft body aircraft along with tissues and rope technology. This is implemented when it comes to the balloon and this is going to be part of the default Fleet. The team showcased some very early work when it comes to the balloon tissue work and it shows how the balloon falls inside itself when it is deflated

The next Focus Microsoft mentioned has had a mini request over the years to improve many systems to be available with different aircraft in the simulator and in this new version of the simulator they've done that. The signal has improved electronics, pneumatic fuel, and hydraulic systems along with improved value systems and a wear and tear system where aircraft can get dirty over time. We have an improved payload and passenger system, a deeper or wider avionics package, and a Cockpit Tablet to be available with all default aircraft. The team mentions they have pretty much improved on all the current systems of the Sim in 2020 and are bringing new ones on board for 2024.

One of the main focuses the team talked about was the digital twin. Microsoft Flight Simulator 2020 looks amazing but they are trying to improve the environment with some new tech to increase the fidelity while flying.

The team hasn't worked out how to incorporate their photographic scenery into the whole world and then use current machine learning Tech to enhance the terrain Services by adding 3D rocks, 3D trees, surface materials, and detail and map tessellations but it broke this down and showed us how they plan on doing it with the new sim. The areas of the world where Microsoft could not get to in the past are now accessible as they can turn 2D into 3D and enhance areas where they're not able to gain accurate data. Using these techniques they will be able to bring the world's surface to the next level.

On top of that, they have new technology to improve the static world with improvements to ground detail, enhanced tree diversity, improved Cliffs, and 3D ground materials. This will be scattered all around. Now that's the static world but when it comes to the dynamic world, the Sim will have a full season set. They'll have the northern and southern lights, tornadoes, and improved storms. When it comes to the living world they're bringing tons of animals worldwide. Ship traffic is going to be included, which is a new system, Acura aircraft, live traffic with which they did mention they are modeling these aircraft at the moment and they're trying to include a bunch of deliveries.

There's also improved vehicle traffic and basically, all the things users have been asking for will be polished in the new sim completely compared to what we see in the 2020 edition.

Microsoft was pretty open when it came to the development of this new simulator and they have been listening to the community on all the features they wanted either by the community requesting these or seeing what third parties have done, using the same type of principles and incorporating them into the new sim. They are taking this Sim to a whole new level.

The biggest and most important gameplay features and improvements that Microsoft Flight Simulator 2024 possesses include 16 pilot Lifestyles where you can realistically experience the lifestyle of several aviation jobs.

Microsoft Flight Simulator 2024 aims to be the biggest and most ambitious title in the series to date. Microsoft Flight Simulator 2024 is coming to PC via Windows and Steam, Xbox series X, and Xbox series S in 2024.

New improvements

At the recent Flight Sim expo Jorg Neumann gave a lot more details about the new Sim and also touched on the subject of what's happening and the reason why they're moving away from the 2020 version. The reason is that they've pretty much reached the limit of what they can do with a version 2020.

Microsoft Flight Simulator 2024 is broken down into three different course sections that are called the focus.

In terms of focus one, this is called the Aviation activity system. Why are they doing this? Well, the reason for that is pretty obvious: some of it is a little bit unexpected but the main reason turns out that Microsoft Flight Simulator 2020 so far has had 12 million different users. That's a lot of people playing the game at the largest point in the franchise's history and it's always been big but never quite this big. Now Microsoft had a look at those numbers and they think that there's around about 3 million users that they consider the core users or the core simmers and these are people who play at the cinema regularly (regular flight simmers and very heavy Gamers) and they found out that surprisingly, one of the most common things that these people want is to see more activities within the Sim.

Moving on to focus two this is Core Sim and Technology, perhaps the biggest reason for the move from 2020 to 2024. One of the things they want to improve is the client size. For those of us who've been playing this Sim for quite a while, you'll soon find that this CM is 150 gigabytes, 200 or 250 gigabytes in size depending on what you've installed and how many upgrades or updates you've downloaded. Now there won't be a new client to be much smaller and to achieve this; they're going to put more of the client in the cloud.

With the current edition of the flight simulator, you know that terrain and photogrammetry are stored in the cloud. This is why we can get such a lovely-looking Sim. They're going to take this a step further and put some of the application, the game itself, in the cloud as well and this means that the installation is going to be much smaller and that download times are going to be much smaller.

Also, in Focus Two, there's a new physics and aerodynamics engine. The new engine is going to give craters and Microsoft itself more controlled surfaces on the plane so we're moving from fairly limited control surfaces up to absolutely tons of them on the planes. Additionally, the physics is now going to be covering rigid, as well as soft body physics, as well as tissue and aerobics physics. The latter of these two are going to be used in the hot air balloons.

Now you won't see this type of physics anywhere in any Sim or any game. You only see this type of thing simulated in some really hardcore simulations but this is going to be in a Flight Sim 2024. One thing to note here is that when this balloon collapses down you'll notice that the surface doesn't clip through itself. The ridge surface detection here is so that as the balloon collapses, when it comes in contact with other parts of this material surface it will react correctly and accordingly, and yes, this looks pretty impressive.

Another nice thing that was great to hear is that the new Sim engine in Flight Sim 2024 is going to be multi-core. This means all the physics and everything else is going to be multi-threaded and won't be relying on just a single thread or just a few threads. This has been a massive hold-up for the current edition of the Sim.

There are also some other improved Graphics going on. There are newly improved ground details. Both are going to get 3D tessellated ground materials. This means a distortion of snow then we've got vegetation-enhanced tree diversity. This means that trees appear in the correct regions now and not the standardized generic trees appearing everywhere.

We also have improved Cliffs. We've got bounded Cliffs and sloppy-type Cliffs. This looks much better.

Moving on, this newest edition is full of seasons. Now this is something that Microsoft did promise for Flight Simulator 2020 and because they made that promise they're trying to look at a way of including these Seasons into the existing edition of Flight Simulator so it is definitely available in the 2024 Edition.

The 2024 Edition is going to have Aurora Borealis. It's rather extreme-looking weather in the form of tornadoes and supercells as well as some impressive-looking storms as well.

Beyond that, we've got the living planet or living world. In version 2020 there were some animals you can find there but they're pretty sparse, they're not too many of them all clustered together but what Microsoft has done is make these into a much larger herd and we start seeing migration going on.

This sort of activity would also extend to live ship traffic, as well as live air traffic. Live air traffic in the 2020 version is in a bit of a mess because this version is not up to it. But then in the 2024 version, there's going to be improved traffic and that means that the crazy traffic activity you see on the surface will go away.

An improved Thin Client that will reduce installation and loading times as well as reduce the footprint on HDDS and internet download usage. The improved client will also help keep the PC version's minimum specification requirements low while still maintaining backward compatibility with the game's Cloud servers.

The game's engine will feature massive performance enhancements and allow aircraft creators more control of their chosen aircraft.

Microsoft flight simulator 2024 will have you fly in Dynamic worlds with fully realized immersive weather effects like tornadoes, storms, full seasons, and even in Aurora Borealis. To increase the immersion even further, the texture details for the ground, mountains, and trees have been improved to be more realistic. On top of that, there will be animal herds, worldwide ship traffic, real-time air traffic, and improved traffic control to give players the feeling that they are flying in a living world.

There will be more in-depth systems involved when piloting aircraft like electrical, hydraulic, fuel, and pneumatic systems, payload and passenger systems, failure and wear-and-tear systems, avionic packages with increased wideness and depth, and a cockpit tablet by default.

Review Questions

1. Provide a brief overview of the history of Microsoft Flight Simulator, highlighting the key improvements and advancements made in each major version.

2. Discuss the significant changes and new features introduced in Microsoft Flight Simulator 2024 compared to the previous version.

3. How has the realism and immersion of the Microsoft Flight Simulator series evolved over time, and what are the latest advancements in this area?

CHAPTER 3
PRINCIPLES OF FLIGHT

In flight, manipulation of the airplane's orientation about all three axes is performed via the primary flight controls which only include the Elevator (Pitch), Ailerons and Spoilerons (Roll), and rudder (Yaw).

Elevator

The elevator pitches the airplane's nose up and down about the lateral axis.

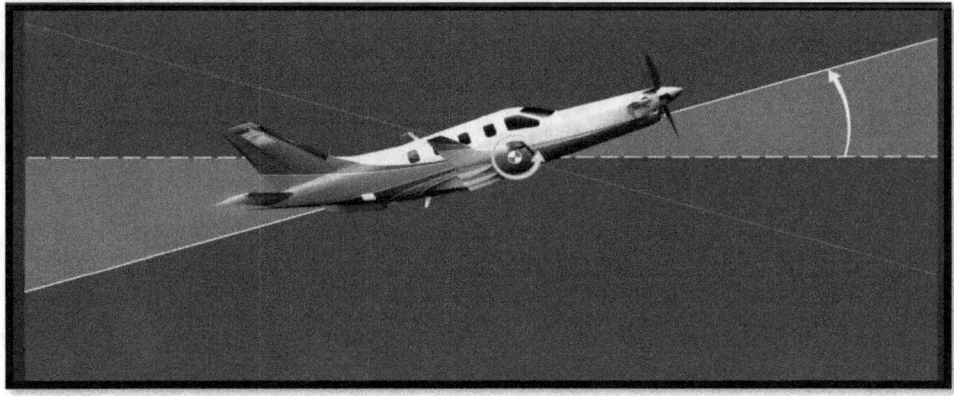

Ailerons and Spoilerons

The TBMS ailerons roll the TBM about the longitudinal axes, meanwhile integrated spoilerons augment roll control by spoiling lifts on the descending wing and at the same time counteracting adverse yaw created by the lifting aileron.

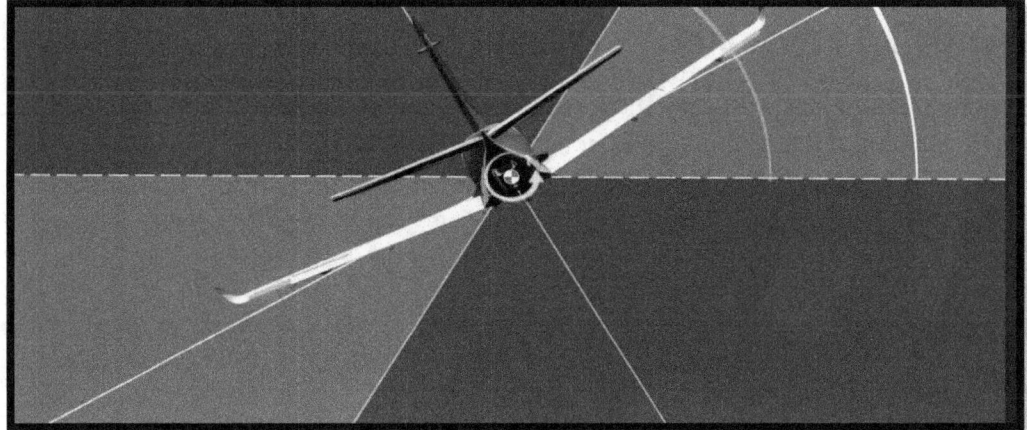

Rudder

Yaw coordination about the vertical axis is maintained with a rudder. Adjusting the airplane's orientation with a wrong primary flight control leads to uncoordinated flight.

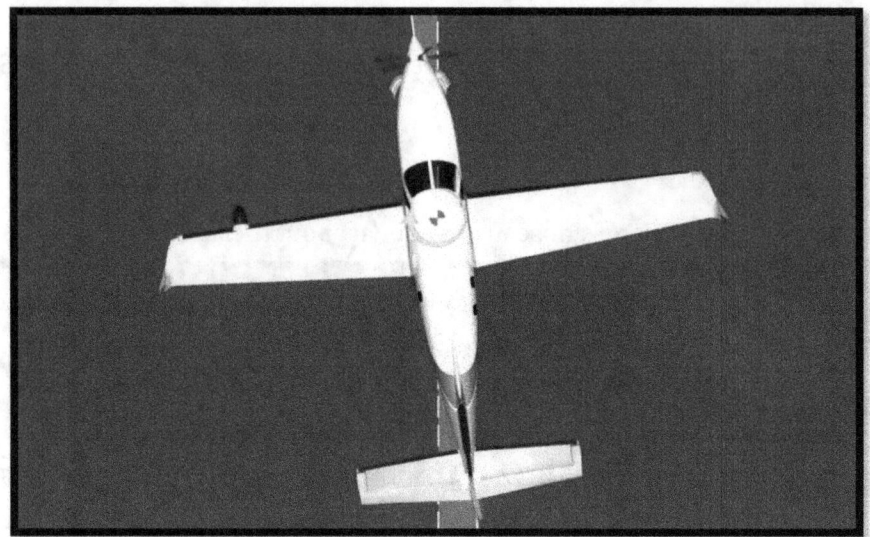

Primary flight controls

The primary flight control/pitch is the elevator.
The primary flight controls for TBM roll control are the Ailerons and interconnected Spoilerons.
The most neglected primary flight control is a rudder which either maintains or returns the aircraft to coordinated flight.
Note: Trim is not a primary flight control.

Starting flight position

Coordinated straight-level flight is the base from which all airborne maneuvers begin. One must first have the ability to maintain constant heading and altitude, moreover, one must demonstrate the ability to address subtle displacements in the aircraft's orientation in all three axes with the appropriate primary flight controls to promptly restore the desired flight path.

Forces of flight

There are 4 forces of flight: weight, lift, thrust, and drag.

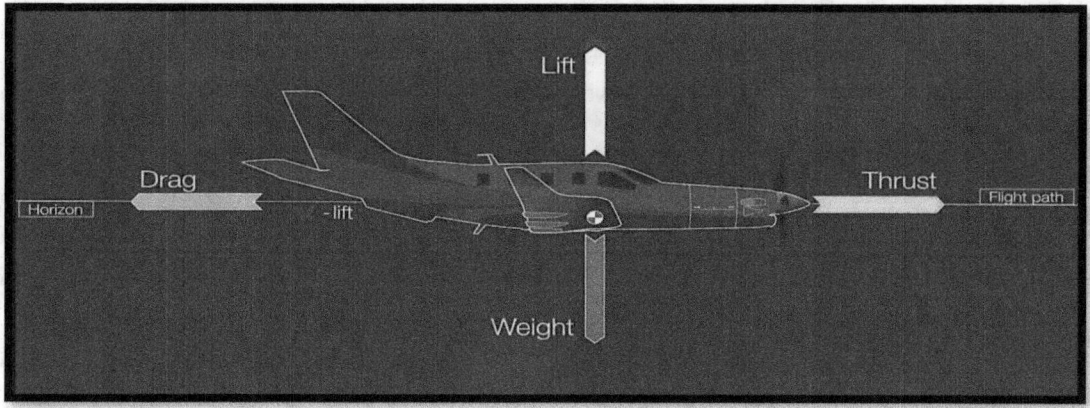

Weight

Weight always pulls the aircraft towards the center of the earth.

Lift

Counteracting weight is a lift that acts perpendicular to the relative wind perpendicular to the flight path. Total lifting force is greater than weight for it must also compensate for the negative lifting force created by the horizontal stabilizer.

Thrust

The thrust axis of most singular airplanes is not exactly aligned with a fuselage which helps compensate for left-turning tendencies, therefore, for simplicity, thrust pulls the aircraft forward in line and parallel to the longitudinal axis of the aircraft.

Drag

Drag also acts parallel to the flight path or relative wind by a river direction.

When climbing

Weight acts towards the center of the earth but during climb a percentage of the weight has an F component which opposes thrust.

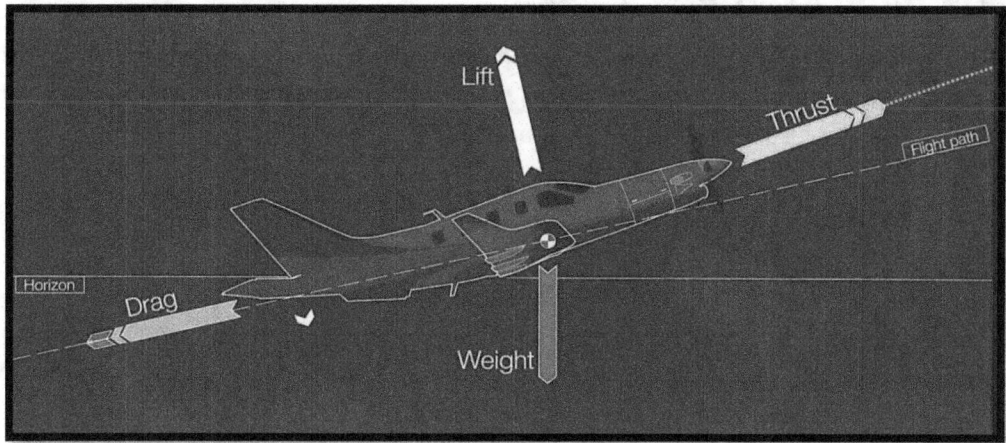

Lift remains perpendicular to the flight path or relative wind.

During climb an angle attack is created between the thrust line and the flight path which provides a vertical component, increasing total lift during a stabilized climb. Climb performance is limited to the amount of excess thrust available at a given speed.

During Descent

At the top of a descent point, the TBM pitches over to begin the descent. Since weight acts towards the center of the earth, a forward component is created that complements the thrust vector.

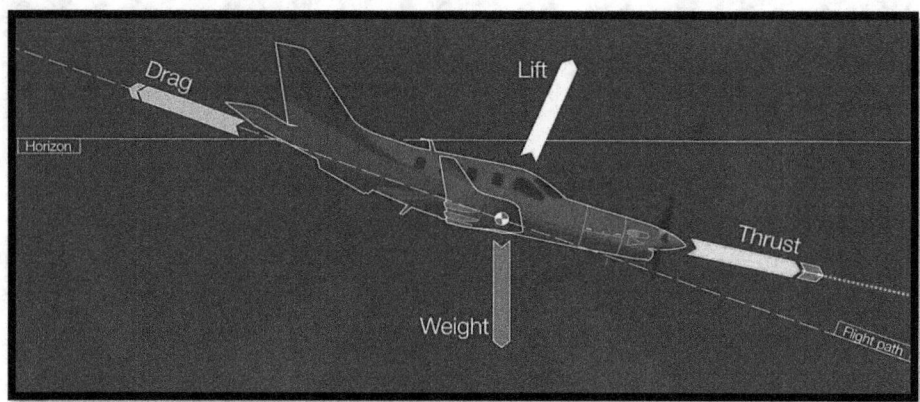

Airspeed will be allowed to accelerate to a desired value, for example, 250 knots pitch or a combination of pitch and power can be used to bring the forces into balance. Since the descent phase of flight is normally flown with the autopilot on, the appropriate pitch mode is the vertical speed with power adjustments used to manipulate indicated airspeed. If one were hand flying, the pitch can be adjusted to hold the indicated airspeed while power adjustments allow control of the descent rate.

Fundamental principles of flight

The fundamental principles of flight are learned, tuned, and demonstrated throughout preliminary flight training. How much time has passed since you reviewed these principles and considered their effects on the aircraft you routinely fly?

Weak skill sets and/or overdependence on all flight control systems can reduce a pilot's sensitivity towards a coordinated flight. A sound foundation built on these basic principles is a key ingredient to maintaining and enhancing aircraft control.

In-Flight User Interface

Once you're in the simulated world in Microsoft Flight Simulator you can look at the user interface by dragging your mouse to the top.

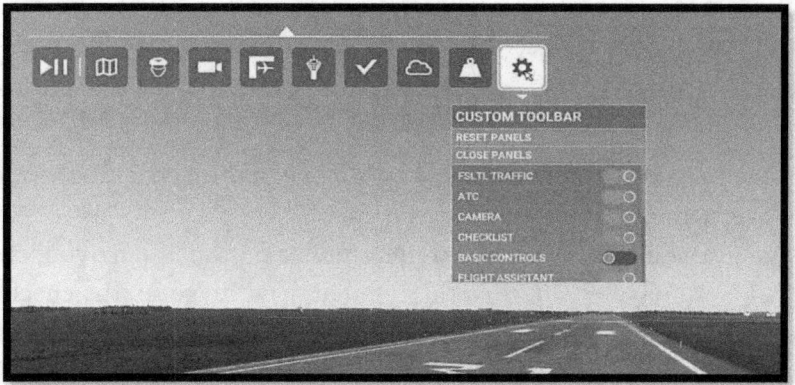

Here, we've got:

- a Custom toolbar option
- Weight and Balance menu,
- the weather on the Fly
- a checklist
- ATC menu
- FSL TL Traffic menu for add-ons
- some camera options (which include External views, Cockpit view, Showcase)
- the Flight Assistant which is the AI Control on your plane
- we can look at your map (a VFR map)
- An option to actively pause the simulation.

Review Questions

1. Explain the function and importance of the primary flight controls (elevator, ailerons, and rudder) in controlling an aircraft.

2. Describe the four fundamental forces of flight (weight, lift, thrust, and drag) and how they interact to enable an aircraft to take off, climb, and land.

3. How does the in-flight user interface in Microsoft Flight Simulator 2024 help pilots understand and manage the principles of flight during a simulation?

CHAPTER 4

AIRCRAFT PREPARATION AND STARTUP

In this chapter, we're going to show you how to use the built-in checklist in Microsoft Flight Simulator to get you set up.

The first thing you can do is hold down the right mouse button. It'll let you look around the cockpit which is beautifully done here in this simulator but to get to the checklists just hold your mouse up to the top and move over to the check mark or you can press SHIFT + C on your keyboard and we're going to start with the pre-flight inspection of the cockpit.

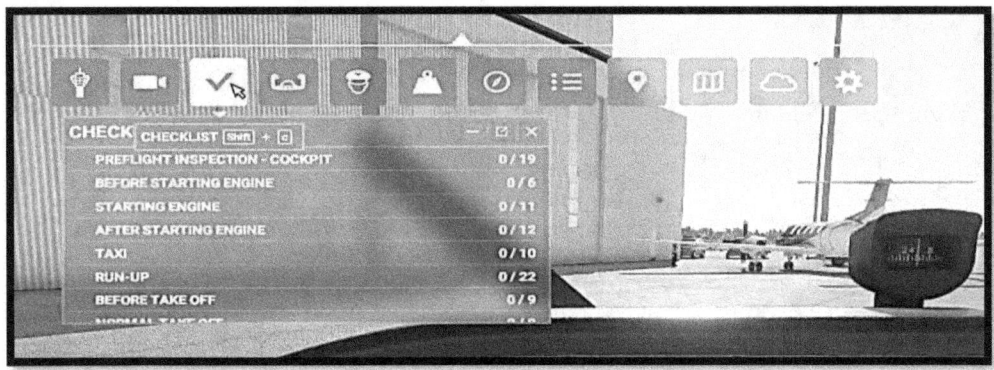

Pre-flight inspection of the cockpit

Here, you have the different items that you'll go through. Click on the item and when you've done it you click "Tick item." The first thing we have is Aircraft documents. For Parking brakes, there's an eyeball symbol here and this means it's a switch in the cockpit that you can manipulate. Hit the eyeball button and it'll highlight and zoom in to the item so we need to set the parking brake. Click it and there you go, the parking brake is now set.

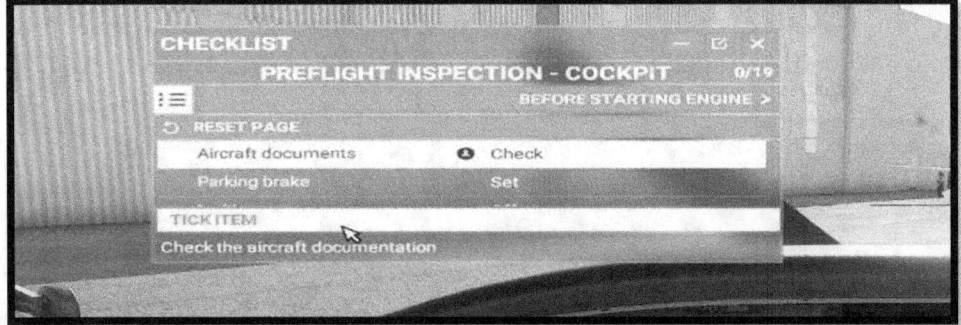

Next up, we'll set Ignition to off and then tick that item. We'll set the Avionics switch (Bus 1 and Bus 2) to off. We'll tick that Battery switch and turn the battery master switch on so we

35

have battery power on the aircraft now. We're going to check the fuel quantity indicators and ensure it's up at 100 percent so we'll tick that item. Next, we will make sure the Low Fuel L and Low Fuel R annunciator lights are off and they are dark.

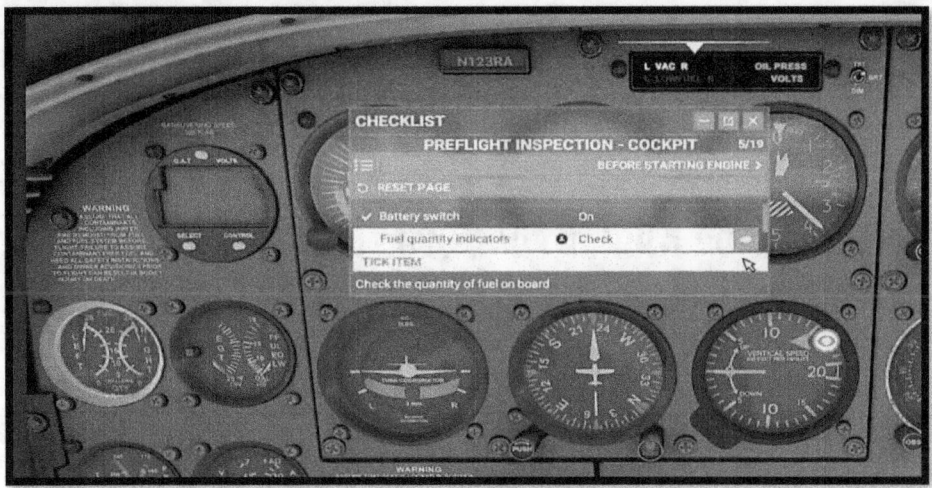

Next, let's turn on the Avionics (Bus 1 And Bus 2) switches and we're listening for a cooling fan. We can hear it so we'll turn the Avionics (Bus 1 And Bus 2) switches off. Static pressure Alt source valve is right next to the throttle It is in the off position when it's in.

We'll test the annunciator lights to make sure all the light bulbs are good so we get any messages we might need in flight about system malfunctions and the fuel selector valve. It's in both so we'll be taking fuel from both of the fuel tanks and the wings. Now we'll make sure the Fuel shutoff valve is open so we'll click that and now it is open.

For flaps, we'll put those down by moving the Flaps Control switch and this will take us outside so you can see the flaps coming down. That's what's going on when you manipulate that flap lever so flaps are now down.

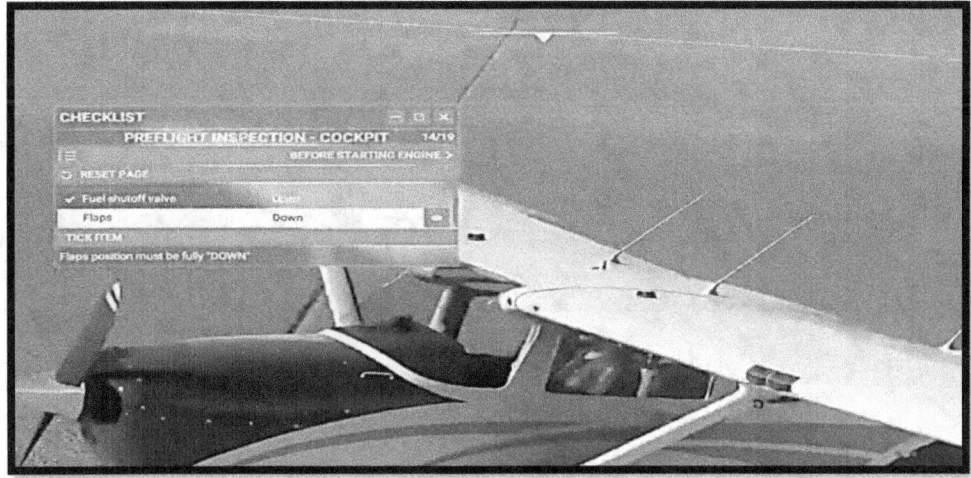

For Pitot Heat we will turn it on. One way you can see if it's working is to look at the ammeter. When you turn it off you'll see how the ammeter moves up a little bit and when you turn it on you'll see it moves down a little bit. That way, you know that the Pitot Heat is working.

We'll turn the Battery master switch off and the elevator trim which is the wheel on the left side below the throttle we're going to move it to Neutral. We're just going to move it to the arrow right here that you always want to be set up for takeoff here in the airplane.

Our pre-flight inspection or the cockpit checklist is complete. We'll move on to the Before Starting Engine checklist.

Before Starting the Engine checklist

The first item is Pre-flight Inspection. if you want to simulate that you can go outside the aircraft and you can, in essence, walk around the plane by scrolling your mouse around. In real life, you would walk and check each of the components according to the POH or the Pilot Operating Handbook but we'll consider that complete.

We'll ensure that our seats and belts are in" Adjust and locked." We'll make sure Electrical equipment is all off (all these switches are in the off position). For the Avionics switch (Bus 1 and 2), you definitely want to have that off before you start. You don't want to cause any problems with your avionics, which are your radio navigation equipment. Make sure the Fuel selector valve is in "Both," the Fuel shutoff valve is open and our engine checklist is complete.

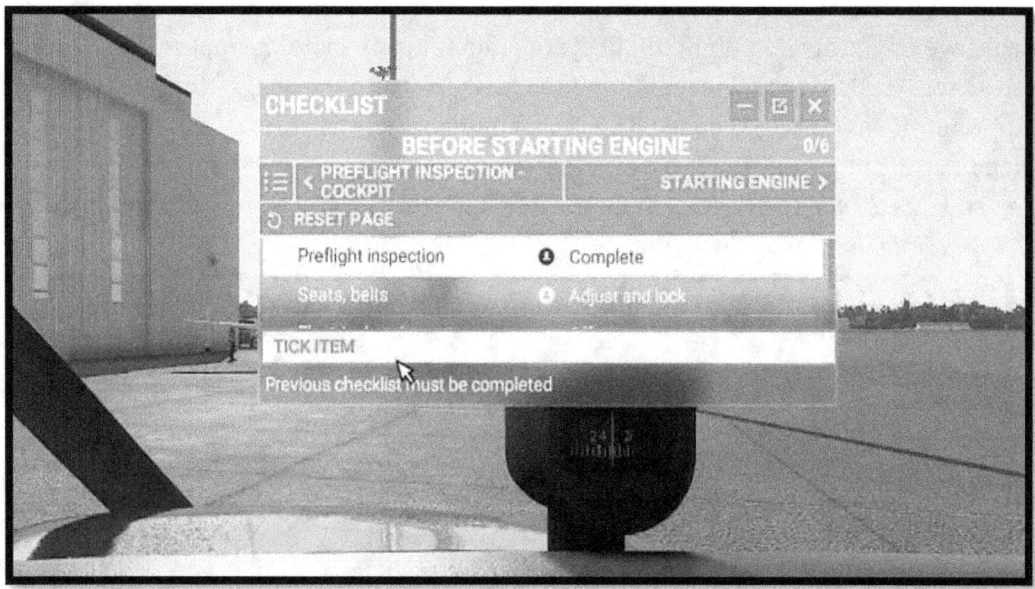

Starting the engine checklist

We'll move on to starting the engine and the first thing we want to do is open the throttle to a quarter of an inch with a little bit of fuel going as soon as we get the fuel pumps going. We'll set Mixture to Idle cutoff so we pull all the way out. We need to check that the propeller area is clear. We'll move on to Battery master and switch to on, switch Beacon to on (this lets other aircraft know we're about to start our engine and people on the ground. We'll set Mixture to Rich so push it in. If you ever forget, recall you pull to lean and you push in to make it rich.

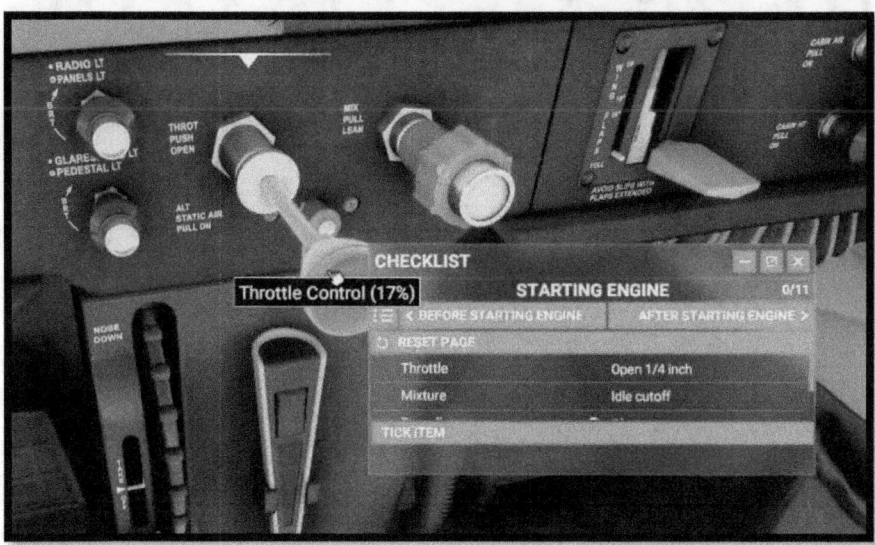

We'll put the AUX fuel pump on for three to five seconds and then turn it off. Another thing we can do is watch the fuel flow up there. It's going to go up a little bit when we turn this on. We'll also make sure we have our feet set on "Ready to break." We'll turn the Parking brake on and Ignition to start so now we'll go ahead and start the engine after ensuring we're all clear. We'll use the mouse wheel, push in the Mixture to rich as that'll get the fuel going, and then pull our throttle back to get our RPMs right here under a thousand.

After Starting Engine

Go through these items here. Make sure it was rich when the engine started and after starting the engine, set the Throttle to "Adjust to 1000 RPM." That's complete.
Moving on to the Oil pressure check, we'll check right here for our oil pressure and make sure it's in an acceptable range. We'll switch the alternator on and the Ammeter to "Check." For the Avionics switch (Bus 1 and Bus 2) we'll set it to on and then set our GPS equipment to on. We'll ensure our Radios are on and then Transponders, we're going to switch it to standby. We'll set Flaps to "Up." You can also hit the F5 key on your keyboard to do that. For the Heading indicator, we'll put that to "Set." You want to check that with the magnetic compass.

It's showing 2, 3, 0; (just add a zero to the end of the number you see there) and it should match up here, so that's right at 2, 3, 0 on the heading indicator as well so we're good to go. If you need to change that you can roll your mouse wheel over the Tune directional gyro heading but we're at 2, 3, 0 and that is perfect.

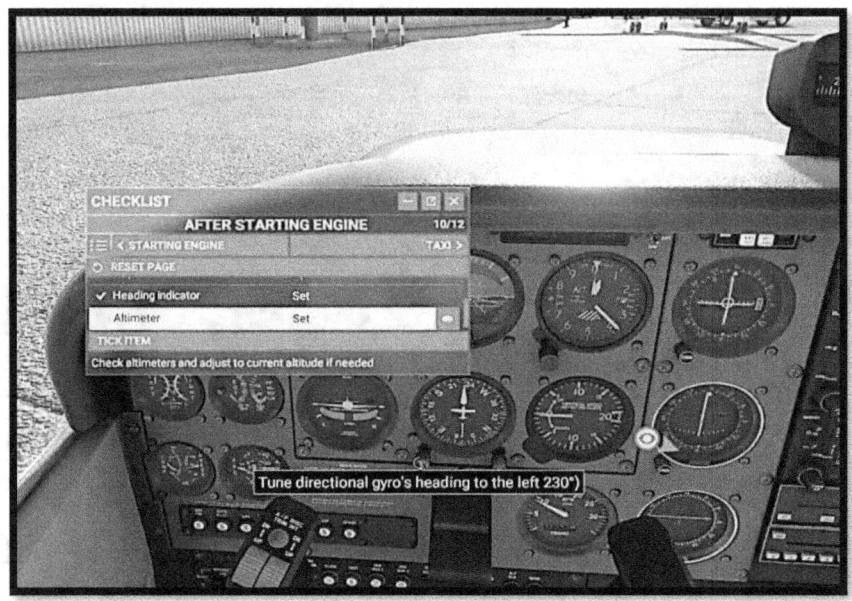

We'll have the Altimeter set and how we'll do that is go here to the Air Traffic Control, tune to the Atis 118.0, and listen. It shows in the Altimeter Calibration window here but it'll also give you a digital readout as you try to adjust the altimeter calibration knob. The attitude indicator is also set and we're level with the horizon where it should be.

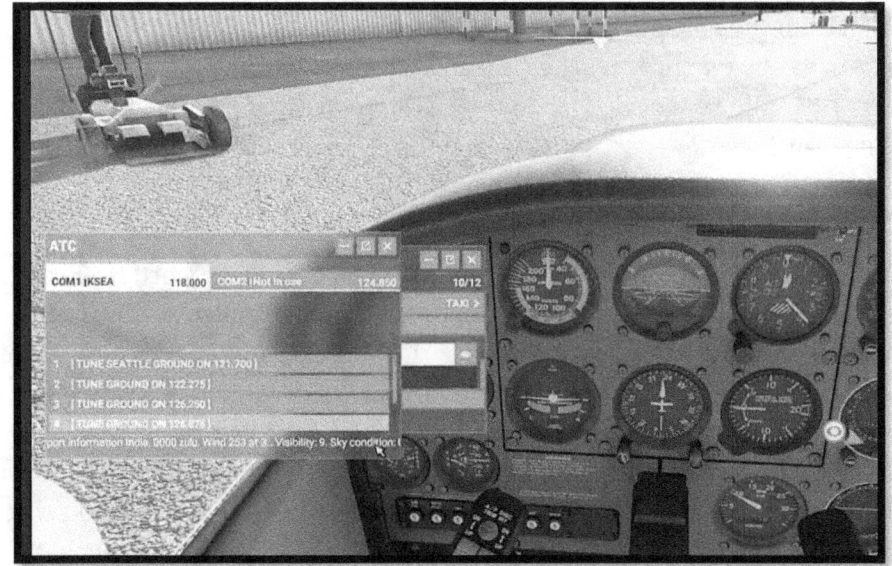

After the starting engine checklist is complete, that concludes how to perform your pre-flight and start up the engine using the built-in checklist of Microsoft Flight Simulator.

Starting Options

Let's go ahead and take a look at some of our starting options when selecting a flight. You would first come in here into the world map and you would pick your destination and your departure location.

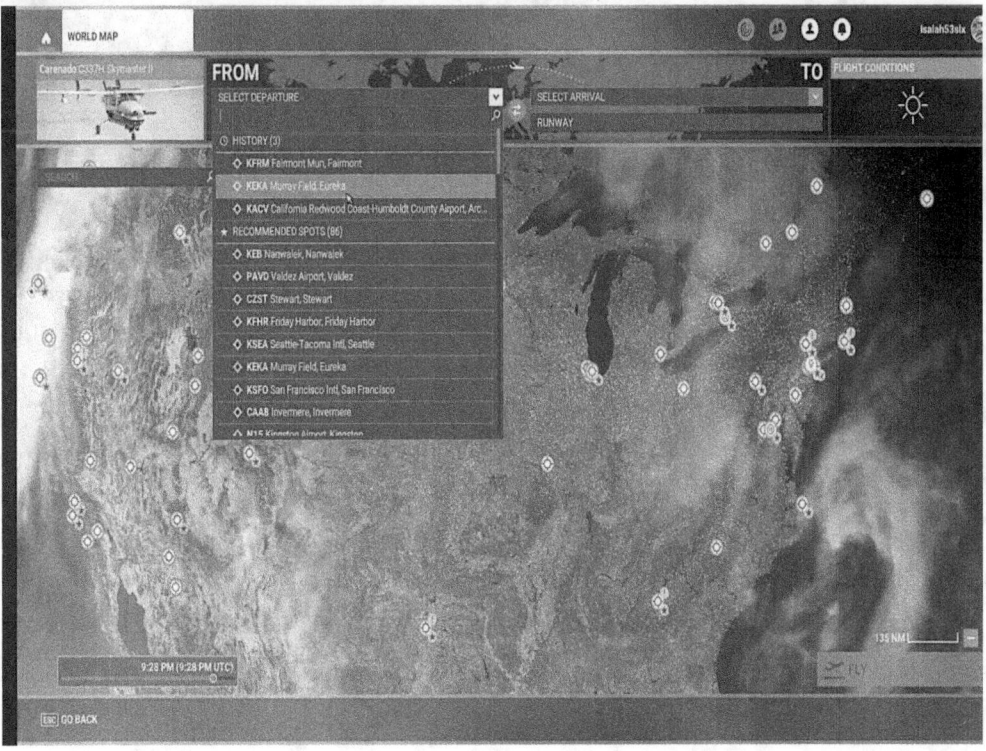

You can go anywhere you want. As you pick a location you can set it as your departure or your arrival or you can pull down this drop-down menu and do a search; you can put in a previous airport, pick the runway or you can pick a ramp parking area or fuel box parking then select your arrival airport and the runway. You've got your VFR options or IFR. You can select your aircraft at the top left corner, there are liveries to choose from and you can change your weight and your balance failures customization.

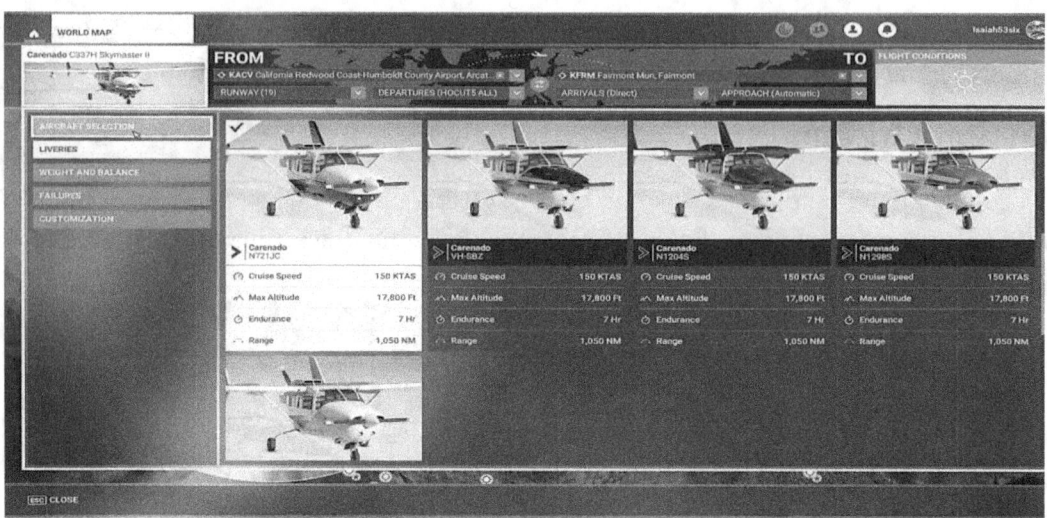

Over here on the right you have the option to adjust your flight conditions and change your time of day whether you want live weather or real-time. If live weather is selected you can turn it off by changing the time of day and then you can change the date. You have your Cloud layers, precipitation temperature, and humidity. Here, you have multiplayer options. There are some Air Traffic settings and then your weather and a button that lets you select a preset or custom. When you're satisfied with your selections, click on "Fly."

Review Questions

1. Highlight the key areas and systems that pilots should check before starting the engine.

2. Explain the proper procedures for starting the aircraft's engines.

3. Discuss the importance of following the correct aircraft preparation and startup protocols within the simulation.

CHAPTER 5

BASIC FLIGHT CONTROLS

This chapter is about basic controls for Microsoft Flight Simulator. We will also show you how to look up buttons.

Basic controls

The first thing we'll talk about is cameras. It's your views that enable you to look left and right, look at the panels, get outside of the airplane so that you can view it from the outside (this is very helpful especially if you're new), and be inside the cockpit.

The next is the throttle. That's like the gas pedal in a car. It makes you go faster and it's the power in an aircraft.

Next is the brakes. There are a few different brakes; parking brakes are set and if you hit that full power you're just going to stay right there on the runway. You have to know the button to take off the parking brake and then you also need to know the button for braking so when you come in to land you don't overrun the runway.

Next is yaw. This one confuses a lot of people who aren't in aviation. It's the left and right movement of the airplane, usually when you're in the air you turn differently than when you're on the ground which is moving the rudder in the very back and you do that with your foot pedals so that's yaw.

Next is flaps. Flaps slow you down but they also give you more lift so you float better. You use this on take off so you get off the runway faster and you use it on landing so that as you're floating, you slow down and you land nice and soft.

Next is the yoke or the stick. It's how you steer the airplane. You'll use it with the ailerons and with the elevator.

Landing gear. This is something that is only on certain aircraft like the big ones. Every aircraft has landing gear but some have retractable landing gear so they'll come up into the airplane and knowing that button will help you so that when you're flying and you bring in the landing gear you fly faster and then when you bring it down it slows you down and prepares you for landing.

Trim is another one that can make somebody's life easier. When you're flying along sometimes you have to use the stick to stay flat and level. If you use the trim, eventually you're going to be able to let go of the stick and the airplane will still fly straight.

Controllers

Note that you can use a keyboard and mouse but we do not suggest it. Try to find a gaming controller of some sort that is compatible with your computer and that will make your life way easier. If you do have a stick or yoke that's fantastic. It's going to work phenomenally for you.

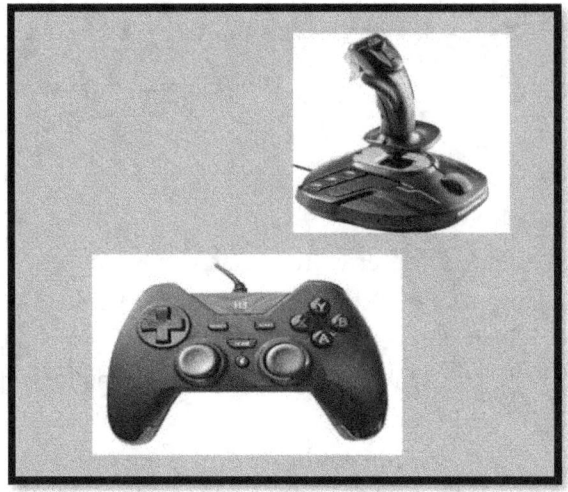

How to look up buttons

Now we're going to show you how to look up buttons. You remember throttle is important but let's say you can't remember what button it was associated with. Click the Escape button, go to Controls and this is where you can find every control that you need.

First, you want to be in the right input so let's say we're looking it up on the keyboard, we'll come down here to "search by name" and enter throttle and we get to see everything that is assigned to the keyboard that has throttle in it but what we're going to worry about is decrease and increase throttle. We suggest you come to Essentials. The shortcut for increasing throttle is to hold down F3 and to decrease throttle you hold down F2.

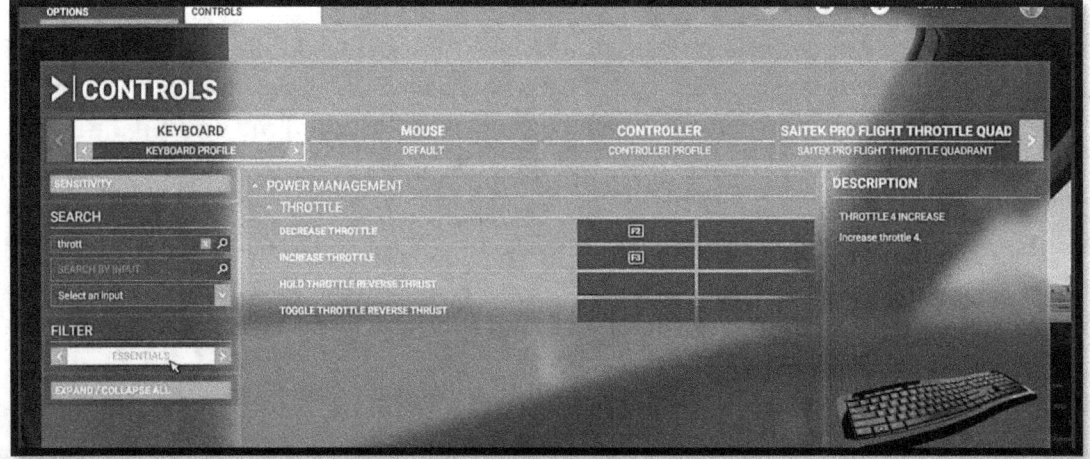

If you come up to the inputs you'll get to the controller and once again, you'll find the throttle. In Essentials you can see decrease and increase throttle; A is to increase throttle B is to decrease throttle.

Before we move on we'll go over the controller, the mouse, and keyboard inputs. If you do have something special like a stick or thrustmaster you can set buttons the same way you can see everything is labeled. If you want to set something like throttle, for instance, you could click here and search by input then click a button that you want to be associated with, let's say button 11, and validate it.

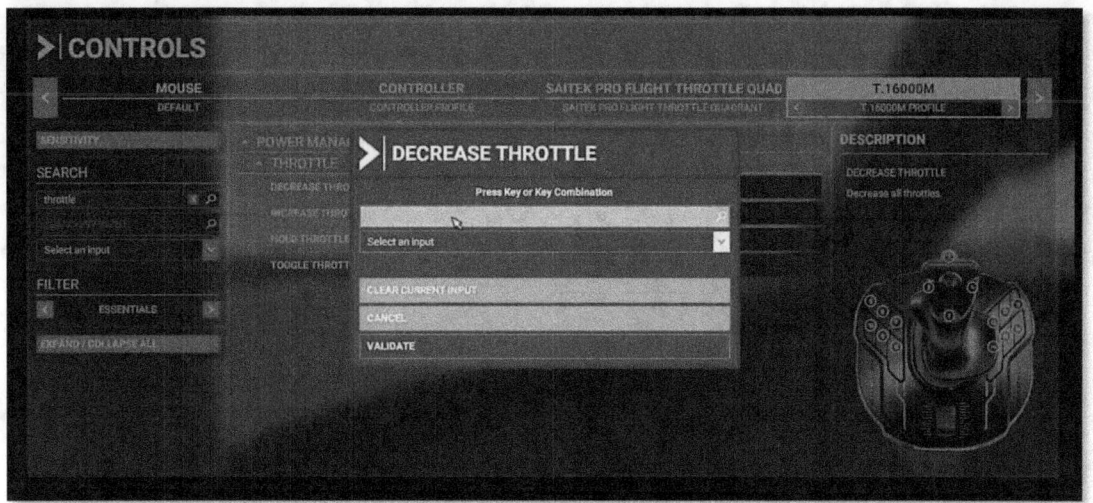

Now you can see that joystick button 11 is now the throttle and that's how you go about setting it if you have something other than the controller or the mouse. You can also still search by the input as well if you don't know what it's assigned to make sure that you don't have two things that are assigned to the same button. You only want one thing associated with each control.

Views

Now we're going to talk about views and we're going to start with keyboard and mouse. To look around you use the mouse. You can right-click and move right, left, up or down, you can look anywhere you want but you have to hold down that right-click button.

Another thing that you can do is the up arrow, down arrow, and side-to-side left and right arrow and it moves you like that. If you do want to do a quick look one way or the other, that's going to be Control with the arrow button, so CTRL+left makes you look left while CTRL+right makes you look right, CTRL+up makes you look up and CTRL+down will make you look back. Those are the basic views while you're flying inside the cockpit with a keyboard and mouse.

To get outside of the cockpit you're going to push the End button and this gets you outside. Once again you can do the same thing with your mouse. You can right-click and move side to side; it is inverted and a little bit confusing but that's something that you can go into the controls panel and invert as well.

For the other views that you have on the keyboard, once again you can click CTRL and if you click down you look behind you, if you do CTRL+up it looks directly down. CTRL+left gets you looking right and with CTRL+right you'll look left so it is inverted but then you can go into the Control panel and invert it so that it feels a little bit more natural for you. Those are the basic views that you have with a keyboard and mouse.

Now let's talk about it with the controller. For the controller, their views are all controlled with the d-pad. When we're outside, if we push up it looks down, we push down it looks behind us, we push left it looks left and when we push right it looks right. That's very easy and you can find it in the menu button, the button with the two boxes. Click that button and it will bring you back inside the cockpit.

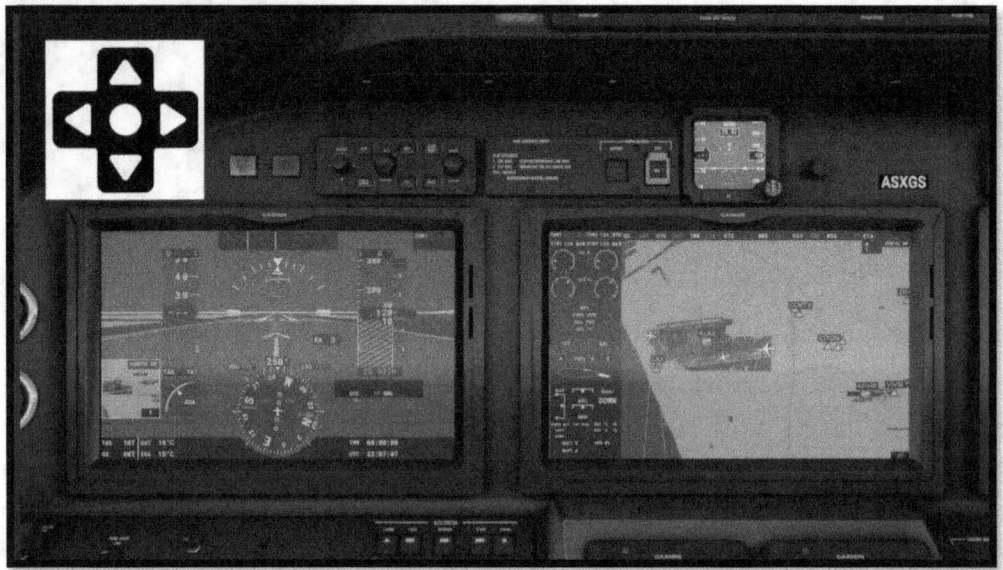

When it comes to views the controller makes it very easy. You can click the up and it gets closer and eventually, it gets very close then you can click down and it goes back. So the d-pad makes it very easy and then the menu button gives you the external and internal views.

The throttle

The next thing that we're going to talk about is the throttle and the throttle is what makes the airplane go faster or slower. It's the gas pedal for the aircraft. Recall that in the keyboard section, F2 decreases the throttle and F3 increases the throttle. For the controller, decreasing the throttle is B while increasing the throttle is A.

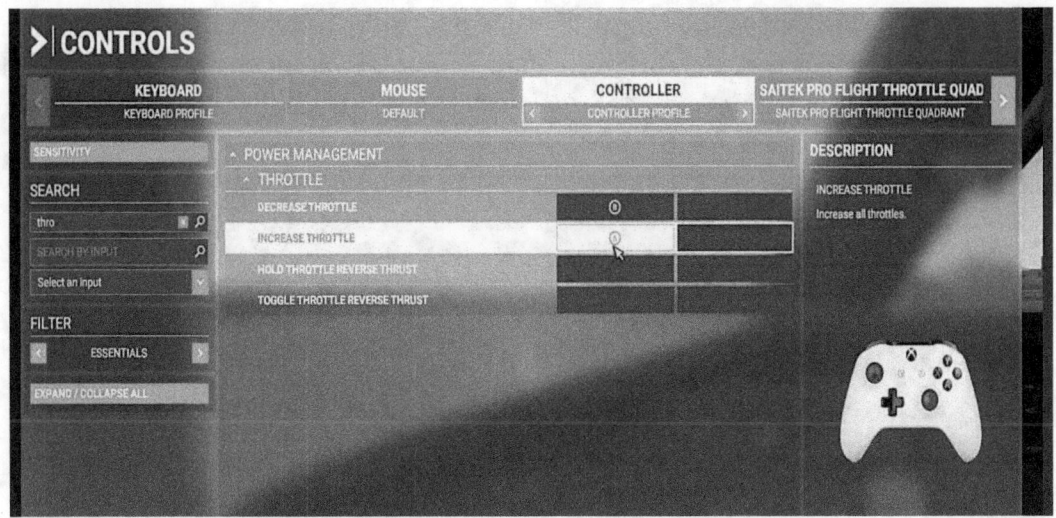

When you increase and decrease the throttle it's going to do both at the same time. Clicking F3 moves it slightly and if we hold it down it starts moving a lot more. We can then hold it down at F2 and it comes back. Now with the controller, clicking A takes it forward, and clicking B it's going back. You'll see it's not like a gas pedal in a car; you set it and forget it and it stays there at a certain percentage.

We can go all the way to one hundred percent and it stays that way or bring it back let's say to about fifty percent and it stays that way so when you fly you don't necessarily always stay one hundred percent the entire time. If you have other systems then just go into the Control panel like we did and look up increase and decrease throttle.

Brakes

The next thing on the list is brakes. There are only two that we need to worry about and that's brakes and toggle parking brakes. There's a left and a right so you can brake with one wheel which is either the right or the left but we're not going to worry about that.

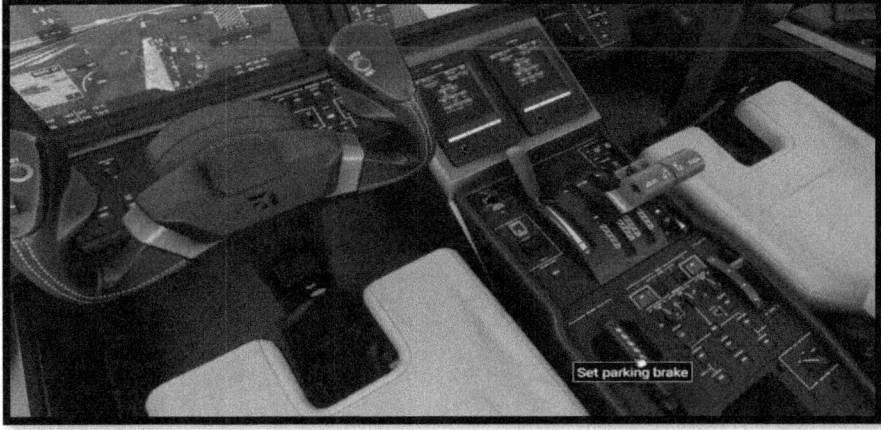

Brakes are what you use when you start to land or while you're taxiing. A toggle parking brake is used when you park; you set the parking brake so it doesn't roll anywhere. Now we're going to set it to essentials and come over to the controller. Here we see that the brakes are Y and the toggle parking brakes are Y + B.

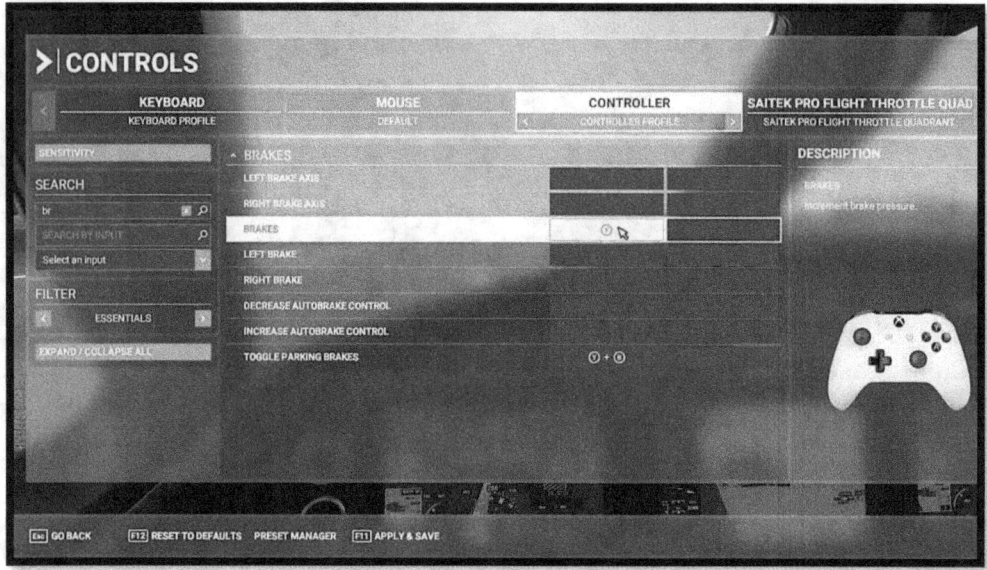

If you hit CTRL + Num Del you'll see it go down as that is for the parking brakes or you'll click Y + B. If you have the parking brake on and you try to put the throttle in, you can't go anywhere. If you hit Y+B or Ctrl + Num Del you'll start moving. If you hit Num Del which is for brake, you'll see you're beginning to slow down.

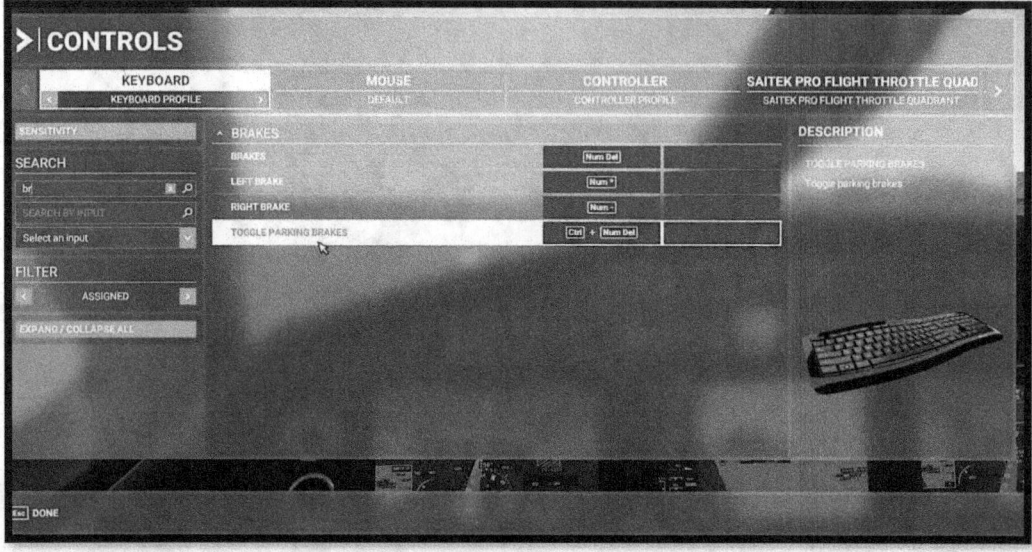

Yaw

The next one is yaw and yaw is for steering on the ground. On the keyboard Essentials, you can use Num 0 or the Enter button. Num 0 does left while the Enter button does right. If you come over to the controller and look at yaw, we have a left trigger (LT) and a right trigger (RT).

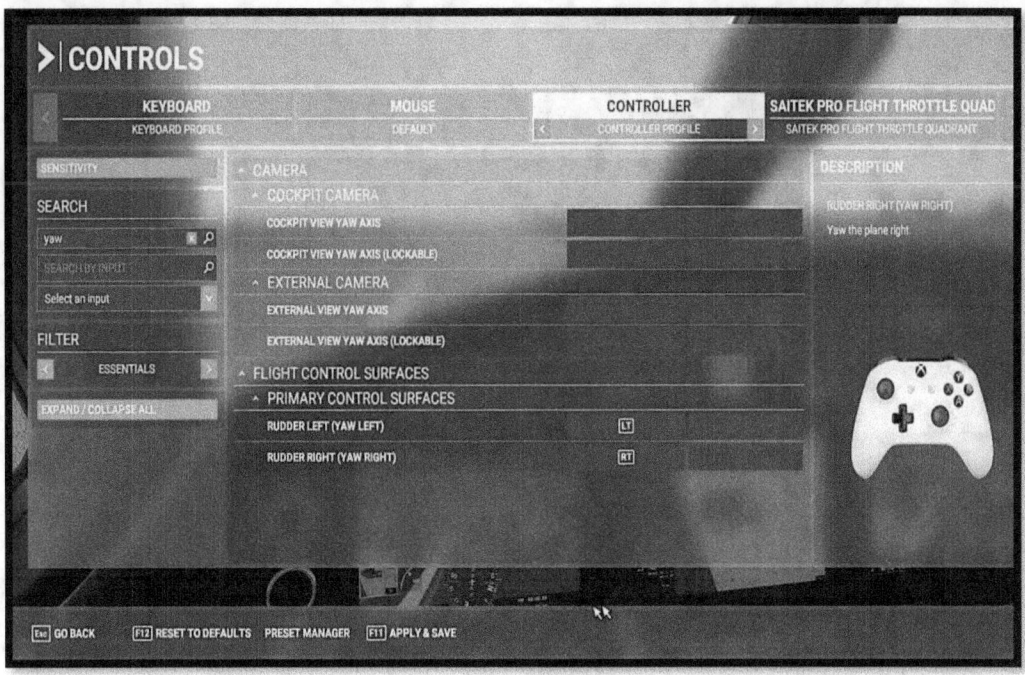

Let's go ahead and see that in action. Back in the cockpit, the rudder pedals push that forward, Num 0 makes us turn left and the Enter button makes us turn right. You can also do it with the controller's left and right triggers and for this, you can go partial or fully extended with the trigger. Note that we only do this when we are taxiing on the ground and you don't want to go too fast taxing. You should go very slowly unless you're going to take off, then you do full power and try to stay on the centerline.

Roll and Pitch

One thing we should have talked about before takeoff is that roll and pitch. Roll makes you go left and right. You need to type in Aileron right to roll right (Num 6)or Aileron left to roll left (Num 4) in the keyboard section. For the elevator which is going up or going down, pitching up or pitching down, it is Num 2 and Num 8.

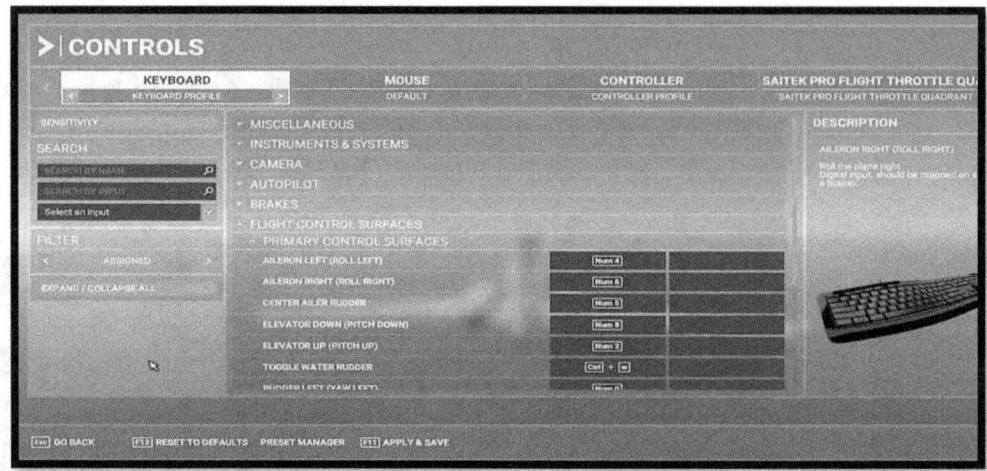

For the controller, it's much easier. We'll go to Essentials, Flight Controls Surfaces primary > Primary and here we will find the Aileron. It's often set for the left so it's the left stick just moving it left and right and then for the elevator, moving it forward and back will push you up and down.

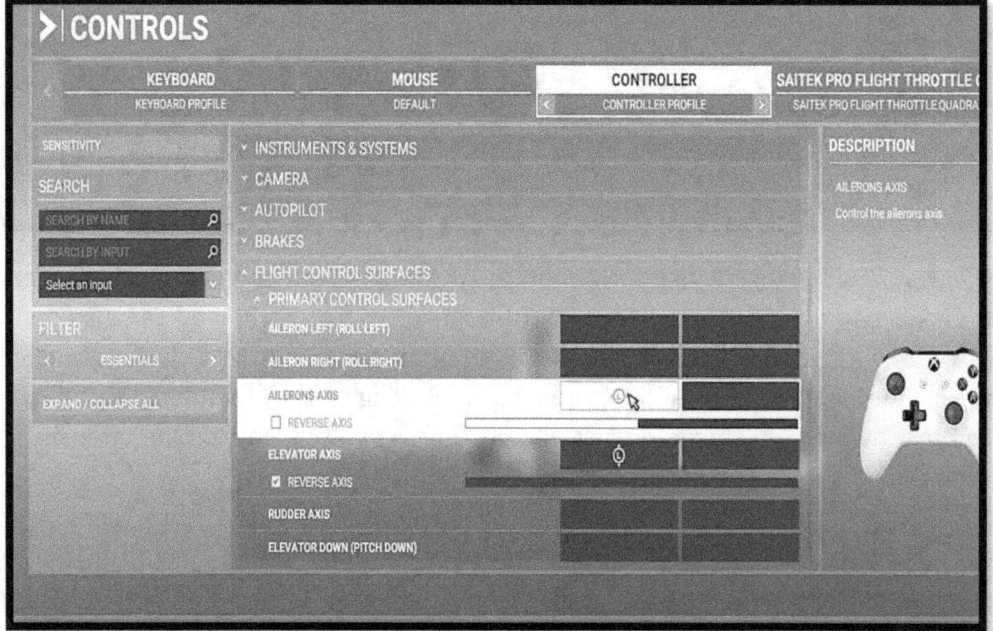

Flaps

The next thing we need to worry about on the ground is decreasing and increasing flaps. F6 decreases it while F7 increases it. On the controller, the left bumper (LB) is to decrease while the right bumper (RB) is to increase.

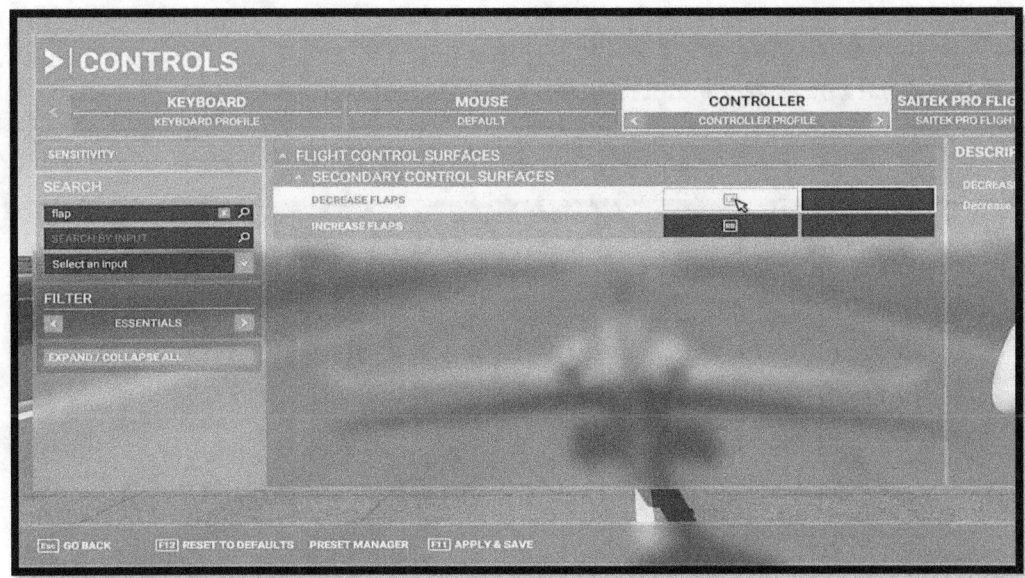

Landing gear

The control for landing gear using the controller is the left stick (LS) so you'll press the left stick in. For the keyboard, the landing gear is G.

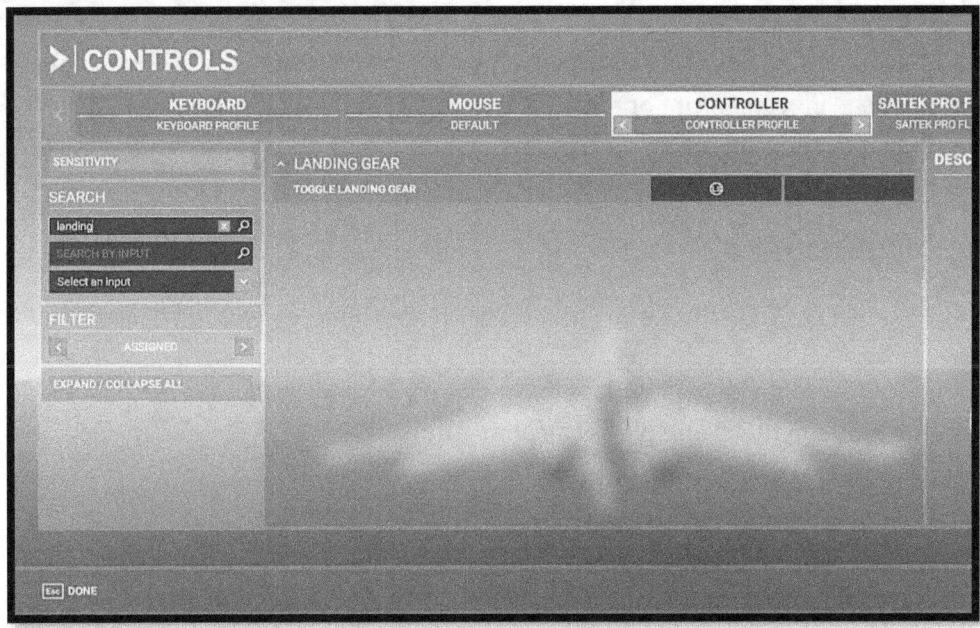

Trim

The last thing that you need to know for the basics is trim and you could get away without using trim but it would be very annoying. Trim allows you to let go of the stick and the airplane will cruise along without having to do so much input.

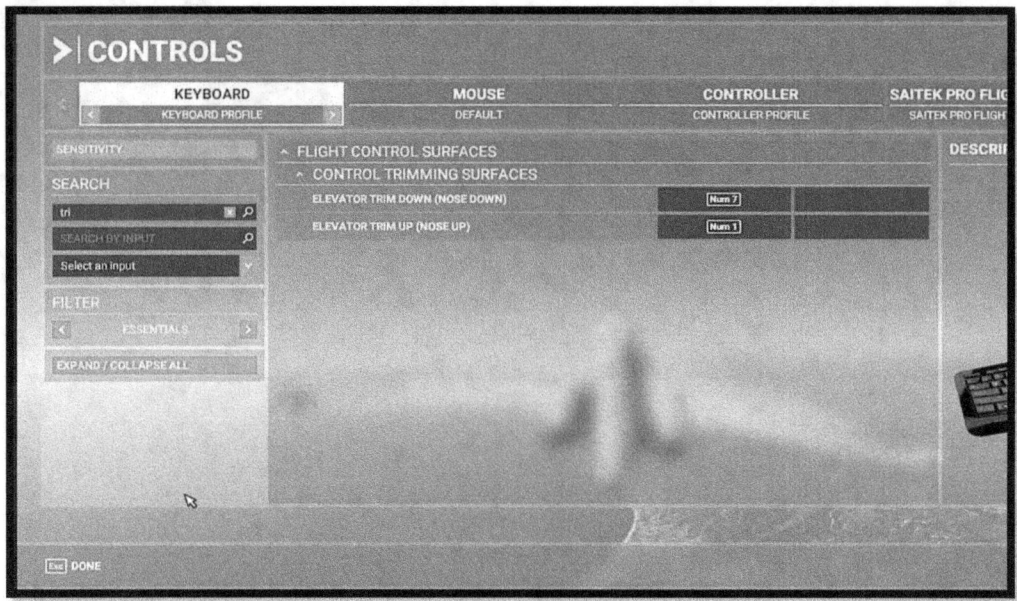

We have Elevator Trim Down and Elevator Trim Up. Although there are other types of trim you want to do the Elevator Trim or the NOSE UP or NOSE DOWN and we have it set for Num 1 or Num 7, that is, the trim Num 7 will make the nose point down and Num 1 will make the nose point up. On the controller, we have the Y + d-pad up and the Y + d-pad down.

Review Questions

1. Provide an overview of the basic flight controls available in Microsoft Flight Simulator 2024.
2. Describe the different views that players can access within the simulation.
3. Explain the fundamental principles of aircraft control.

CHAPTER 6
CAMERA SETUP

In this chapter, we are going to focus on camera setup. The camera setup in Microsoft Flight Simulator is in-depth and in some places not intuitive, however, we are going to help you get the basics nailed and also show you some advanced things.

Aircraft preparation

Make sure that you've fired up the simulator and you've got all of your peripherals plugged in because you may want to map some controls during this illustration

Before we start, we'd like you to click on the world map at the top left, click on the aircraft, choose airliners, and choose the A320neo, everyone has this. Then at the top right choose Flight conditions, turn the Multiplayer off, Air Traffic off, and choose Preset. Choose Clear Skies, pick 12 p.m., and choose LOWI which is LOWI Innsbruck, and Runway 26 as the starting point. Click Fly.

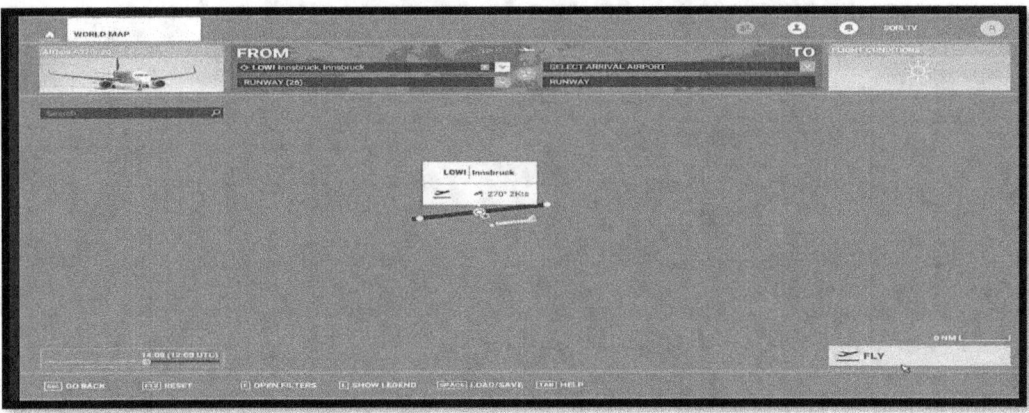

If you did all that right you should now be sitting in the A320 at Innsbruck. You may be wondering why we chose the A320 right? Well, the A320 is a reasonably complex aircraft that comes with some default cameras that you'll be interested in seeing particularly around the instrument views. Every aircraft comes with default cameras in Microsoft Flight Simulator but you can also map your own custom ones and we'll show you how to do that later.

Camera controls

The first thing you'll want to do is know how to just briefly look around, hold down the right mouse button and you should be able to just pan around the cockpit, use the mouse wheel, and zoom in and out. Having zoomed in and out and moved the mouse around, the control space will take you back to the default view.

Camera Controls

There are three main camera modes in Microsoft Flight Simulator.
- There's the cockpit camera.
- There's the external camera which is accessible by pressing the End key. It will show you the basic controls of the aircraft, flaps, altitude, airspeed, and that kind of thing. Press the End key again and you go back into the cockpit.
- If you press the Insert key that will take you to the drone camera and the drone camera is something that you can move and fly around quite easily like a drone. Press the Insert key again and go back to the cockpit.

Quick views

We're now going to focus on the cockpit. First, we have quick views. If you hold the Control key and hold left or right it will quickly look to the left or the right. Press the back arrow key and it will look behind you, press the forward arrow key and it will slightly look up.

If you go to the General settings, under Camera, the quick view function can either be set into a hold mode where you have to hold the keys down, or into a toggle mode where you simply press it once and it will hold that position until you press it again. It's up to you which option you want to go for.

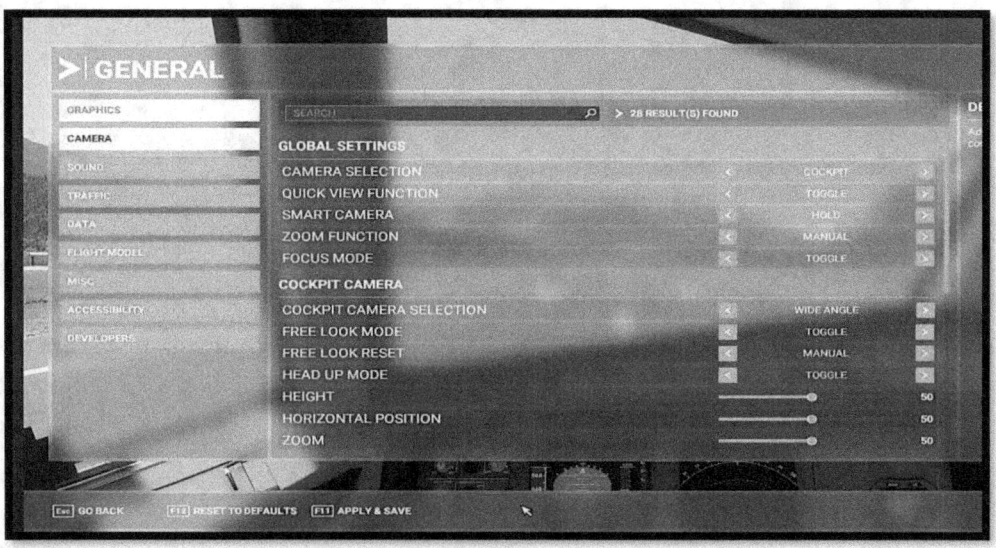

Instrument views

Next, we'll take a look at instrument views. Instrument views are essentially views on various parts of your instruments. Depending on the aircraft you're flying some of them will not be implemented on the airbus. We've got about seven instrument views and to access them you press Ctrl 1, 2, 3, 4, 5, 6, 7. Ctrl 8 goes to the overhead, and Ctrl 9 brings you back here and 0 brings you back here so 9 and 0 are not implemented but for example, on the Dreamliner, CTRL 9 has two overhead views.

Also, when you press one of the instrument views, say Ctrl 2, you can then press the A key to cycle through the instrument views in order or SHIFT + A to go back in order. The instrument views can all be mapped to various buttons on your devices.

Cockpit camera controls

How do you move the camera around inside of the cockpit? Let's look at the keyboard mappings for that, however, before we do that there's one thing that we suggest that you do and that is to press Escape, go to Controls then click on your keyboard which should be on the default mapping. Choose "All" so we can see all the mappings camera, and cockpit camera, and scroll down until you see the options here that say Translate Cockpit View Forward and Backward.

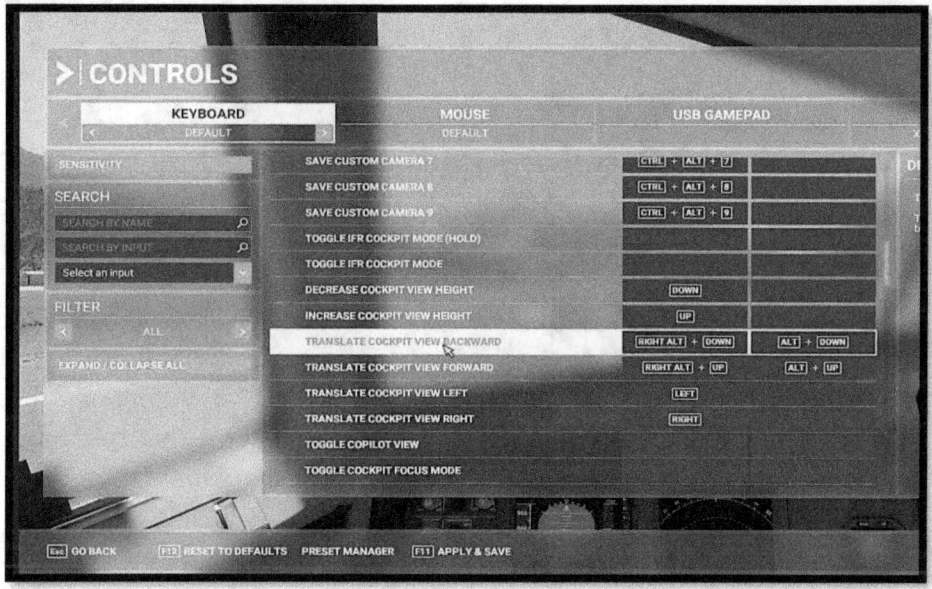

The first column will go forward and backward and the second column translates forward and backward in a 45-degree vertical slope which is very odd. Also, the right Alt key is being used by default in mappings and we strongly urge you not to use the right Alt key because in different countries, different keyboards windows will interpret the right Alt key differently, sometimes it's all graph and sometimes there's a left control Alt. It all behaved very strangely and we strongly suggest that you get rid of it. So what we'll do is click on it, and click Clear, it'll then ask us to make a new keyboard profile which we'll do and what we'll do next is move these over to the Alt sections so we'll click on that and then replace it with Alt + Down and Alt + Up then clear those two. Now you should have Left Alt + Down and Up. Do not use the right

Alt key. We strongly urge you not to do that. Click Apply now and when you go back you should be able to use the left Alt + Up to go forwards and backward with the arrow keys.

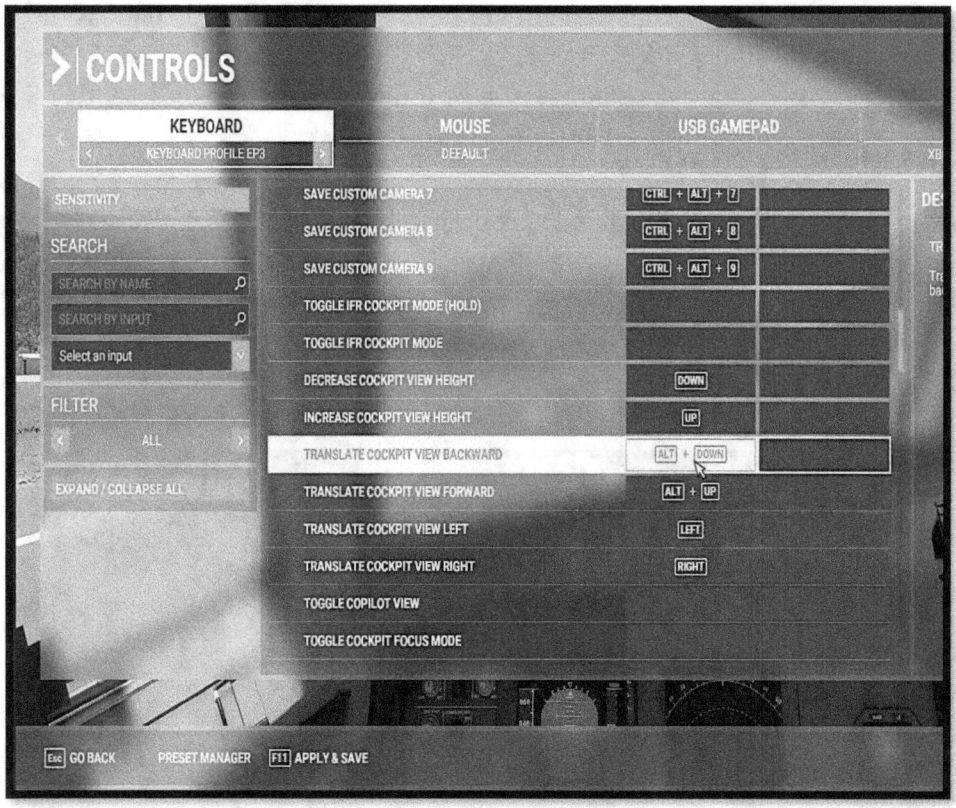

Additionally, we can hold the Alt key and go left and right, which gives us forwards, backward, left, and right. If we then hold the SHIFT key we can go up and down on our rotation and right and left so the only thing now is the vertical up and down and this is simply done by using the arrow keys to go up and down. Left and right also work on the default arrow keys so now we've got the default arrow keys, the ALT arrow keys, and the SHIFT arrow keys.

Custom views

What that means is that we can position the camera pretty much anywhere we want, for example, we could look to the right, hold the ALT key, move forward, hold the SHIFT key, and move down. Then if we wanted to, we could bring the mouse wheel out and just zoom in, and now we could save that as a custom camera view.

One thing we've noticed while playing this Sim is that when you're coming in on approach or when you're texting or when you're just sitting in the cockpit on cruise, you often want to have slightly different camera views. Now Microsoft Flight Simulator does help you in this regard a little bit. For example, if you press the space key it gives you what's called an elevated position which can be useful particularly if your nose is high and you're looking down at the landing and you can't quite see what's going on. You can just quickly press the space key. There's also something called IFR mode that you can toggle which is not mapped by default but you can map a button or a key to it and that will give you the kind of view which is focusing on the instruments and is slightly more zoomed in, however, you can't beat a custom view.

To create a custom view (we have 10 of them in total), you program them by pressing CTRL+ALT and then the numbers from 1 to 0. You access them by pressing ALT on its own from 1 to 0.

Let's say you're slightly forward up but you want to be able to read all the instruments. Now you'll press CTRL+ALT and then pick a number, let's say 1 for this so we have CTRL+ALT+1. You'll program that in and then press the CTRL space key to just go back to your default position. When we press ALT+1, we get that action. You could put that on one of your peripherals, on a button or if you have a stream deck you could just punch in ALT+1 in the stream deck and call it main view or landing view. That's one of the custom cameras.

Let's say we want to create another one. For example, you want something that looks down at the FMC but you're the kind of person that would much prefer it to be up here like a captain's view so you might want to just scroll around, probably move forward a touch, and then just scroll down and zoom in. We'll put that into number two, for this example. Now we'll do CTRL+ALT+2 then go back to our main view. When we press ALT+2 we get that.

So why have custom views and normal instrument views?

Instrument views which are accessible with controls 1, 2, 3, and 4, are automatically programmed for you in every aircraft that you fly whereas custom views are things that you will have to do yourself. You can't take these custom views that you've just done here and apply them to your Cessna 172. You have your Instrument views pre-programmed but you won't have any custom views pre-programmed; custom views give you all the versatility that you need inside the cockpit, however, it doesn't feel like we can have custom views externally at the moment as these only seem to apply to cockpit cameras but they're very useful.

Now what we suggest you do is set up your cameras so that you've got a good view like a nice default view. You can just roll with the default view or set yourself up with a standard flying position. Make sure you've got some programmed for your instruments so you can quickly access all your instrumentation then take your favorite ones and just map them onto your peripherals.

Before we go on to talk about the external camera and the drone camera and how to use them, let's have a quick look at two things: the camera settings and the camera hotbar.

Camera settings

To access the camera settings first press Escape, go to General, and click on Camera. A lot of the options that are defaulted for cameras can be found in this Camera section.

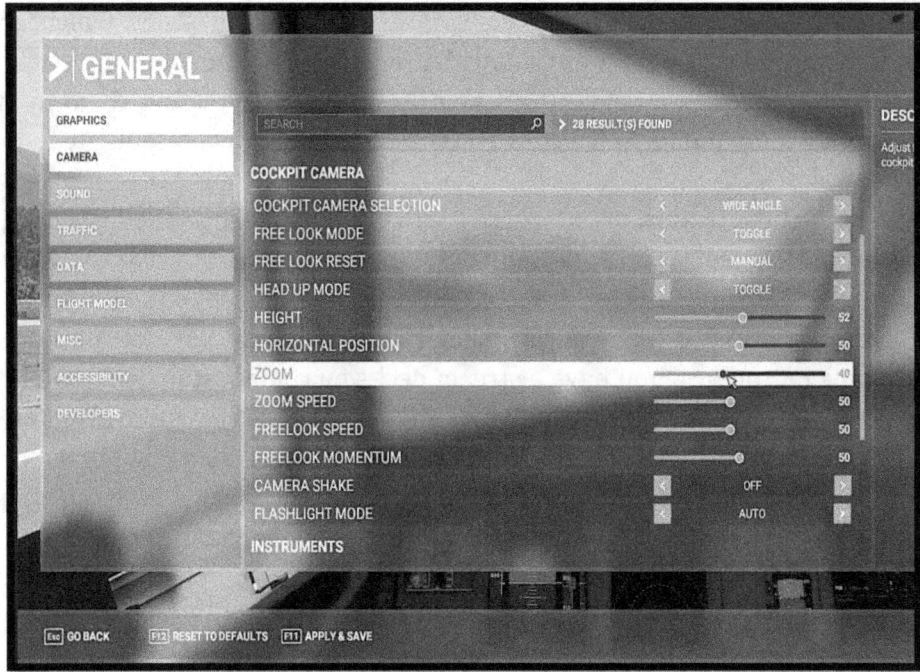

For example, if we scroll down and look at the cockpit camera we've got the zoom which is the current zoom. You can change the zoom for the default camera or you could change the horizontal position but we wouldn't recommend it and then you can change the default height so if you think that the default camera is a bit low just come here and tweak it. When you're flying around in some bouncy IFR conditions you might find that their camera headshake is a bit too much; you can turn it off here. The flashlight mode is for if you spawn in the cockpits and it's dark outside you'll have a little flashlight automatically turned on but you can turn that off here.

There are some things like the instruments and that's for whether you want the instrument cameras to be toggleable or you have to hold them and there are various options around the Chase Camera. Just go through them and tweak them however you feel is comfortable for you.

Camera Toolbar

If you move your mouse to the top you get a little icon called the Hotbar or the toolbar and there is an option here for camera. One thing to note is that by default it seems to spawn in with this. What's going on here is this box is expandable so make sure you expand it otherwise you're going to miss out on a whole bunch of options.

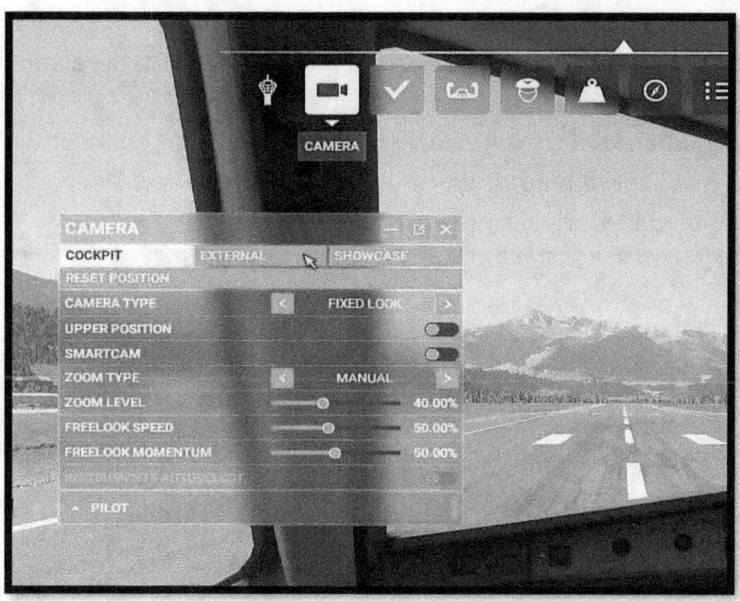

The camera is split into Cockpits, External, And Showcase. The showcase is basically the drone camera but here you can adjust some of the settings that we just saw back there you've also got the presets such as the instrument presets that we took you through (Ctrl 1, 2, 3, 4), they're all in here but now you know how to do them with hotkeys or you can map them to your peripherals.

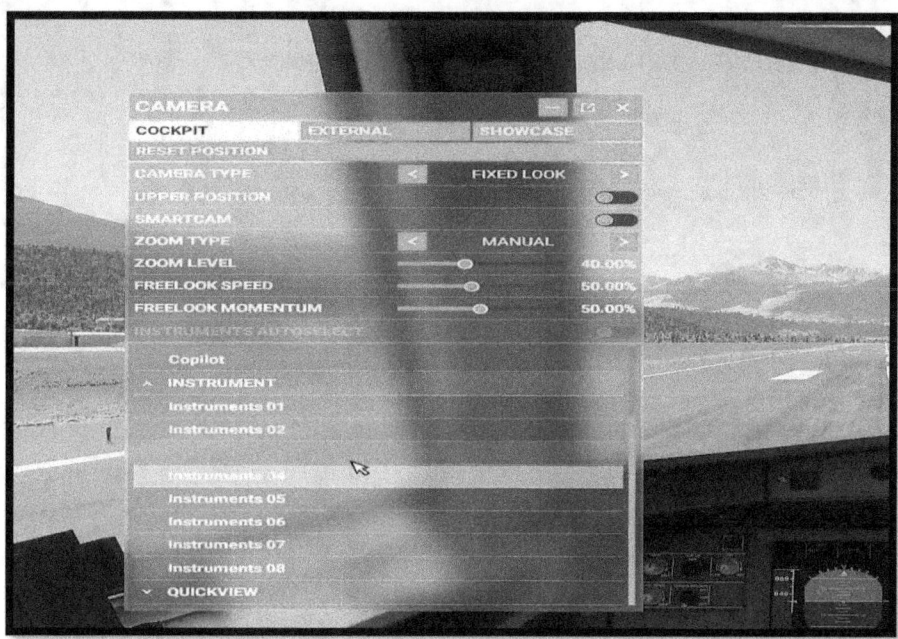

You've got the standard pilot view, the close pilot view, the landing, and the copilot view. You can click through them here if you want to. Also, if you get stuck and your camera's pointing at the ground and you've no idea what's going on just come up to here and use this to reset the position and get yourself back into the cockpit.

There are a bunch of quick views that we've taken you through, some of which are mapped on the control key but these tend to work better as you can see. They're not useful in the Airbus but they do tend to work better in the GA aircraft.

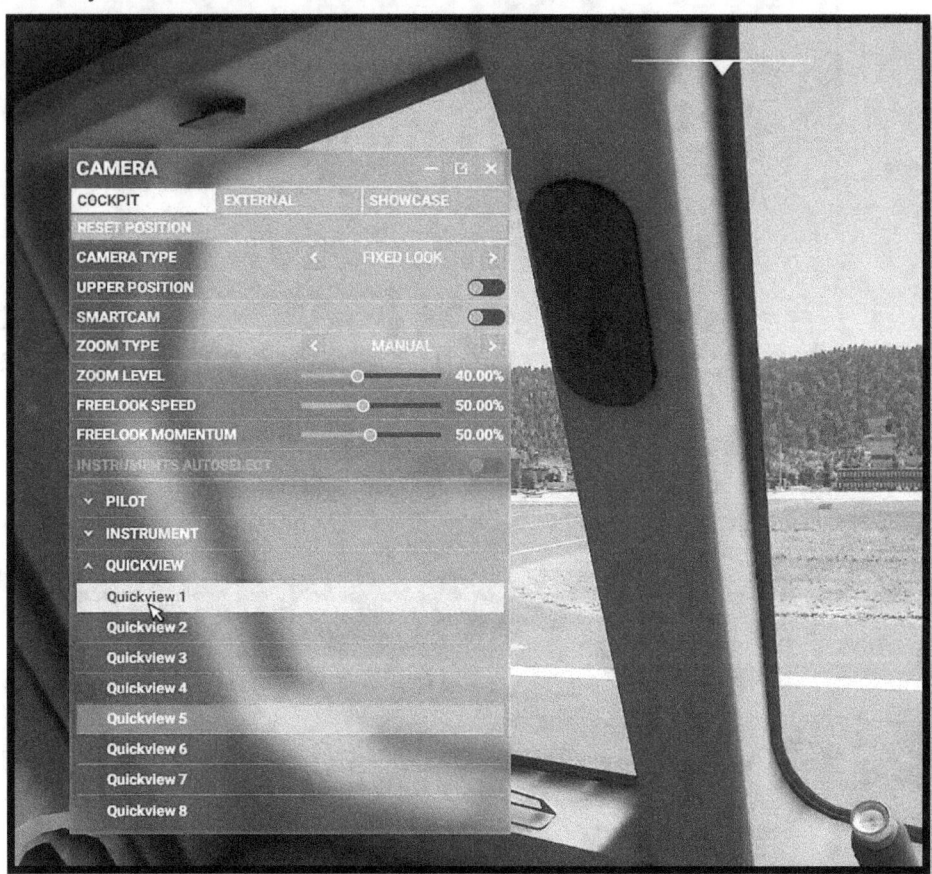

The External camera

You can access the external camera by simply pressing the End key or you can come up into the hotbar and just click on External. The external camera is interesting for a number of reasons: You've got full access to the controls while you're in the external camera. You can see where you're going, and what speed you're doing so you can fly around in this camera.

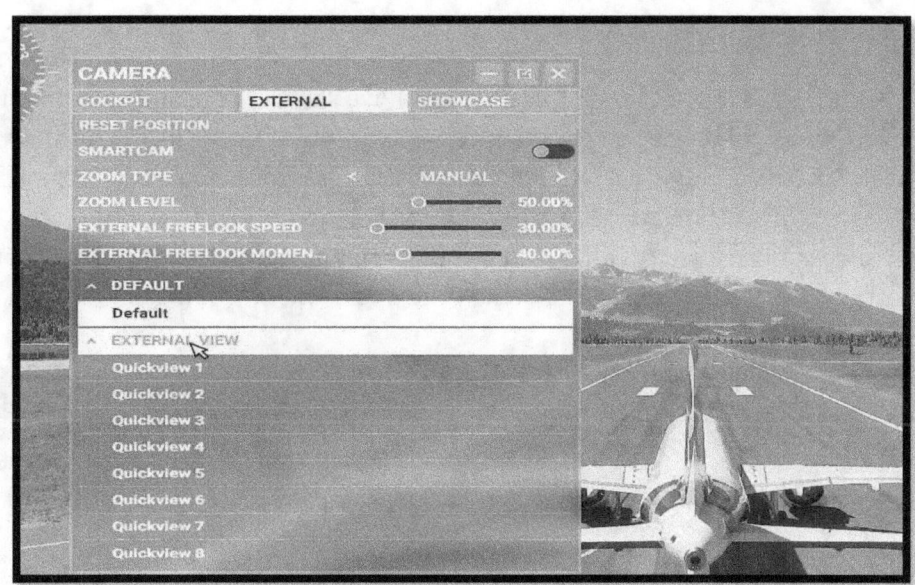

There are a number of external views that are available and these are called quickviews; four of these are maps and four of them are not. You can go into the settings and map them but Quickview 1 will give you a view to the right of the aircraft, Quickview 2 from the front, 3 from the left and 4 over the top, 5, 6, 7, and 8 to 45 degree angle mappings which are not mapped by default. For example, if we want to do a quick view we can press CTRL, and then left, right, up, and down on the arrow keys will access the quickviews.

Accessing and customizing the fixed cameras

What is interesting though is that here there are no fixed cameras but there are cameras and they're mapped by defaults in the key bindings but they're not available here. The fixed cameras are accessed by CTRL+SHIFT and then 1, 2, 3, 5, 5, 6, 7, 8, 9, 0, and that's how you access the fixed cameras. Press them again and it'll go back to the standard external view.

Now the most obvious questions leading on from that are can you customize the fixed cameras? If we go to one of these cameras here, can we move the camera, zoom the camera, or change it in any way? Unfortunately, you can't adjust the fixed cameras in any way.

The next question you may ask yourself is can I go from being in the cockpit to the gear view? The answer is yes, you can but not in the way you might think because what you have to do is if you're in the cockpit and you press CTRL+SHIFT+4, what that does is give you the instrumentation views. What you need to do is press the End key then CTRL+SHIFT+4. You need to change camera mode to external and then use the keys for that so it's not quite a chase plane or anything like that where you can be in the cockpit and then immediately switch to an external camera view.

The Showcase Camera

This neatly brings us to the Showcase Camera which we said is the drone camera. Under the showcase, you have a whole bunch of external cameras which we've just been through, and then if you click on the drone you get the drone camera with the drone options. Where things get interesting is that you do have a bunch of options here to do with the drone focus that you can adjust. You can make it so that the drone is focused on a particular thing, you can adjust the depth of field, you can make it focus on just the plane and blur things in the background, just get creative with this.

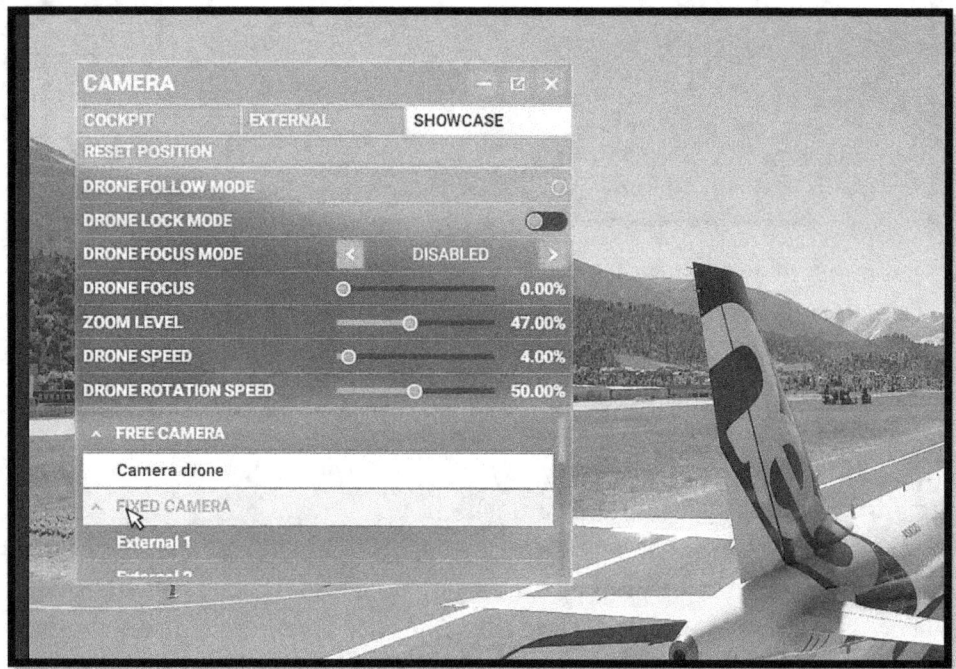

The drone controls are W A so that's A and D, W and S to go forwards or backward so you can translate around. Then you've got R and F to go up and down. On the numeric keypad, assuming you've got one, 4 and 6 will rotate and 8 and 2 will pitch. Between those, if you use both hands you can get it to fly around and when you're flying around you can go to a drone camera when you're on a cruise and get a nice view of things if only you'll remember what keys to press.

There is a better way, of course. You can map keys to your stream deck or to your controls or whatever you want to do but the best option is to plug an Xbox controller in. If you plug an Xbox controller into your Sim, the drone camera becomes fantastic. You can use the two thumb sticks to scroll around, hold the Y key to zoom in and out and you can set the speed of the drone movement as well.

For example, let's say you're flying around and you think this is a bit too quick. You can hold the A key down and adjust the speed to make it a lovely slow pan or even just speed it up a little bit. You can left-click with your thumb stick and it will lock on to the plane itself so no matter which way you move, it will always be pointing at the plane. There are so many cool things that you can do when you plug an Xbox controller in for the drone cam, we strongly recommend you buy one if you want to use the drone cam because it is completely game-changing and easy.

How far can the drone camera fly? Let's say it's currently in Follow Mode. If you right-click with your thumb it will disengage from Follow Mode; the aircraft can fly away from the drone by default and the drone will follow with it but if you increase the speed at which you fly and you just keep the speed going you can fly quite a long way.

There is a reset option that will bring the drone cam back. If you look in the settings, you can either map something to that or change something like that but we strongly recommend you have a reset because you can get quite lost with the drone. It's fantastic fun and if you love making videos you're going to love that camera.

We've covered a lot in this section but then just try to remember that it has camera modes, it has Cockpit mode, it has External mode and it has Showcase/Drone mode. Also, you have to move between the modes before you try to move any of the cameras.

Finally, to answer one question, does it support track IR? Yes. If you're lucky enough to have track IR. You can use head tracking and here you're just moving your head around, up and down, left and right and you can just pause it if you have a pause on your tracker, and then the camera will disengage and snap back to the center. It's good to have track IR, particularly for GA flying because to look around the cockpit is fantastic.

Review Questions

1. Explain the different types of camera views available in Microsoft Flight Simulator 2024 and how they can be used to enhance the pilot's situational awareness.
2. Describe the process of customizing the camera settings, including the ability to create and save custom camera views.
3. How does the external camera and the showcase camera feature in Microsoft Flight Simulator 2024 allow users to capture and share their flying experiences?

CHAPTER 7

HOW AN AIRLINER COCKPIT WORKS

In this chapter, we are going to show you how the cockpit or flight deck of a jet airliner works. The flight deck implies a bigger space with room to move or walk around, as opposed to a cockpit with just enough space for seats that pilots might climb into.

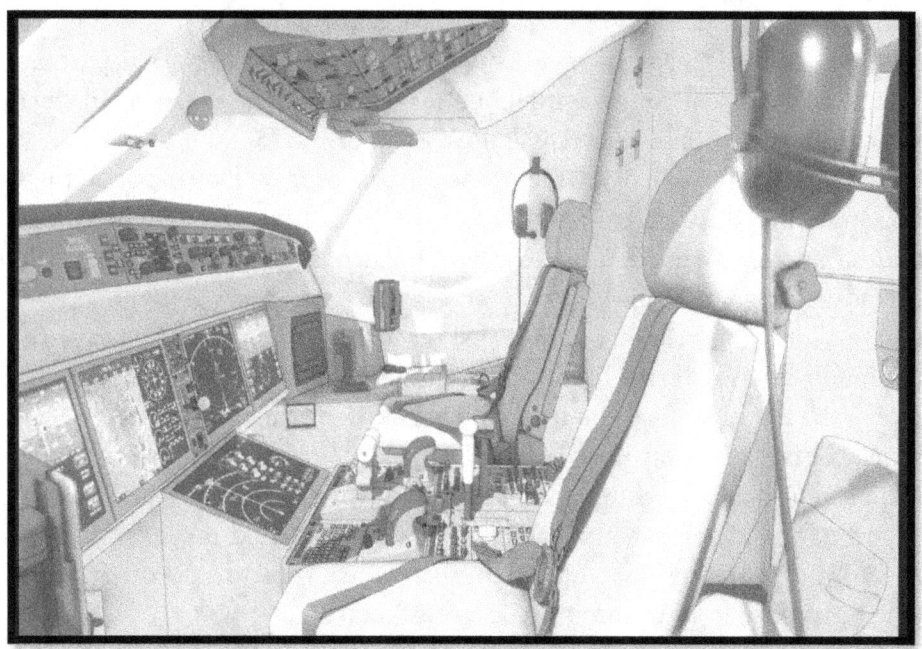

Starting at the back wall of the flight deck, there are hat clips and the pilots' wardrobe closet. On the other side, there's a jump seat that slides and folds out. There's a crash ax nearby, as well as a flashlight, oxygen cylinder, and portable breathing equipment. Detailed circuit breaker panels are situated near the back wall on both sides.

Seating arrangements

The pilot and copilot seats move back and to the side for entry. They have a five-point harness, and ample adjustments for proper access to flight controls, as well as comfort. There are heated foot mats on the floor. Eye-level locators between front windshields indicate proper seat position, ensuring optimal visibility for all flight deck operations.

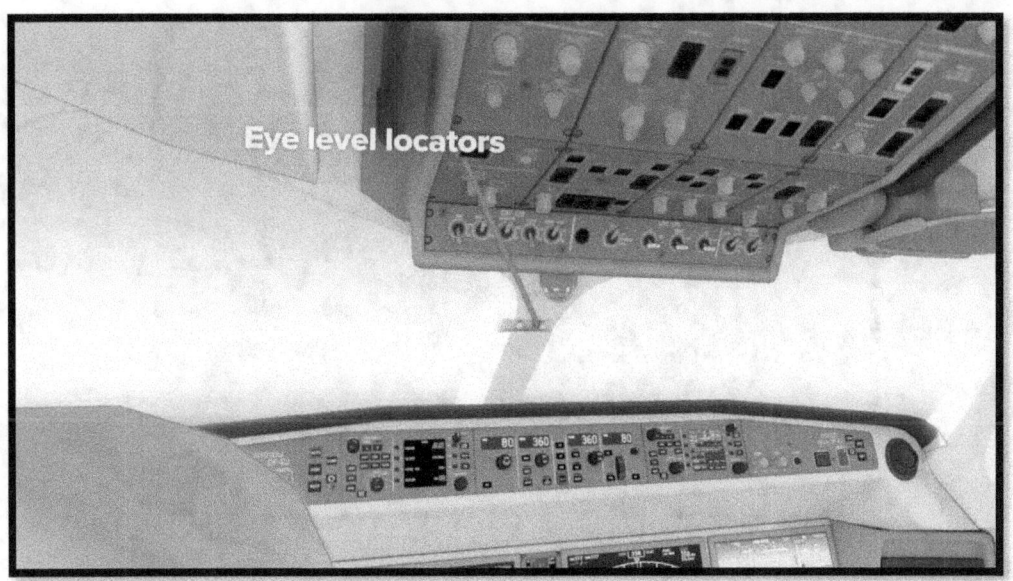

Eye level locators

The ideal position is reached when the white sphere is completely hidden by the front red sphere, as viewed by the person adjusting the seat. The armrest on the outside of each seat has tilt and vertical adjustment knobs for unobstructed arm mobility when using the sidestick or tiller.

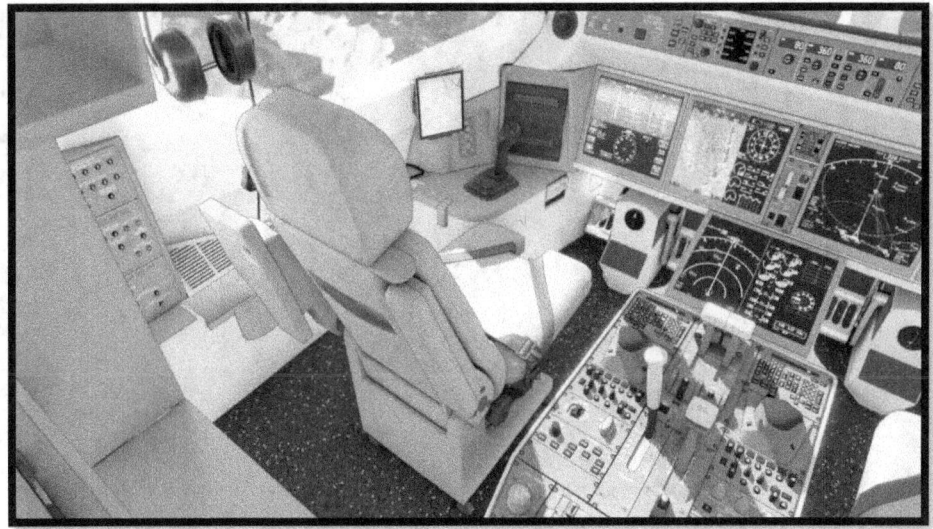

There's a small step near the inside shoulder of each seat back for access to an overhead escape hatch. A compartment holds an emergency rope that the flight deck crew can use to slide down the side of the plane.

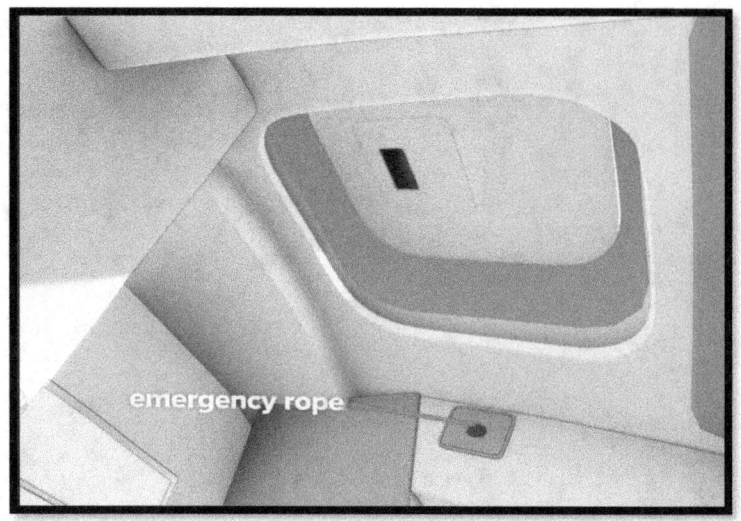

Sidetick

A sidetick controller on each side gives the pilot or copilot control over the roll and pitch of the aircraft. An autopilot/priority switch disconnects autopilot if it's engaged. With autopilot off, holding the button gives this sidestick priority.

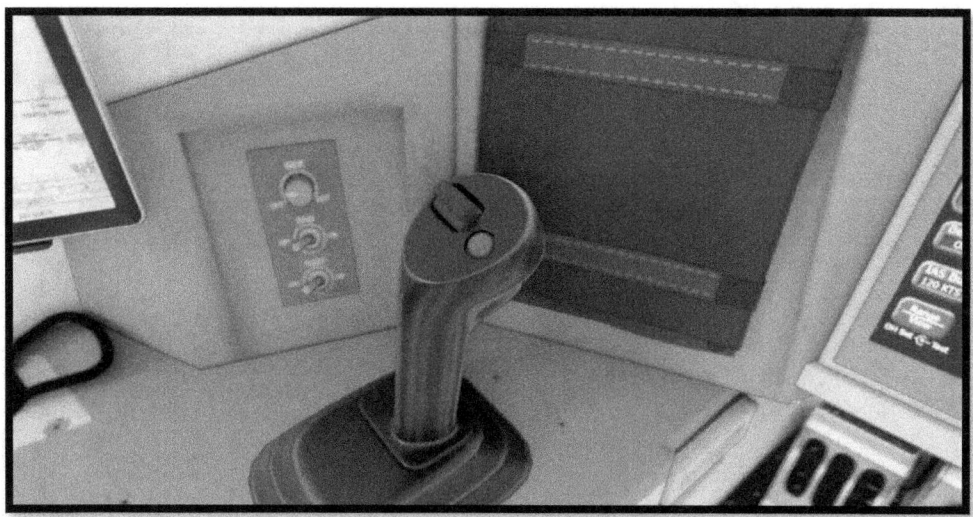

A pitch trim switch can set the auto-trim rate for the horizontal stabilizer, or allow manual trim adjustment in direct mode. There's a switch at the front of the stick for radio or intercom communication.

Steering

While taxiing under 30 knots, a steering tiller can be used to turn the nose landing gear up to 80 degrees in either direction. To avoid damage to the nose landing gear, rotation is limited from 80 degrees down to 9 degrees max as speed increases from 30 to 100 knots and above.

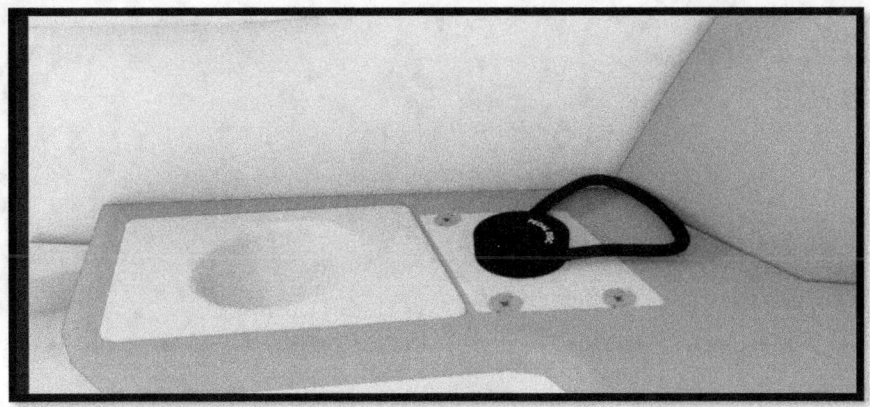

Rudder pedals can be used at any time to rotate the nose landing gear, but are limited to a maximum of 9 degrees. In the past, the flight bag at each seating position held airplane-specific operation manuals, navigation charts, checklists, and so on. Electronic tablet devices have replaced most of these items in recent years. Some airplanes may also have a head-up display, allowing the pilot or copilot to view relevant, real-time information like runway alignment, airspeed, altitude, and more.

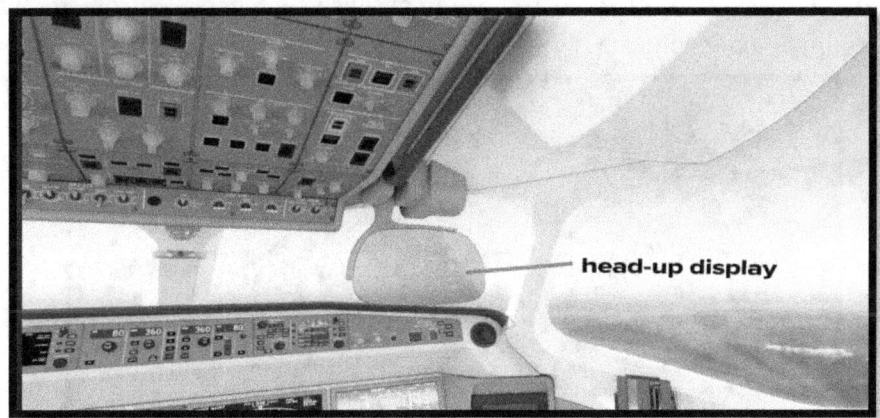

head-up display

Rudder pedals

With feet in the lower position, rudder pedals move forward and back for rudder control. Moving feet to the upper position allows the pedals to rotate, engaging the left and right main landing gear brakes.

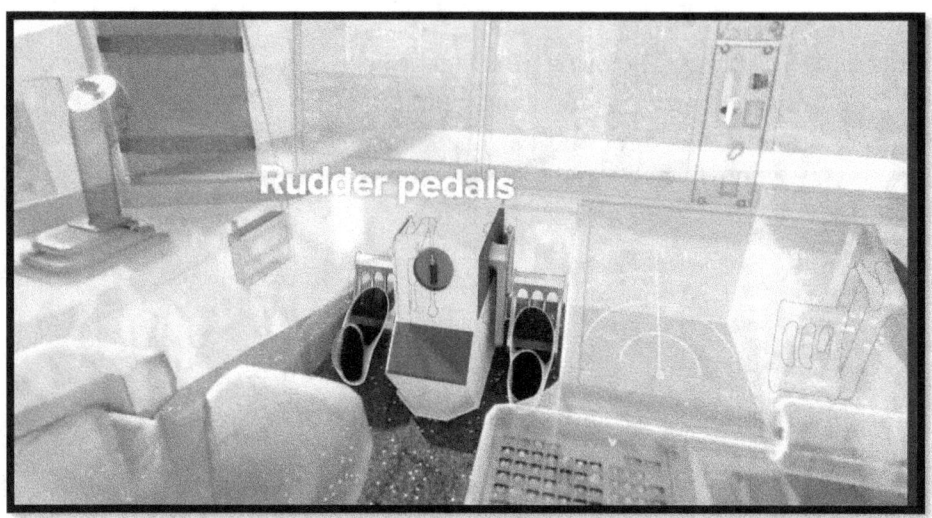

A mechanical linkage ensures the pedals on both sides move together. Pilots can adjust the pedal position with a knob at the front.

Control panels

Now, let's have a look at the control panels, starting with the overhead panel. Many of the switches in these panels have lights that convey important info, something like the warning lights in a car's dashboard. However, unlike simple car warning lights, when pilots interact with these switches, their lighting status can be updated. A fire module sits in the center. The switches glow red when a fire is detected. Some of these switches are protected with doors that must be flipped open for access.

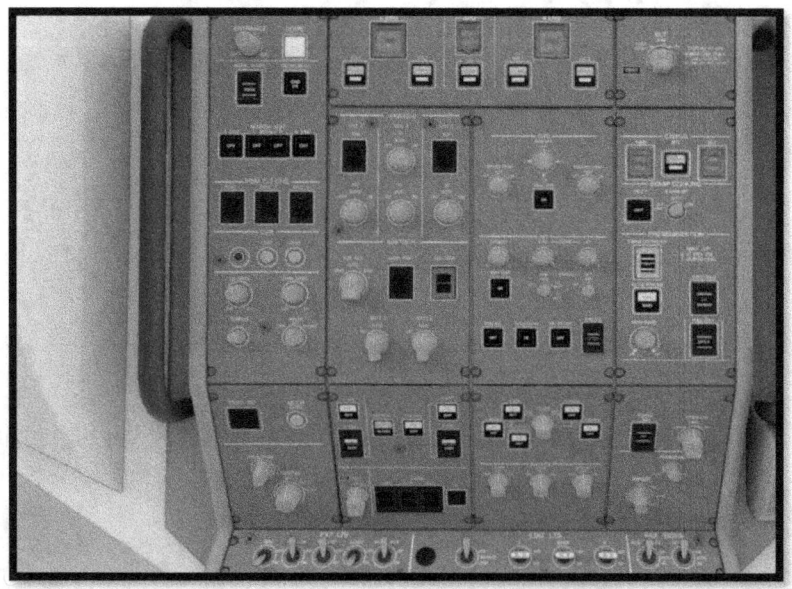

Pressing a fire switch helps mitigate fire spread and damage by shutting off fuel to the respective engine, and arming fire extinguisher bottles, among other things. Once armed, nearby switches discharge specific fire-extinguishing bottles when pressed.

Let's move to the left-outboard module. Starting at the back, the entrance knob and DOM switch control flight deck lighting.

The protected AURAL WARN switch allows the audible warning system to be silenced if there's an issue with the aural system. This system handles the many warning sounds and phrases that alert pilots to critical events.

WINDOW HEAT and PROBE HEAT toggle de-icing functionality for windows and external temperature measuring devices or probes.

PRIMARY FLIGHT CONTROL computers can be individually disabled using any of the three protected switches here.

The CVR section handles the cockpit voice recorder, which records not only sounds inside the flight deck but also all connected audio channels both internal and external.

The next panel section has knobs to control lighting brightness for circuit breaker panels, overhead panels, the compass, and more. Turning this knob to the "STORM" setting illuminates the complete flight deck, all panels, and DIM lights to maximum intensity.

The next panel controls communication during plane servicing. With the SERVICE INTERCOM switch on, all flight deck and service intercom channels are opened. The call button sounds like a horn in the external service panel area. At the end of this module, there are the captain's side reading light and windshield wiper controls.

The Hydraulic Section

Now, let's move to the left inboard module. The HYDRAULIC section has controls for various hydraulic system scenarios since there are three separate hydraulic systems in the plane for safety and redundancy. This panel allows various configurations so these systems can work as normal, or supplement each other in varying conditions.

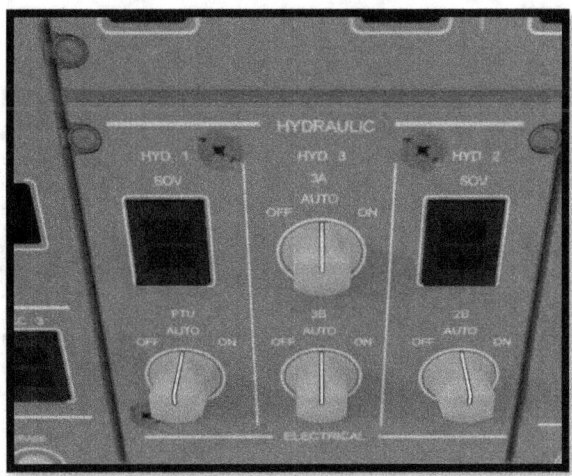

The Electrical Section

The Electrical section has a knob for various electrical system scenarios. For example, the ESS setting powers only essential systems. The guarded switch next to this knob turns off power to select CABIN systems, which can be useful for isolating sources of smoke in the cabin, whether from electrical arcing or some other source.

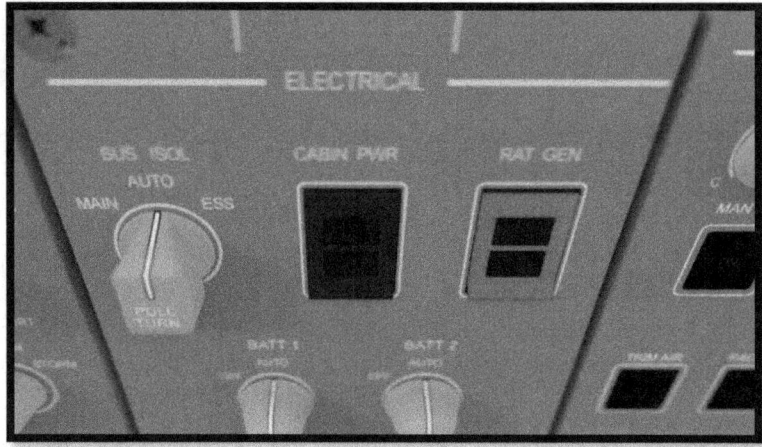

The guarded RAT switch allows the flight crew to manually deploy the Ram Air Turbine or RAT. Under normal conditions, the RAT will deploy automatically if power is lost in flight.

Battery knobs control onboard battery packs one and two. The L and R GEN switches toggle engine-driven electrical power generators. Each has a protected DISCONNECT switch to disconnect the generator shaft from the engine, if, for example, leaving a malfunctioning generator connected could lead to engine damage.

The APU switch can disconnect the auxiliary power unit from the system in case of an electrical fault. The EXT switch allows the crew to toggle the external power connection. The APU pull-turn switch functions something like a car ignition. The START setting is held for 3 seconds to start the APU. Once started, the switch reverts to the RUN position. The APU FAIL light illuminates for any electrical, fire, or starting issues.

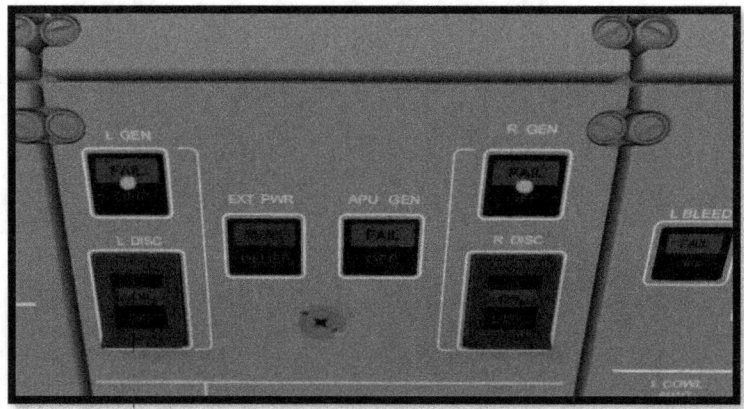

The Terrain Awareness and Warning System, TAWS, has protected switches to turn off aural warnings associated with landing gear, terrain detection, and flaps. The GS switch turns off aural warnings related to Glideslope which is the pre-calculated path of descent in the flight control system.

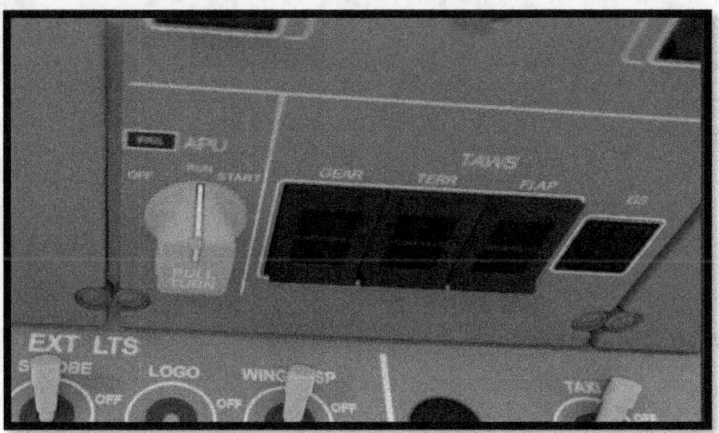

The Fuel Sub-section

Moving to the right inboard module, we see the FUEL sub-section. With the MANUAL TRANSFER switch in "OFF" mode, the fuel system functions as normal. The other settings allow the flight crew to select specific fuel tank configurations. Left and Right boost pump switches control supplemental, electrically powered fuel pumps, where the system under normal operation relies on engine-driven pumps as the primary source of fuel pressure.

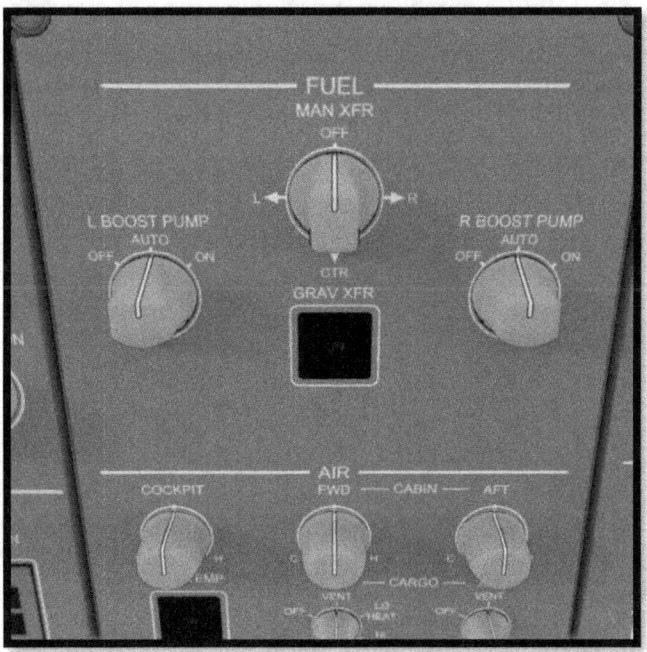

The GRAVITY TRANSFER switch opens valves so that fuel can move between tanks by gravity alone. The AIR section has climate controls at the top, and also ventilation settings for cargo compartments.

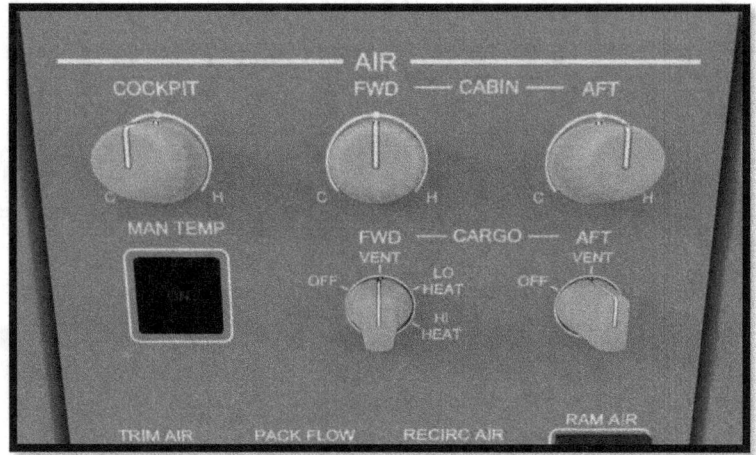

The TRIM AIR switch toggles valves that allow air from the engine bleed air system into the climate control system.

When the PACK FLOW switch is active, the air conditioning units or packs enter high flow mode, which can be useful for clearing smoke or odors. There's a switch for recirculating air fans.

The guarded RAM AIR switch can open external ports at low altitudes for flight deck or cabin ventilation. Left and Right PACK switches grant manual control over air conditioning packs, which otherwise operate automatically based on desired climate control settings. CROSSBLEED, LEFT, and RIGHT BLEED switches grant manual control for engine bleed air valves, and APU bleed air.

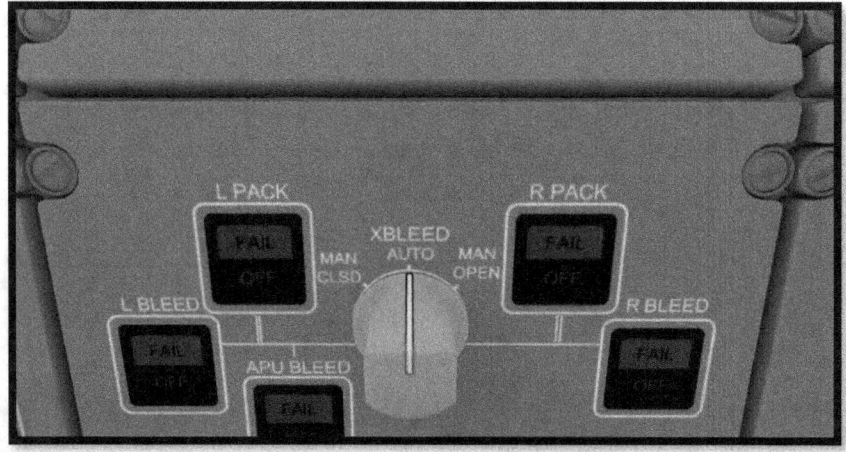

The ANTI-ICE section controls de-icing capabilities in the left and right engine cowling and wings.

Emergency section

The ELT or Emergency Locator Transmitter pull-turn knob can test and arm the ELT.

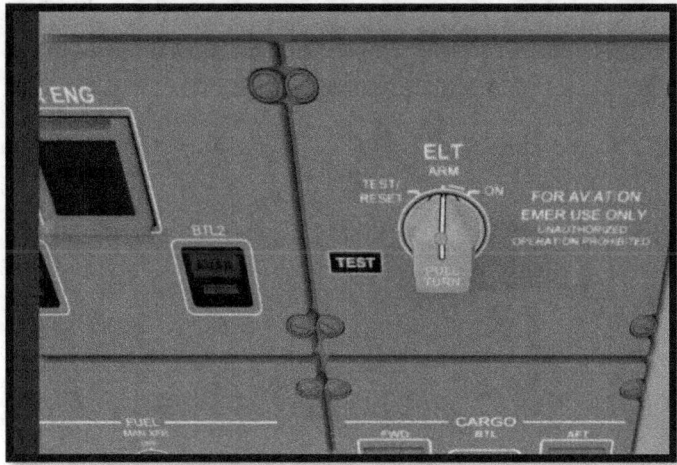

The CARGO section handles fire reporting and deploying fire extinguishing bottles in the cargo areas.

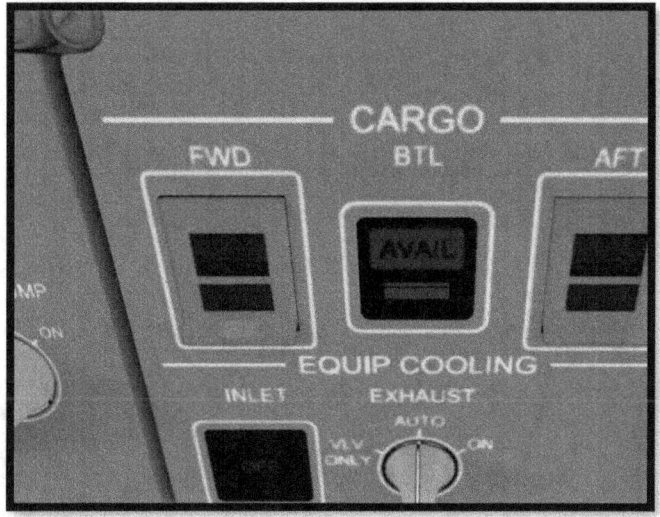

EQUIPMENT COOLING refers to cooling systems for equipment bays. The INLET switch controls cooling fans and an external valve to take in outside air. There's also a switch for exhaust air produced by the equipment cooling system.

The Pressurization Section

In the PRESSURIZATION section, there's a guarded switch for emergency depressurization of passenger and flight crew areas. The AUTO PRESS switch allows manual pressurization control, which is usually an automated process. In manual mode, the dial beneath sets the pressurization rate.

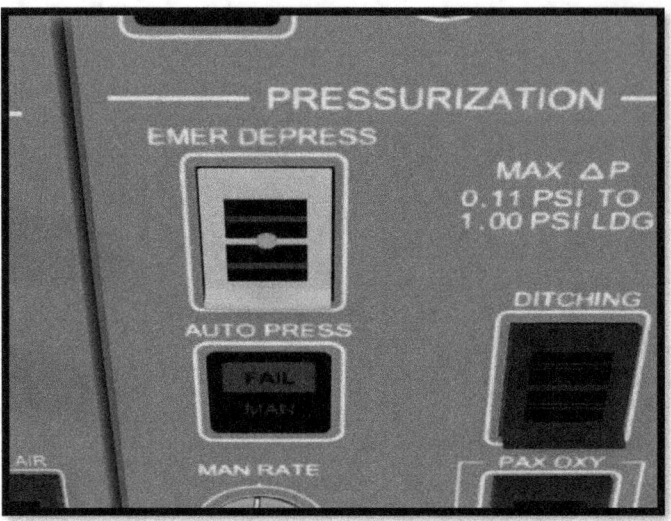

The guarded DITCHING switch activates a ditching sequence. Ditching is a controlled emergency water landing in an aircraft not designed for such. The ditching sequence closes all valves below the aircraft flotation line, except for the RAM AIR valve.

The PAX OXY switch deploys passenger oxygen masks. At the end of this section, there's a switch to toggle the EVACUATION HORN and a pull-turn switch for EVACUATION LIGHTING. Beyond that, we see the Copilot side windshield wiper and reading light switches.

Lights section

Starting from the pilot's side, there are External Lighting Control Switches (LTS) for NAVIGATION, BEACON, STROBE, and LOGO lights. The Landing Lights section has a Taxi lights switch, and special switches with triple LED indicators for LEFT, RIGHT, and NOSE landing gear lights.

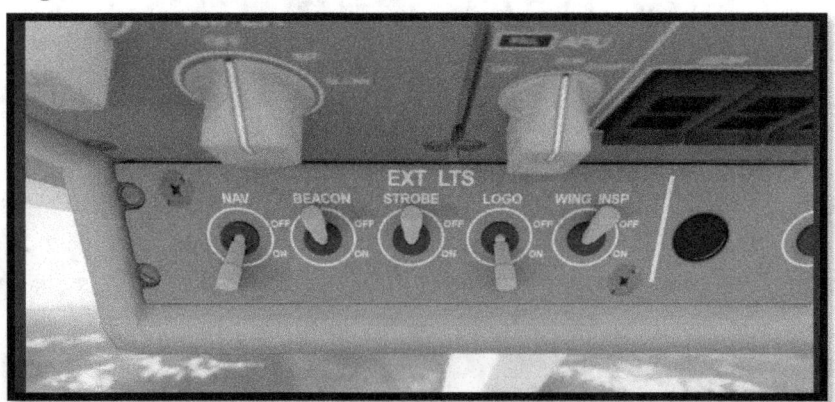

73

A pair of switches in the PAX LIGHTS section control the seat belt and no personal electronic devices warning signs in the passenger cabin.

Glare shield

The glare shield control layout is mostly symmetrical from side to side. Starting at the captain's side, the two leftmost dials control brightness for main displays 1 and 2 beneath. The CHRONO button controls a basic stopwatch-type function, which can be displayed on the primary flight display.

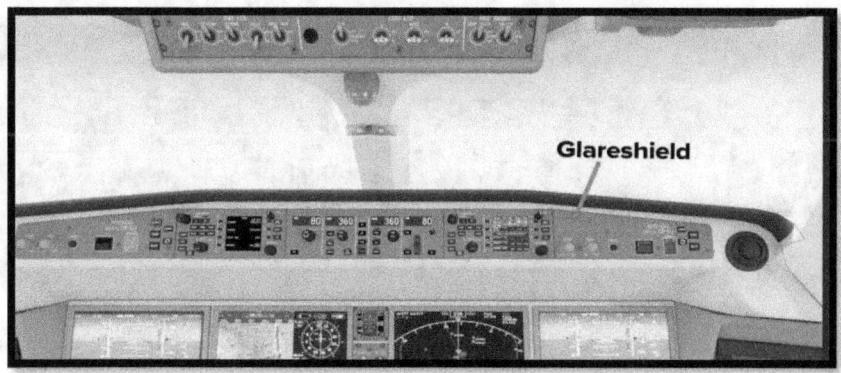

The WARNING/CAUTION master switch shows a red warning or yellow caution alert if either is triggered. The switch must be pressed to acknowledge the alert and re-arm the system for any further alerts. Pressing the SIDESTICK button gives priority to the pilot's sidestick, and deactivates autopilot. An oral "PRIORITY LEFT or PRIORITY RIGHT" message sounds.

The next cluster of buttons is a non-verbal system to supplement pilots' communication with Air Traffic Control. There are options to ACCEPT, STANDBY, REJECT, or LOAD pre-programmed messages into the Flight Management System which can then be quickly accessed in communicating with Air Traffic Control.

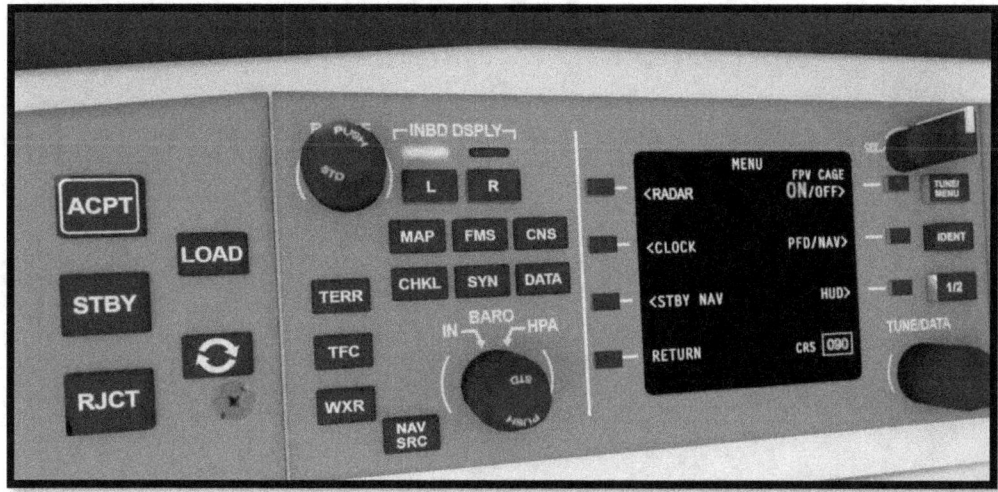

Radio and Control tuning section

The Radio and Control tuning section has knobs and buttons to quickly change displays for relevant info, and a radio panel with many related functions. The L and R buttons correspond to the left and right sides of the main display number two beneath.

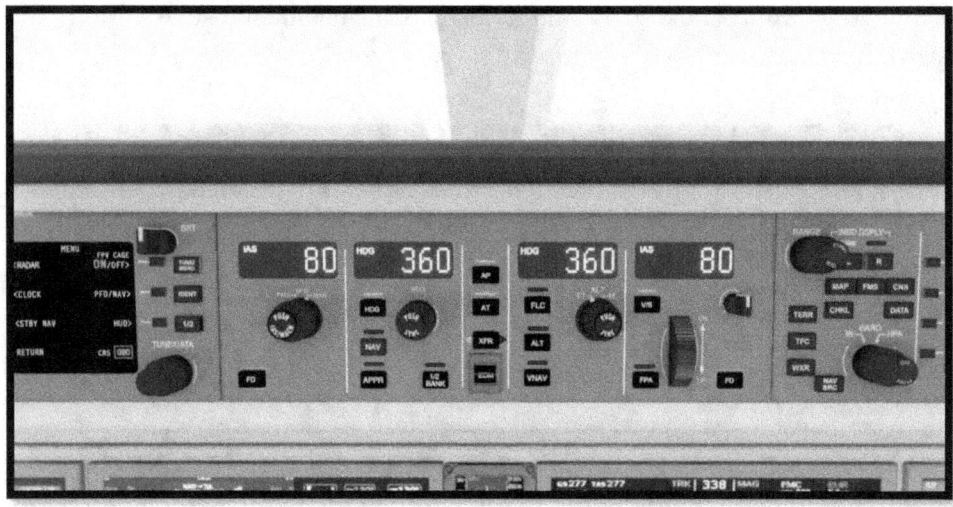

The MAP button displays the last selected map type, of which there are various options. An adjacent knob adjusts the map range.

The FMS button displays Flight Management System details, like position, Flight Plan, performance, route, and more.

The CNS button opens screens related to communication, navigation, and surveillance capabilities afforded by the many special antennas and systems on the craft.

CHKL opens the electronic checklist. SYN opens synoptic pages, which are simplified real-time diagrams of critical systems, showing, for example, the status of the hydraulic or fuel system and major components at a glance.

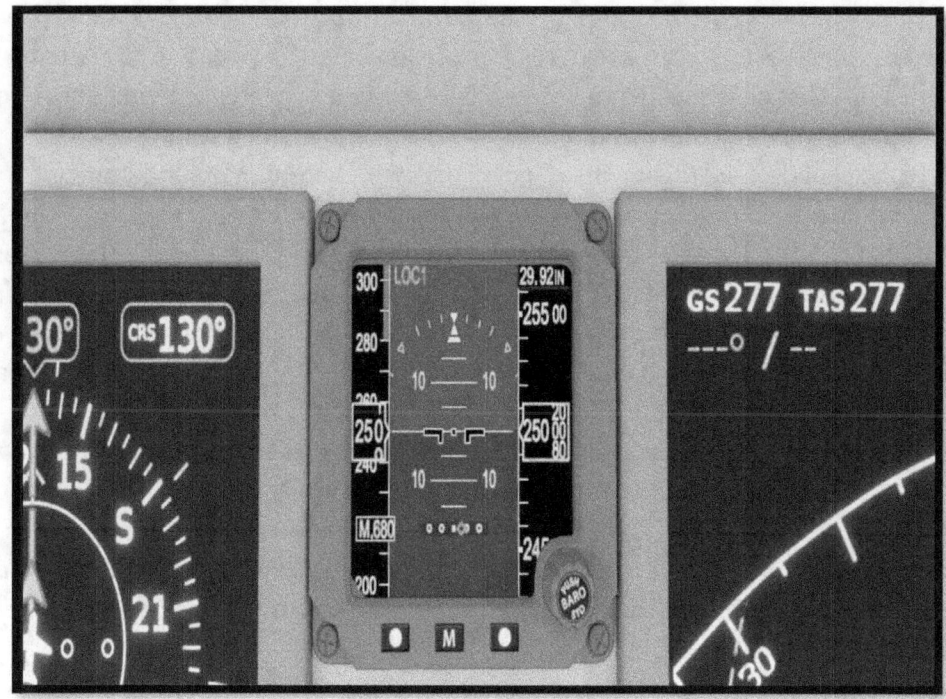

DATA displays the last selected data page, which can be items like important documents or aeronautical charts. Terrain, Traffic Alerts, and Weather switches bring up overlays corresponding to those systems. The BARO switch changes how barometric pressure is displayed.

The small screen has surrounding buttons for quick access to features that affect how items are displayed on primary screens below, including weather radar, navigation details, and so on. The TUNE/MENU button and dial are also for navigating settings and menus on this screen. IDENT broadcasts aircraft identification to air traffic control for 18 seconds.

Flight Control Panel

The Flight Control Panel sits at the center of the glare shield and is used to input and monitor flight data in the Automatic Flight Control system. The FD switch displays pitch and roll commands from the Flight Guidance system on the primary displays.

The SPD switch selects between various ways of measuring airspeed, and how that info appears on nearby flight control displays.

The HDG button displays the heading on the flight control display. The dial tunes to the desired heading, which is an angular measurement from North at 0 degrees, clockwise to 359 degrees.

NAV selects between various available ways of measuring lateral, or side-to-side movement as the aircraft travels its flight path. The APPROACH button selects between various approach systems, where airplanes and airports have different available equipment setups.

Aircraft can choose to rely on their own data for airport approach or some blended procedure where airports have systems in place to relay precision guide information to the craft. The ½ BANK switch limits bank angle in a turn, especially at higher speeds, to avoid uncomfortable g-forces on passengers and crew, and to mitigate the likelihood of a stall.

Switches in the center of the flight control panel deal with autopilot and related functionality. The AP switch toggles autopilot. The AT switch toggles autothrottle capability. The XFR or transfer switch determines data channels and sensors used for the flight director system. The guarded EDM switch activates emergency descent mode and is not a special guarded switch to play electronic dance music for impromptu sky raves. On the copilot's side, an FLC switch determines how flight level change is maintained. Pilots generally select to maintain horizontal airspeed for climbs, but vertical airspeed for descents.

The ALT inner dial sets the desired altitude, and the outer dial sets measurements in feet or meters. The ALT switch holds the aircraft at its current altitude.

The VNAV, VS, and FPA switches are different modes to auto-calculate pitch commands. VNAV uses data from the flight plan. VS uses the desired vertical speed to generate pitch commands, which the crew can set using the nearby dial. The FPA switch uses a desired flight path angle which can also be set with the dial.

Main instrument panel

Four large, interchangeable screens can be customized to show things like flight parameters, navigation and communications info, approach and weather charts, synoptic pages for critical systems and component status, electronic checklists, maintenance data, and more. A small Integrated Standby Instrument in the center can supply the necessary info to fly on emergency power with no other available displays. It has nearby buttons and a dial for customization.

Landing gear and brakes

The landing gear lever extends or retracts landing gear, and must be pulled out to operate. In the event of a malfunction, the guarded Alternate Gear release switch electrically disengages uplocks so landing gear can naturally free-fall to the down and locked position.

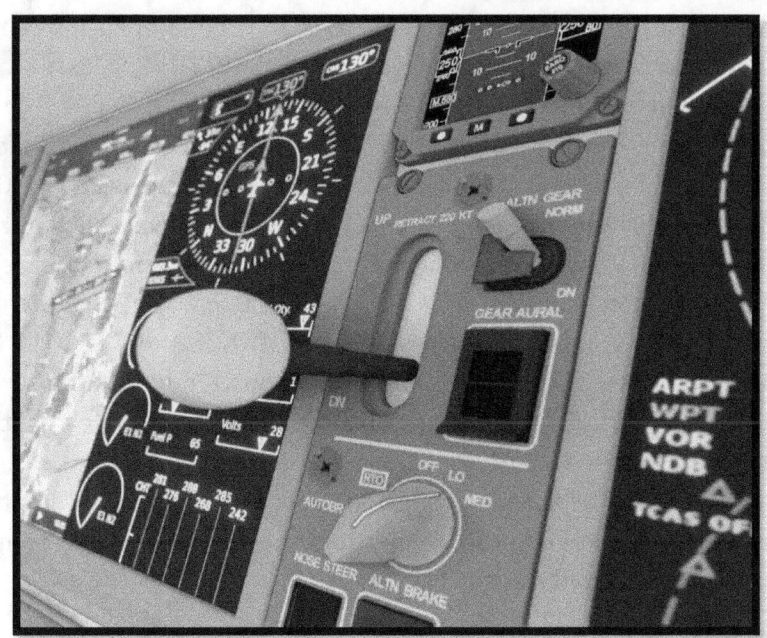

The guarded Gear Aural switch mutes the GEAR aural warning. The AUTOBRAKE switch has settings to maintain a constant deceleration during landing. The RTO setting controls braking for a rejected takeoff scenario, where the plane has to stop on the runway instead of taking off.

The protected ALTERNATE BRAKE switch grants full manual brake control, without automated braking assists. The NOSE STEER switch toggles nose wheel steering capability.

Center pedestal

The center pedestal is situated between both pilot seats and houses various system input devices and controls for throttle and flight control surfaces.

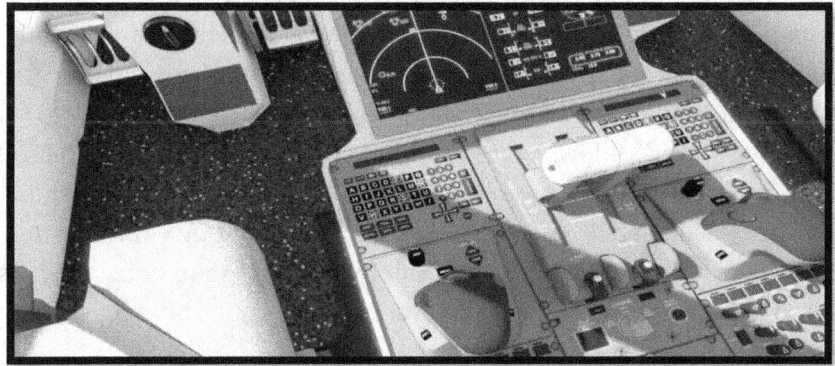

Starting towards the front of the plane, there's a keyboard for interacting with the Flight Management System and display screens. The buttons along the top are connected to the flight management system as well. MSG displays relevant system alerts. ROUTE opens the pre-programmed flight route. The Direct to Dialog button offers a streamlined way of changing or adding waypoints to the flight plan. The DEPARTURE/ARRIVAL button shows the respective flight plan info depending on the phase of the flight.

Beneath the keyboard, there are more buttons for flight system access. MAP shows a map and flight plan overlay. FMS opens flight management system settings. CNS shows a communications and navigation screen. The checklist button shows relevant checklists. SYN brings up synoptic pages. DATA can show charts, videos, docs, and database info. CAS can show or hide messages from the Engine Indicating and Crew Alert System or EICAS. This system monitors many critical engine processes. The CANCEL and EXECUTE buttons in the top right can approve or cancel flight plan modifications. The trackball-style mouse and surrounding buttons and knobs provide robust interaction with the flight management system and display units.

There are buttons to select which display to interact with, a stacked knob for scrolling through lists and settings, and Push to Talk buttons at either side of the palm rest to open communication through selected transmit channels.

Audio Control Panel

The audio control panel handles the many available radio communication channels. Call buttons along the top let the crew select which antenna to use for broadcast. Very High-Frequency antennas are best for "line of sight" communications and can be blocked by buildings or mountains. High-frequency antennas can penetrate some obstacles but are prone to distortion from atmospheric conditions like solar flares, geomagnetic storms, and so on. SATCOM is the satellite communication channel that may be ideal in places with limited VHF and HF equipment. CAB opens communication between pilots and flight attendants in the cabin.

Volume switches pop up to activate respective listening channels. Pilots can listen on any number of channels. The PTT and INT rocker switch selects between external communication and internal channels reserved for communication between pilots, or to ground crew.

The next 3 dials let pilots listen in on various radio beacons and guidance systems that transmit info to the aircraft. Many of these channels transmit in Morse code. ID is a constant three-letter broadcast. VOICE allows voice transmissions through this channel. NAV 1, 2, and 3 are channels related to Flight Management systems and usually transmit audio for specific airport identification, among other things. DME is the distance measuring equipment channel. MKR is the marker beacon channel that aircraft can use to determine distance from a selected beacon, usually located along runways. PA is the public broadcast channel that lets the crew broadcast to passengers in the cabin.

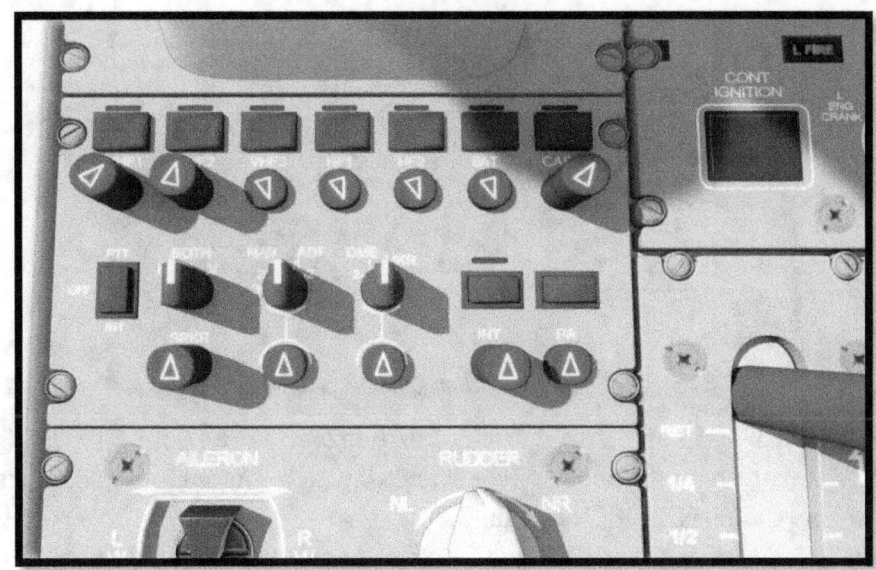

Trim Control Panel

The trim control panel has a split aileron trim switch that's spring-loaded to the center position, for adjusting aileron trim.

The surrounding LWD and RWD labels stand for left wing down and right wing down respectively. The rudder trim switch is also spring-loaded, and the surrounding labels indicate Nose Left or Nose Right.

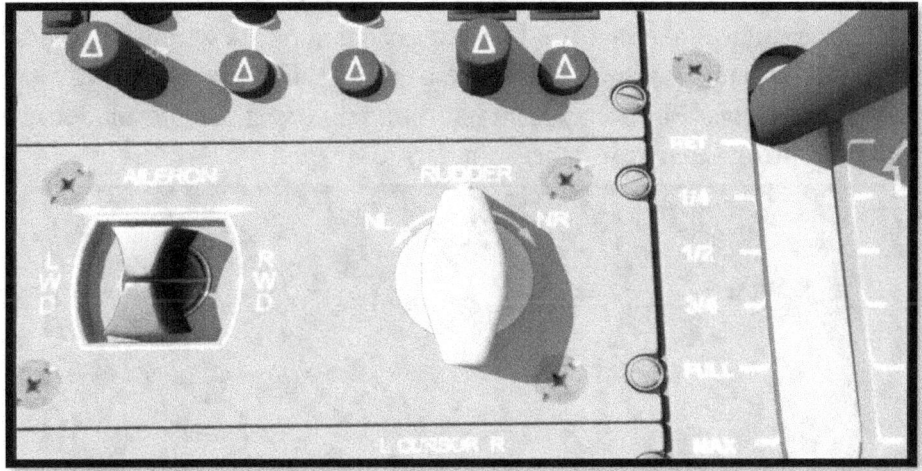

Reversion Switch Panel

The reversion switch panel ensures critical info will appear on displays, especially in the event of a primary flight display failure. The DISPLAY switch has three set scenarios to quickly switch certain digital info panels to particular displays, based on which displays are still available.

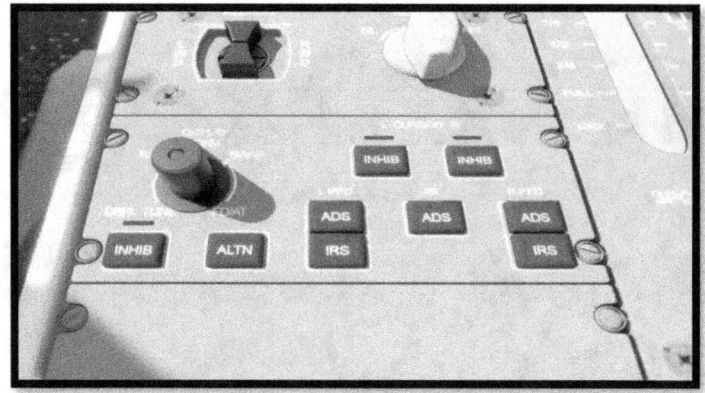

The INHIBIT switch disables display tuning customization. The FLIGHT DIRECTOR and AUTOTHROTTLE alternate source switch changes which channel this data uses, from multiple available channels, again, for redundancy.

The LEFT and RIGHT CURSOR INHIBIT switches disable the respective trackball and buttons. LEFT and RIGHT PRIMARY FLIGHT DISPLAYS control respective display screens. ISI is the small display in the center. The ADS switches let the crew cycle through info from various sources in the AIR DATA SYSTEM, like air temperature probes, angle of attack sensors, and so on.

IRS switches cycle data from INTERNAL REFERENCE UNITS. These units have accelerometers and laser gyros to measure things like aircraft attitude, and heading, among others. The park brake pull-turn switch sets the parking brake. At the back of the center pedestal, there's an interphone that can be used to communicate with passengers or other flight crew. An onboard paper printer is situated behind a thin slot in front of the interphone, with its associated buttons. Pilots may print out things like weather information, clearances from Air Traffic Control, and performance numbers for takeoff.

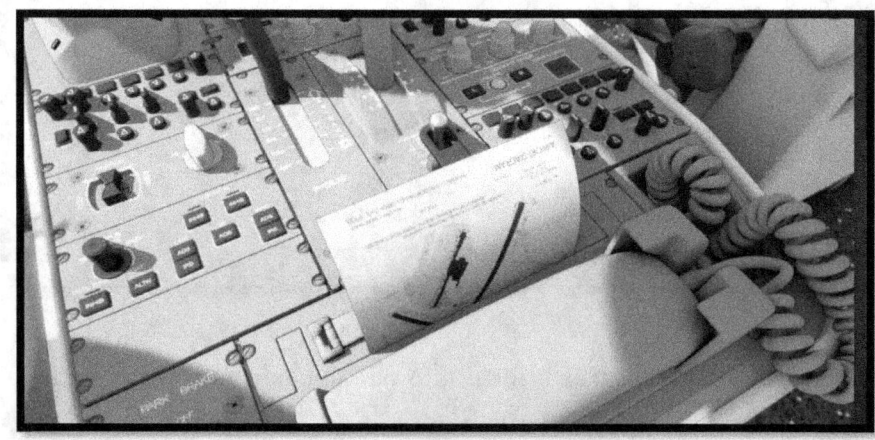

Multi-function spoilers can be extended with the flight spoiler lever in direct mode, though like other systems, spoilers often function automatically as directed by the flight control system. The slat/flap lever has a release handle on top to advance past gated positions 2 and 4. There's also a protected DEPLOY switch to override the system and force deploy slats and flaps to position 3.

The engine panel has a switch for CONTINUOUS IGNITION. This setting is generally automated but can be manually toggled by the crew. Continuous ignition guards against engine flameout due to various events like heavy weather or turbulence. The START switch in AUTO mode lets the engine start sequence be directed by automated systems. L or R crank lets the crew dry crank the engine, or crank engines as part of a manual start sequence.

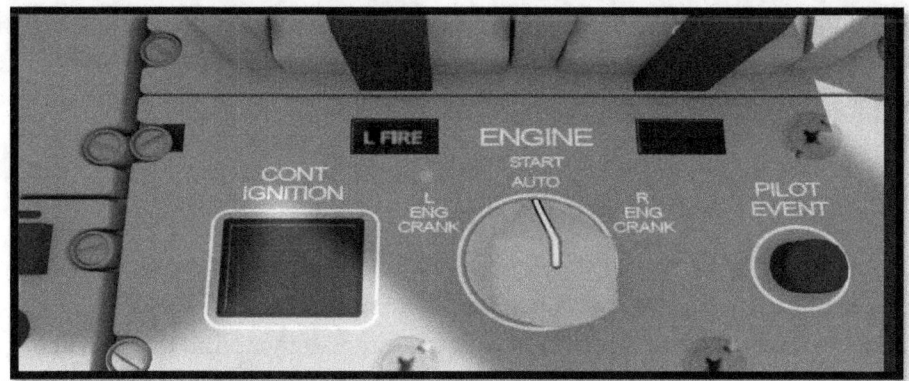

There are fire indicator lights for the left and right engines. The PILOT EVENT switch, when pressed in, marks Flight Data Recorder info for future maintenance investigation.

Throttle Quadrant Assembly

Throttle Quadrant Assembly Switches at the base of the throttle quadrant assembly initiate the LEFT or RIGHT engine start sequence. Throttle levers for each engine reach maximum throttle as they move forward. Finger pull levers on the front of each throttle lever allow rearward travel into the thrust reverser section.

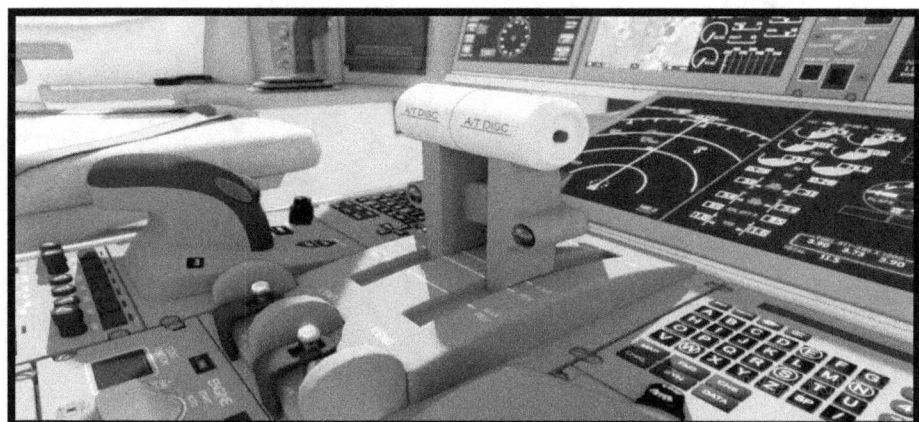

A button on the side of each lever toggles AUTOTHROTTLE on or off. TOGA switches at the side toggle take-off or go-around modes. TAKE OFF mode increases the throttle for takeoff based on automated flight plan data. GO AROUND mode is an alternate automated throttle process to maintain flight, for example, in an aborted landing scenario.

The copilot side has some of the same modules as the pilot's side, with the addition of a lighting panel, and the cockpit door panel. The stacked DISPLAY knobs control brightness for various displays. The INTEGRAL stacked knob controls lighting brightness for many panels in the flight deck with its outer ring, and glare shield panel brightness with the inner knob. The FLOOD switch controls instrument panel flood lights.

In the cockpit door panel, LEFT and RIGHT buttons toggle display for surveillance cameras on the other side of the door. The UNLOCK button unlocks the door. There's a keypad just outside the flight deck door with an emergency code that crew members may use to force unlock the door after a time delay. During the time delay, the red switch on this panel can deny the emergency open request.

Review Questions

1. Provide an overview of the key components and layout of a typical airliner cockpit, including the seating arrangement and primary control systems.
2. Explain the purpose and functionality of the various systems found in an airliner cockpit.
3. How does the detailed representation of the airliner cockpit in Microsoft Flight Simulator 2024 contribute to the overall simulation experience?

CHAPTER 8

ELECTRICAL AND HYDRAULIC SYSTEMS

In this chapter, we're going to be taking a look at an aircraft's hydraulic and electrical systems, explaining how they work and how they designed it the way they did.

Electrical Systems on an aircraft

In this section, we're going to look at the electrical systems on an aircraft. We'll explain all the units and what everything is. You'll have a pretty good understanding of how it changes based on the different types of purpose.

Getting familiar with the terms

The first thing you're going to need to know is that when we are talking about electrical systems, you're going to hear the following terms a lot:

- Voltage: this is your electrical pressure.
- Amperage: is going to be your electrical current or flow.
- Power: is simply when you take the two together and make it do something whether it's a limited light bulb or defrosting your propeller.

The easiest way to keep these two things together or keep them apart is to always think about them in terms of a dam. When you have a tall dam, with water behind the dam, if you were to take a little hole and drill a hole in the bottom down here you'd have a bunch of water that comes spurting out. Now depending on how much water you have backed up here it's the height of this that determines how hard that water is going to try to push itself out. That pressure of water is the equivalent of your voltage.

The next one you're going to see of course is that hole is going to have different sizes. If it's a pretty big hole a lot of that water at that pressure is going to come gushing out. Now the amount of water that comes gushing out at the same time is the equivalent of your amperage. Finally, if we were to put somebody standing right here, for example, we're putting their face in that little hole. The bigger the hole the more work that's going to get done and that's going to blast that person out pretty much downstream there; that's equivalent to be the power. If you always think about those three items in terms of that you're going to have a pretty successful time.

Understanding Current

The other thing we're going to take a look at is the difference between alternating current and direct current.

In alternating current, electrical current alternates, sometimes between 50 or 60 times per second so you still get work done but you don't have a continuous flow.

The other kind of current you're going to see is what we call a direct current. This is when you take all your electricity and you're going to make it flow in the same direction just like we have in our little Dam illustration. On an aircraft, there are a lot of different sources of power and they're all going to be a little different depending on the type of aircraft, the application, and the age of the airplane.

Batteries vs generators

Let's look at Boeing, for example. In this aircraft there are two sources of power: we have the battery which you're going to see in some aircraft and we have what they call generators. Generators are these big things attached to our little engine that generate electrical current based on how fast the engine is turning.

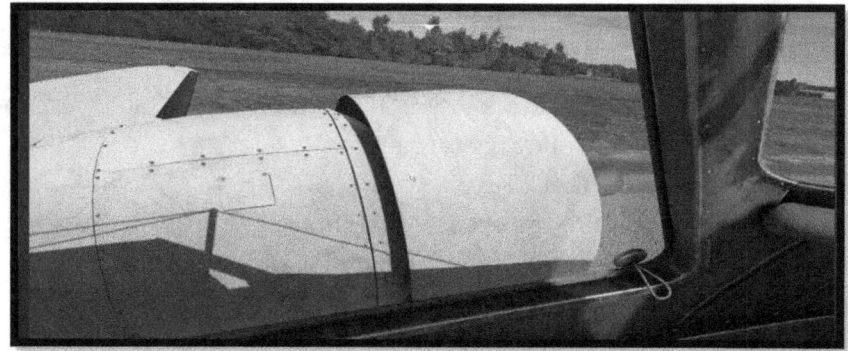

If we come floating down inside the cockpit, you'll notice that we have this handy gauge or little amp meter and you'll notice that it has a negative portion. You'll also notice that it has a positive portion. This tells you how fast you're discharging the battery so a -6 or -7 amps, for instance, is the current flowing out of the battery. If you were to keep the situation exactly as is you would run your battery empty.

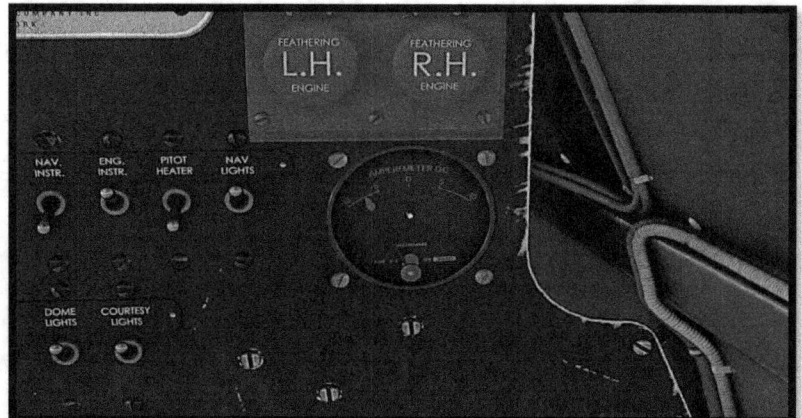

Now depending on the type of aircraft you're operating it'd be a pretty complement. It could be an issue, so one of the things you can do is reduce your electrical load by shutting off various items on board. You'll notice by putting out a couple of those lights and things that take engine instruments off you've reduced your electrical load significantly and gone down to about -4 amps which on most batteries are usually between 40 and 50 amp hours.

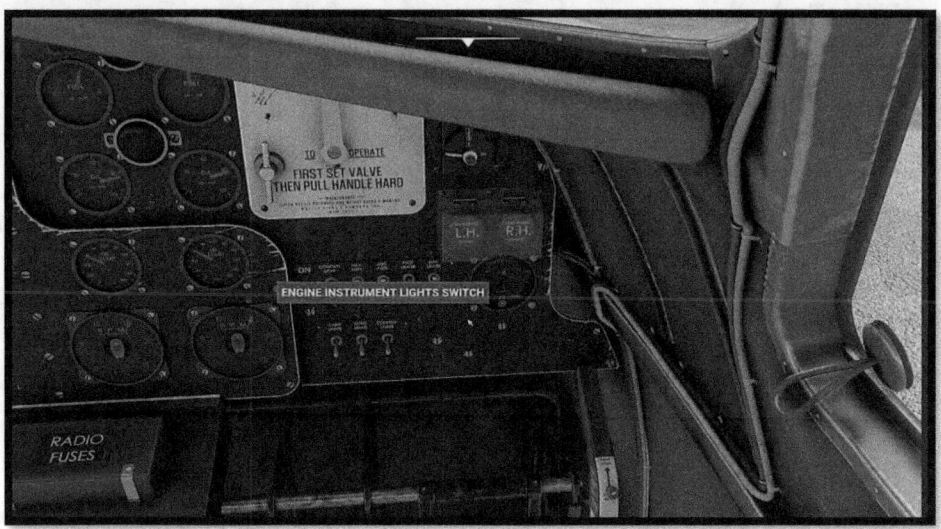

This means you get about 11 or 12 minutes before your battery is completely discharged but the interesting thing about generators and the reason that they're not used anymore is the fact that their power production is completely dependent on how fast it's turning.

Let's say you go ahead and push your throttle full, you can see the engine power coming up a little bit and you're going to notice that all of a sudden your aircraft is now producing positive. You're charging the battery on board. Now if you come in here and start turning on some buttons here, you're trying to increase the electrical load and you'll see that once that electrical load starts to kick in it has an impact on your ability to keep up with the charging of the battery which is why with a lot of these old aircraft you do not run anything until you're ready to go. You're sitting here picking up a lot of temperature just being parked on the ground running those generators.

The interesting thing about generators is they produce a direct current which is the same type of current that your battery is producing so the two are essentially interchangeably electrically on board of the aircraft itself.

This is a little bit of an awkward situation because if this were night time you could run your battery to zero which could be a very big problem depending on what's going on. If you need to come in for a landing, for example, you'll go ahead and pull your throttle back, coming in setting yourself up, just coming over the runway, and then all your lights go out. You can imagine the electrical complications that you would experience with that.

It's also worth noting that some of these older aircraft had a single generator. You wouldn't produce generators on both sides. Generators are relatively simple to use and that's one of the reasons why you'll still see them in airplanes such as big turboprops in some cases, what they would do is just run one engine and run the generator while leaving the other engines off just so they can keep some electrical flow going around inside of the aircraft.

As you know, they didn't stick with this design. One of the big evolutions and again, one of the downsides of the generator is the fact that not only does it only produce direct current but it's also relatively heavy. We have these things instead called alternators that produce alternating current which as you probably realize now we can't use that directly, instead we have to convert it into direct current to run certain parts of the aircraft.

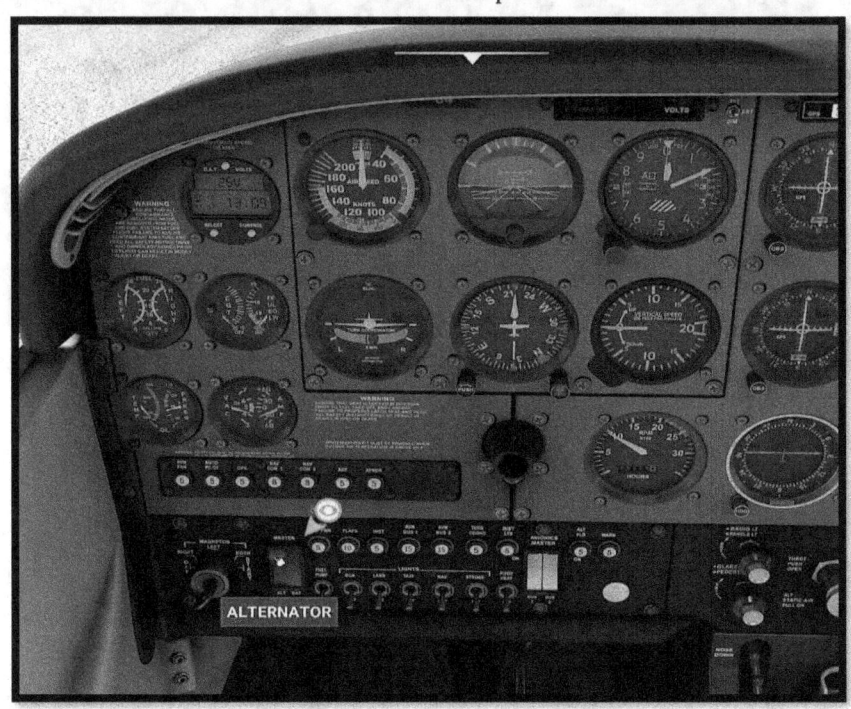

We have a Cessna 172S for this illustration which is a great example of how all this comes together and looking down inside our cockpit we have ourselves our electrical bus. If you're wondering what all those little things are, they're just circuit breakers. An interesting thing is you can pop one of these circuit breakers out in the real world and it would disable that part of the aircraft.

Now what we're going to do is go over to the battery section and engage the battery switch. A couple of different things are going to come on when you do, one of which is the battery. If we hit the avionics switches we're going to see a couple of indications of what our aircraft is up to.

Well, one thing we would like to do is reduce our electrical load a little bit. You'll notice we have a couple of new measurements: we have one that indicates our voltage, in this case, we're at a 25-volt system here which means we're very charged. Most of these aircraft will use dual batteries for the purposes, again you'll take two batteries and add them together so you can get yourself a higher voltage available.

Another thing you're going to observe if you flip your head down here is that we're pulling about 10 to 15 amps which is quite a bit of electricity here even though we're just sitting on the ground. If you're wondering who our winner is here it's going to be our GPS. If we were to come over here and do one of these real fast you can see that just on its own we're only pulling about five or six amps which isn't that bad at all but then we have no indication anymore of what our actual voltage is so we'll go ahead and start up the aircraft here and then we're going to keep it down nice and simple and we're not going to do all those fancy procedures. All we want to do now is get this thing a rumble in here and for that, we'll give it a little bit of power to hold us at about 1000 RPM. Microsoft Flight Sim will randomly erase your hours so be mindful of things like that.

The alternator

Now we've got the things started up, we've got a little bit of RPM, we're just running off the battery and we're still pulling amperage here. If we were to come and flip on the avionics master, everything goes on but we're still at 25 volts which means all the electrical power on this aircraft is still coming out of our little direct current battery. What happens when we turn on the alternator? We'll notice a bunch of things happen: the first thing that happens is that the system voltage now jumps up to 28 volts because our alternator runs at a higher voltage than a battery does. The second thing we'll observe is our amperage down here. We're now charging the battery. The interesting thing that will happen is as we fly this, our amperage will slowly decrease as we continue charging the battery to the point when it's completely charged.

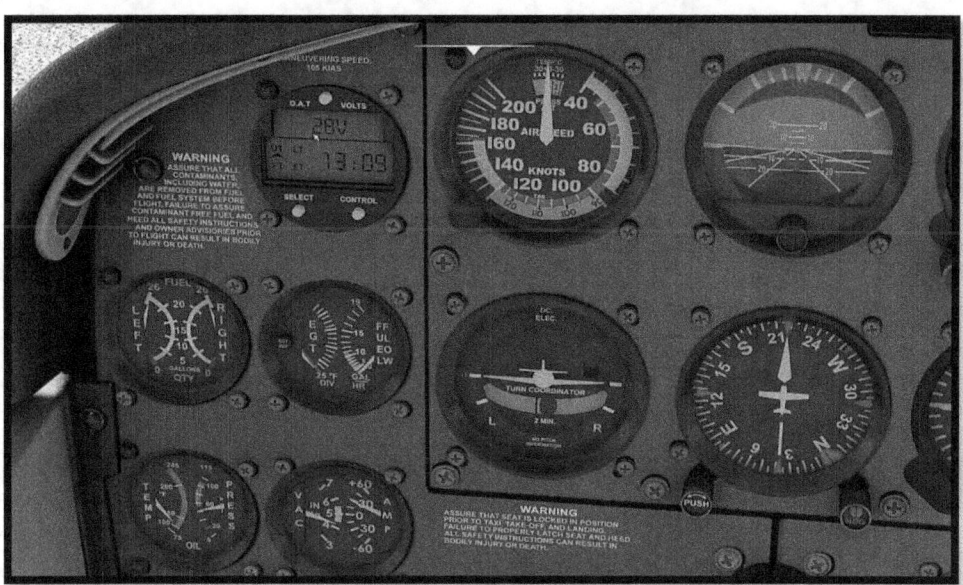

Now you're wondering, didn't we mention a minute ago that in alternating current the electricity goes in a zig-zag direction, and in direct current, it all goes in one direction? How do we get alternating current to be direct current? Well, they have these devices called rectifiers and what they do is take that funky wave and only allow it to come out in one direction so we can recharge our battery.

One of the cool things about these buses is that we can take the battery out of the system completely and the engine's running, all our electronics are on, we can read all our gauges and our system voltage is still at 28 volts even though the battery isn't even electrically connected to anything else on board of this aircraft.

Now the alternator is doing all the work, one of the interesting things is that if we were to pull the throttle way back, our lights would start flickering a little bit and these displays would start cutting in and out because the alternator at such a low RPM is not able to provide enough electrical power to keep all of this good stuff going on so it's quite interesting that we don't get that effect but keep in mind if we're on a generator, a long time ago the generator would have popped right off the line and all these things would go dark instantaneously.

Aircraft with multiple engines

So far we've engaged the battery and the alternator, the battery is now being charged off the alternator and we're still pulling electrical power out of it. If we install this aircraft like this, it's relatively straightforward. We have our source, we have all the consumers, we have our two instrumentations but where things start to get more electrically complicated is when we move into an aircraft that has multiple engines.

For example, we have a Boeing 737 and this aircraft has some electrical needs. We've got the engine itself and the avionics and we have a ton of different types of avionics here. We also have computer systems on board and there are so many different electrical components on this particular aircraft that need electricals in it. If we come over to our little systems display we get a nice little breakdown but on an aircraft this large you have a new problem and that's the fact that you have Alternators on both engines but those two alternators could potentially be working at a different frequency against each other.

Think about it this way: if one right now is on the up wave and the other one is on the down wave, if you were to try to put those two waves together to get one straight wave, this would not be desirable, as a matter of fact, the E2 engines would kick each other off so you have this problem on aircraft like this that the systems have to be synchronized for them to be able to safely go ahead and power. The solution many designers did is to design the systems so that they are independent of each other.

We have one power in one part of the aircraft and the other generator system generators are powering the other side of the aircraft so if we come up here and pop off the right generator, for example, everything pops itself off simultaneously and the reason nothing bad happened to us there is because our left generator now automatically kicked in and started providing power for the other side of the aircraft.

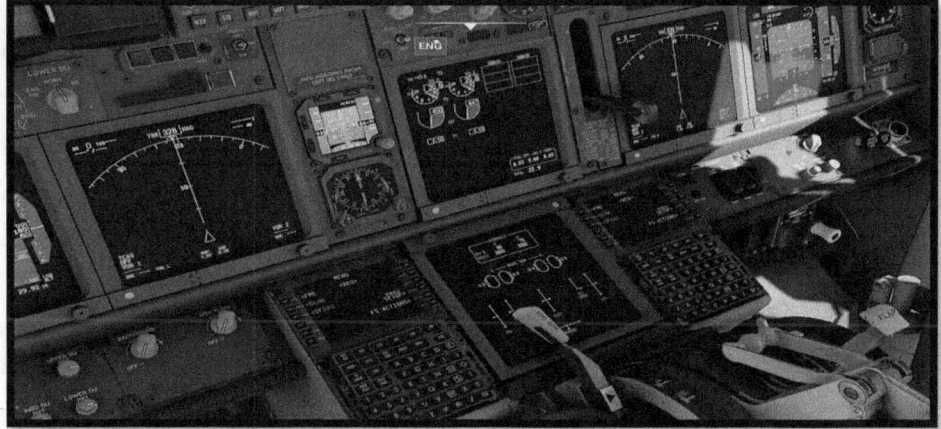

There is this little switch here called bus transfer and this allows us to link the two systems to each other. There's no "On" position here, it's either "Auto" meaning if something bad happens push the button or it's got Off saying please don't do that.

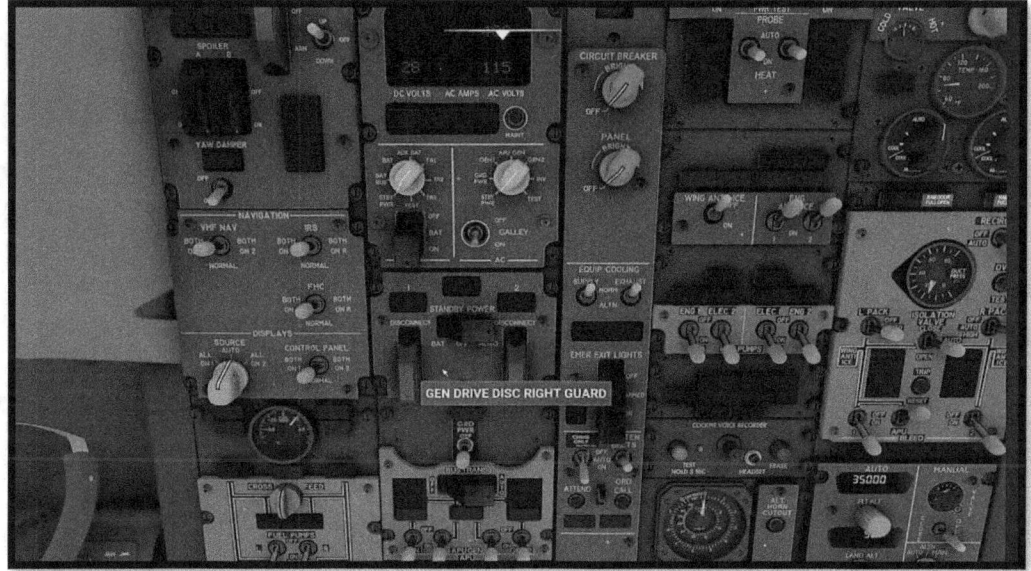

Now if we switch this to the Off position and we go ahead to disengage our generator here, we'll lose half of our aircraft because nothing is powering that side of the airplane. If we were to come over here and close the sucker, this particular generator on this side of the aircraft is now feeding this one as well.

Where it gets kind of interesting on aircraft like this is if you were to float up you'll notice there are two different switches here: we have an AC system and a DC system, and they're separate from each other. If we go to the battery bus we have our TRS which is the different places where we're going to be sending electrical power and we can see how much amperage we're sucking out of it.

On the right-hand side, we have a completely different set here. We have ground power which should be nothing. We have our first generator which is producing about 115. Notice it has a frequency of over a hundred and on generator 2 over here, it's producing about 48 so this one's working hard to power this side.

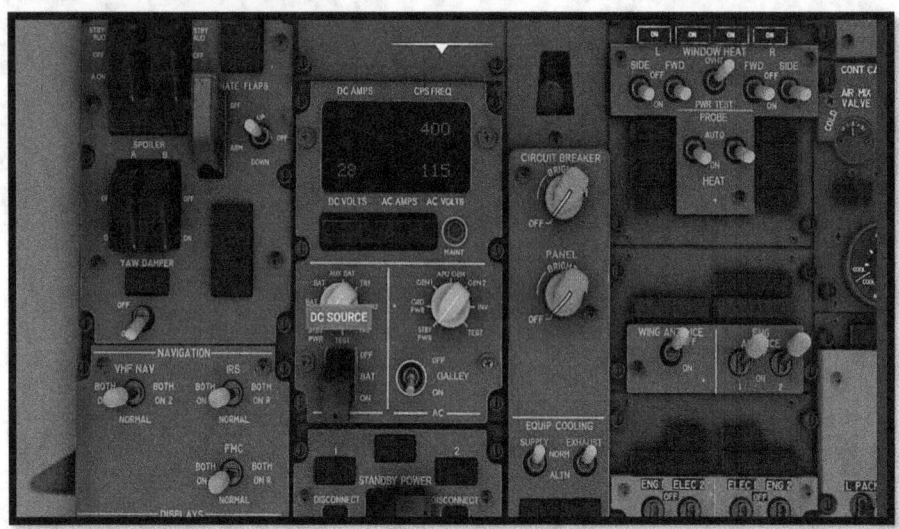

An inverter is a way you can take DC power and convert it into AC and right now, the inverter is not pulling anything and the reason is the fact that we're not pulling off of this. We're going to leave this up here, pop the generator off one side real quick which immediately produces a bunch of angry alarms.

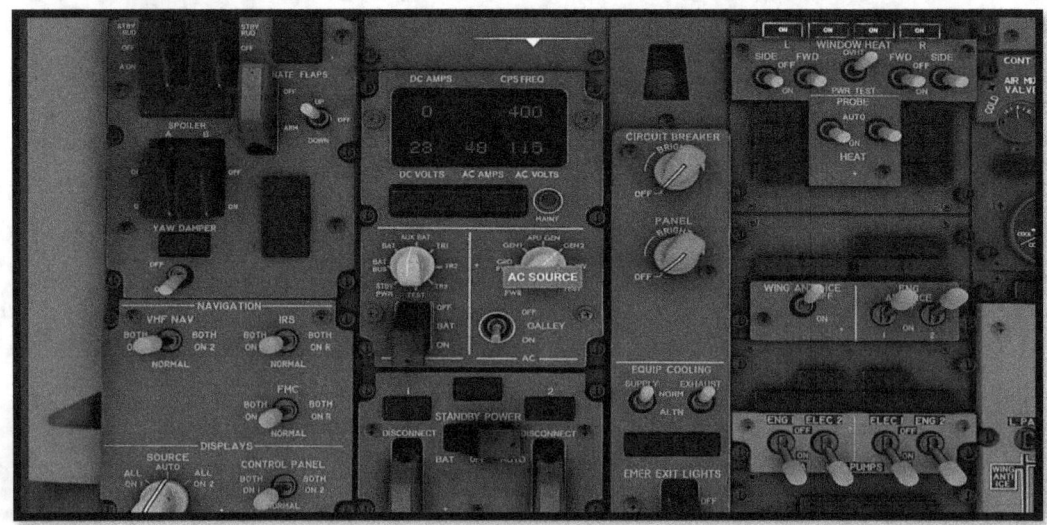

We're going to pop the other generator off and now, our auxiliary battery kicks in and all our electrical pumps and everything fails simultaneously; we're now powering this aircraft off of our particular piece and we can see our inverter here is working hard and the lost voltage is desperately trying to keep everything powered here. If we were to come back here and flip everything back on and then go back to our generator, everything is now working back normally so again, one of the interesting things about these systems is the way that they separate those.

Now you're probably wondering, what if you're in an aircraft with four engines? That gets very complicated and depending on the aircraft you're going to have a different type of system. Going back to the scenario above, our autopilot kicked off, everything clipped off, our flight directors clipped off and everything popped off just to give you an idea of how devastating that can be but the fact that we still have it now should tell you that these aircraft have a backup generator. Yes, they have what they call an Auxiliary Power Unit (APU).

Auxiliary Power Unit

The APU is to give us a little electrical power as well as compressed air either in the emergency that we lose something during flight or if we're in a situation where the aircraft is parked and we just need a little bit of electrical power to keep us going.

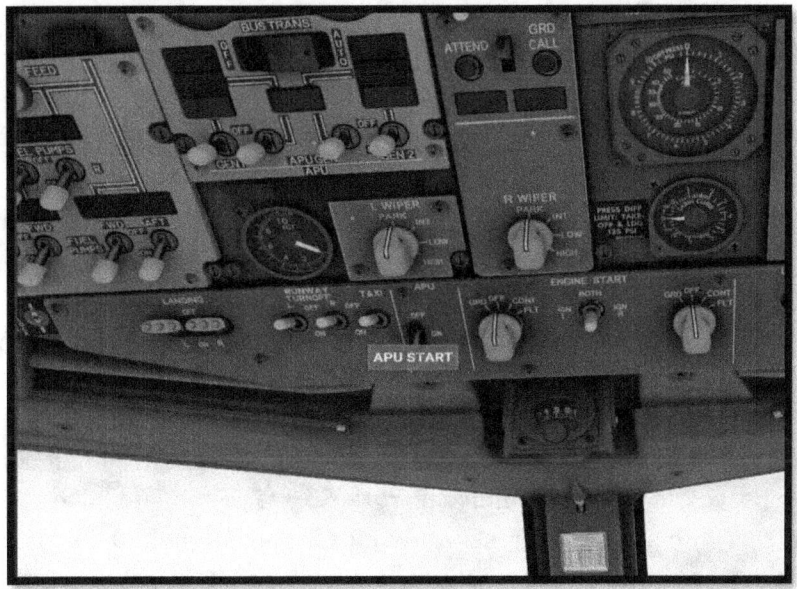

More complicated engines

In a scenario where we have six engines, the electrical system on this aircraft is downright intimidating but it uses the same philosophy as everything we have seen so far. We have all of our Transformer rectifiers, we have a 36-volt bus here, it's a three-battery bus and we have the same techniques here as far as picking what different system we'd like to use. We have the same AZR style, VSY, and all our engine generators but to save the frustration, they designed it so that the engine there has only four generators even though we have six engines in an effort to try to break everything down and make it a little bit simpler.

What is fascinating is that on this aircraft we have what they call a three-phase system which increases the complexity a little bit but makes it a little bit easier. We also have two separate APUs on board which makes this one even more complicated to operate and the other thing is that with the battery or DC system here, we have separate meters for our rectifiers which if you can remember is converting AC to DC in our battery units themselves. We have five batteries on board that all are moderate and completely independent of each other and we have a battery heating system as well to keep the batteries at the correct temperature at high altitudes or something along those lines.

The Hydraulic System

For this demonstration, we're going to be taking a look at the Boeing 737 700 which is one of these lovely pmdg aircraft that goes into a lot of detail. Keep in mind there are other aircraft that have very complicated systems and we'll take a peek at one of those a little later on but for now we're going to stick to this aircraft to understand what's going on and how to deal with it if something comes up in the air.

What is a hydraulic system

An aircraft is fairly large and weighs quite a bit and we have this lovely little yoke that sits behind our lap. You can see how it works on the controls but if the yoke is barely moving (because we have some gigantic control surfaces located around your aircraft), the problem here is we have these very heavy chunks of metal plus we have the slipstream of very high-velocity air combining to make it physically impossible to move these controls by muscle alone. So very large aircraft of a certain size are always going to have systems called Hydraulic.

Although there are electric and pneumatic as well to help push the controls into the position that you desire, if we did not have these systems we'd be in a world of hurt because we may not be able to move the controls to operate the airplane.

A hydraulic system works in the basic principle that if you squeeze a liquid it doesn't like that which now means we can use that to make it work. So, we're going to have a pump which is going to provide us with pressure, a reservoir which is going to hold the hydraulic fluid, and then things like actuators and pistons that are going to be doing all the work of the hydraulic system.

Hydraulic pumps

Now on our aircraft, we have about four different hydraulic pumps available to us. We have system A and system B. You'll notice we have engine-driven as well as electrical pumps.

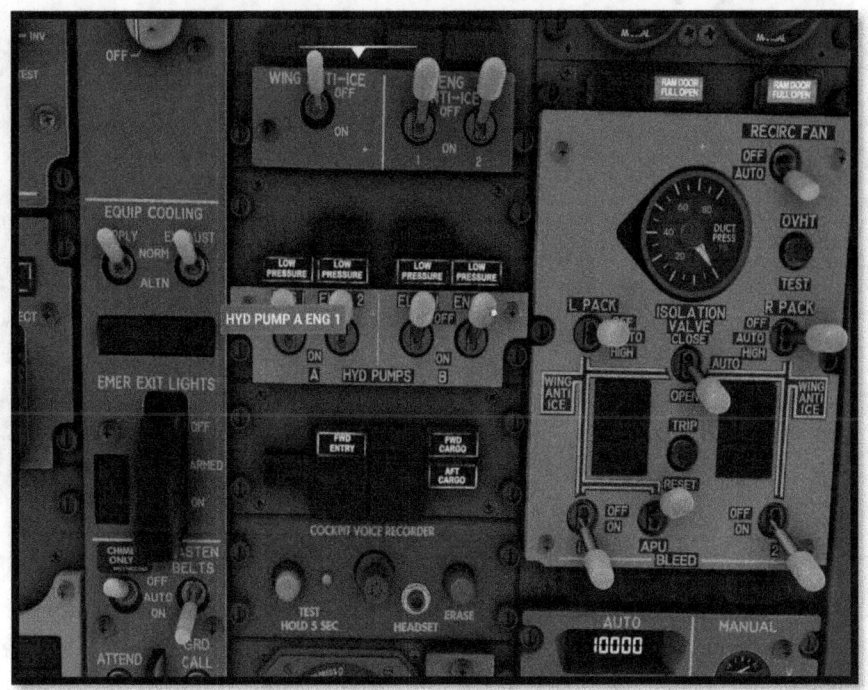

The interesting thing we have here which is very fascinating about this particular design of this aircraft is all these hydraulic pumps are designed to work on the same sets of items and they're designed in such a way that if one set of hydraulic pumps is available and not the other it's going to prioritize where the pressure will go.

After activating the A system, let's say we have plenty of hydraulic quantity and we have a pressure of about 3000 psi. Now if we come back outside and start moving our controls there's no difficulty whatsoever to move the controls themselves around. The Rudder is happily going and then our spoilers and everything seem to be rolling pretty fast; it might be slightly delayed but nothing too bad at all and that is because we are on the A system.

The way that the 737 breaks its hydraulic systems apart is this: you're going to observe the fact that we have two different systems acting on the flight control simultaneously. You'll notice on flight control A, that if we come up here and pop this off real quickly we'd actually be popping the flight controls off of system A and now if we're moving the controls nothing's happening. The reason for that is that we shut off the path of that hydraulic pressure.

Now if we flip back up here and go ahead and slam that thing back closed again and jump back outside we can direct hydraulic pressure back to our actual flight controls themselves so that works directly.

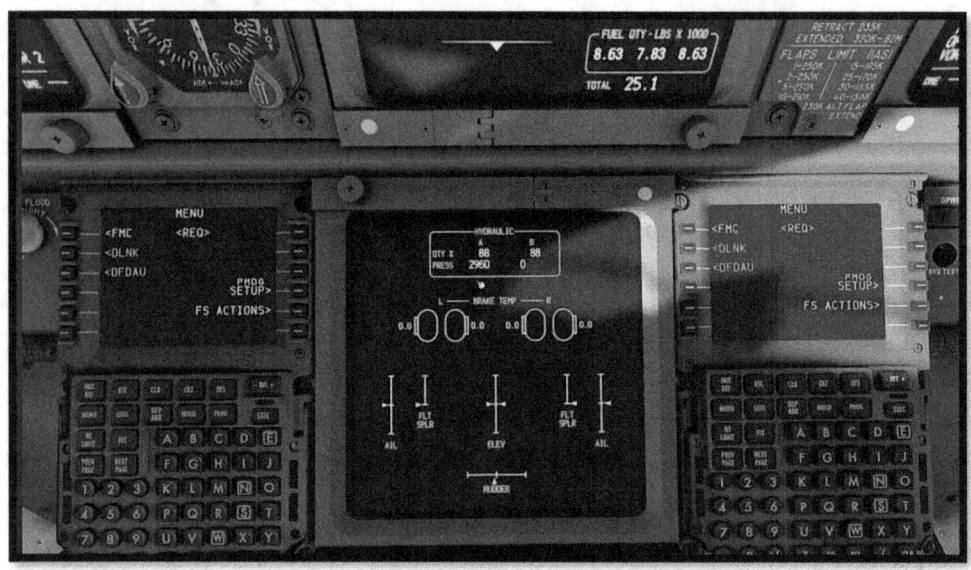

What gets interesting is the other hydraulic components on an aircraft namely our flaps, landing gear, and brakes. If we were to go ahead and deploy some flaps here, keep in mind we're only on system B here, we'll go ahead and give it four clicks of flaps there and we'll notice that the aircraft is sitting there and nothing's happening. Now the aircraft depressurizes a little bit here and that's because the 737 is engineered so that if we lose one hydraulic system we will not be able to put down our flaps. It's system A prioritizing being able to push our controls around. In this particular aircraft what they did to make things a little bit simpler is they gave us an alternative flaps handle. If we turn the sucker on we can now manually crank the flaps. When we say manually we mean it's going to take a lifetime of manual cranking to get this thing to go anywhere.

Review Questions

1. Describe the key components and functions of the electrical system in an aircraft.
2. Explain the purpose and workings of the hydraulic system in an aircraft, and how it integrates with the aircraft's various subsystems.
3. How does Microsoft Flight Simulator 2024 accurately model and simulate the complex electrical and hydraulic systems of different aircraft types, and how can pilots learn to manage these systems effectively?

CHAPTER 9

CATEGORIES OF AIRPLANES IN FLIGHT SIM

In this chapter, we are going to be looking at the easiest and hardest planes to fly in the Sim. We are going to break it out into categories and for each one of those categories, we'll give you a few easy planes to fly and a few difficult planes to fly.

We'll be covering the bush planes, prop planes, turboprops, and jets. We've restricted the list of airplanes to those that come with the Standard version of the game because we want to make sure this list is as inclusive as possible and we know that a lot of you out there who are just getting started are trying it on Xbox game pass and only have the Standard version. We won't look at third-party planes for the same reason and on top of that there would be too many to include because there are so many great planes out there that you can buy.

Bush Planes

These are planes that you would use typically for accessing remote or underdeveloped areas like the north of Canada or the Australian outback. The definition of a bush plane is pretty broad and it can include almost any general aviation airplane but we're specifically talking about the shorter-range airplanes that are piston-based with a high wing and good short runway performance.

Our pick for easiest to fly in this category is the Cub Crafters and NX Cub. It features a glass cockpit that makes it easy for newcomers to pick up the basic concepts of flight and how to read all the different instruments and if you follow the default tutorials you should be pretty comfortable with this one as well.

The NX Cub has a traditional tricycle landing gear which makes it easy when you're on the ground to see where you're going but it also simplifies takeoff and landing when you're flying in and out of short runways. It's fairly slow with its crew speed of about 110 knots making it ideal for learners to practice maneuvers that they'll have to have a good grasp on before flying the bigger and faster planes.

The harder plane to fly in the bush trip category is the X-Cub. It also has a glass cockpit like the NX Cub so navigation is going to be fairly simple. Where the X-Cub gets more difficult to fly is the fact that it's a tail-dragger; it makes visibility out of the cockpit and seeing where you're going much less obvious. For takeoffs, you have to rely on peripheral vision to see where you're going because you can't see straight ahead until you've gotten to a certain airspeed and ideally for landing you're touching down with all three wheels at once. Accomplishing that takes a lot of practice though so you can just land on the main front gear first but it's a different experience and technique than landing most of the other airplanes in the game which have a tricycle landing gear.

The X-Cub doesn't provide a boost in airspeed so if you want to get somewhere faster you'll have to look at the next category of airplane.

Prop Planes

These are the next step up from bush planes. We are also including turbocharged piston engine planes in this category which aren't to be confused with turboprop planes which we'll be looking at soon. Two of the easiest planes to fly in Flight Sim are the Cessna 172 and the Diamond D840. Both airplanes are very stable in good and slightly windy weather conditions making them ideal to start exploring different scenarios in Flight Sim.

They both have the G1000 glass cockpit which makes it easy to get situated and navigate from one place to another with ease. On top of that, the D840 has a very simplified throttle quadrant as well; all you need to worry about is the throttle and it'll take care of the rest for you.

The Cessna 152 is an easy plane to learn on as well and that is true. It is a little bit slower than the other two airplanes and with its traditional steam gauges, it makes for a much larger learning curve for newcomers. Once you've gotten pretty good at flying the Cessna 172 and the D840 you can move on to two harder Prop planes and that's the Beechcraft Bonanza and the Diamond D862.

Both planes have the G1000 cockpit as well but that's about where the comparisons between them end. The Bonanza is a speed demon with a top crew speed of close to 170 knots but it also takes a little bit of practice to manage it properly on takeoff and landing. It's also got a few features that make it a little bit more complex to fly such as retractable landing gear and the prop and mixture controls. They aren't hard things to master but when you're just getting started it's easy to get bogged down in all of the little details and not enjoy the flying experience as much.

It's a similar story for the D862 but it's even more complex because it's got two engines; managing an extra engine doesn't seem like a big deal at first but there are some significant differences. That second power plant makes the D862 a fast airplane as well and you need to plan ahead of time what you're going to be doing with it because everything happens a whole lot faster. Once you've mastered these two more complex Prop planes you're pretty much ready to move on to Turboprops.

Turboprop Planes

A turboprop airplane is a lot closer to being a jet than you might realize. It has a pressurized cabin which means it can travel at a lot higher altitudes than a Prop plane and the engine shares more characteristics with a jet engine than it does with a piston-based engine. There aren't many turboprop options in Flight Sim, there's only the Cessna 28 Grand Caravan, the Dare TBM 930, and the King Air 350. Among the three there's only one that we consider easy to fly and that's the Cessna 28. It feels like a bigger and faster version of the Cessna 172 and it makes for an easier transition because it has the same G1000 glass cockpit.

In terms of airspeed, it's about on par with the Bonanza that we were looking at a few minutes ago but it feels a lot easier to control than the Bonanza. Both the TBM and the King Air are much more difficult to fly. They both have low wings which you'll always find a little bit more challenging if you're used to flying airplanes with high wings but the upgraded avionics of the G3X take a lot of getting used to compared to the G1000 you're probably used to with the Cessnas.

Both airplanes are faster than the Grand Caravan and for short cross-country hops they can get you where you're going in a nick of time but that extra speed comes at the cost of having to plan a little bit more how you're going to fly them and practice a whole lot more to be proficient at flying them. In other words, you can't just load into the cockpit of the TBM or the King Air and expect to be able to fly them from day one.

It's also hard to say which is harder, between the TBM or the King Air. The TBM is faster and seems to have a little bit more kick to its power plant but the King Air has two engines and that always makes things a little bit more complicated and challenging too. Either way, they are both a lot harder to fly than the Grand Caravan.

Jets

Lastly, we are going to give some picks for the easiest and hardest jets to fly in the Sim. We're combining the jet and airliner sections because there are limited choices in the Standard version of the game.

In terms of an easy jet to fly, we are going to recommend using the F-18. The flight model for the F-18 is highly watered down from what you would expect in a real-life airplane but it can be a lot of fun to just take off and start exploring an area and just be able to explore it a lot faster than you can with a general aviation plane. If you want, you can fly low to the ground or between buildings to do your best maverick impersonation. kickoffs in the F18 are pretty easy and the same goes for just flying around somewhere. Landings do take a little bit more work and they take a little bit of getting used to because it is pretty different from landing a general aviation airplane but overall, it isn't too hard and you should be able to get it right with just a few practice runs.

In terms of a more difficult airplane to fly in the jet category, that's where we'd recommend the Airbus A320. The default A320 is missing a lot of features in it and it's not as realistic as possible so this is the only occasion that we're going to recommend that you get a freeware version of the A320.

Types of airspaces

In this section, we're going to be discussing the different types of airspaces. This is an important subject for you to learn because you need to know the different rules, weather minimums, and equipment requirements for each type of airspace. We have different types of air space to keep aircraft separated and to keep us from hitting each other.

There are two basic types of airspace: Controlled and Uncontrolled.

The six classes of airspaces you need to be familiar with are:

- Alpha
- Bravo
- Charlie
- Delta
- Echo
- Golf

Unless you've already done so, you will need to memorize the phonetic alphabet. Don't worry about the numbers or the Morse code there but try to memorize this as soon as possible. As we have stated, we have six classes but we have two types (Controlled and Uncontrolled).

Classes A through E are Controlled airspaces. This means we can receive radar services from ATC and if we're receiving those services we're under radar control. Now we will use these services too but it is specifically designed to keep people who are flying on instruments safe. Class G airspace is Uncontrolled airspace; you can remember this by thinking of G as government-free (these are typically not under radar control).

Class Alpha

Now let's take a quick look at each one of these. First, let's take a look at class Alpha airspace. We're not going to spend too much time talking about this one because you need to be on an IFR clearance to be up here among other things but you do need to know that class Alpha airspace goes from 18,000 MSL (pronounced as one eight thousand not eighteen thousand) to Flight Level 600; that's a pressure altitude of sixty thousand feet. Keep in mind that when it comes to altitudes of ten thousand feet and above we need to enunciate them this way. For example, instead of ten thousand, we should say one zero thousand, instead of eleven thousand we'll say one one thousand, and so on. We don't ever want there to be confusion about which altitude ATC wants us at.

If you want a good way to remember class A airspace remember A is for above; this airspace is above where we can go as VFR pilots.

Class Bravo

Let's take a look at class Bravo airspace. Class Bravo airspace is a busy airspace. You'll see this around big airports like Dallas Fort Worth and Chicago O'Hare. A good way to remember this is that B stands for busy. Class Bravo airspace starts at the surface and typically goes up to 10,000 feet AGL. Keep in mind that we need to be specifically cleared by ATC to go in there.

Class Charlie

Class Charlie airspace is crowded but not as busy as class Bravo. It's also shaped like an upside-down wedding cake. It is smaller though and that upper level is typically only 10 miles in diameter. This airspace starts at the surface and goes up to 4,000 feet AGL. Remember, C is crowded and we also have to communicate with ATC before we can go in here.

Class Delta

Class Delta airspace is shaped like a cylinder. It's usually five miles in diameter and it surrounds smaller towered airfields. This airspace starts at the surface and goes up to 2500 feet AGL. The D here stands for dialogue because we need to talk to their tower before we can go into their airspace.

Class Echo

You can remember this airspace by thinking E is for everywhere else, that's because Class Echo airspace is a controlled airspace that's not designated as Alpha, Bravo, Charlie, or Delta. Most of the time Echo starts at 1200 agl and goes up to the bottom of class Alpha. Sometimes in busier areas, Echo will start at 700 AGL, though the biggest thing new pilots forget is that Class Echo is a controlled airspace. Just remember we can get radar services here so that makes a controlled airspace.

Class Golf

The last type of airspace we're going to look at today is Class Golf. As we already mentioned, G is government-free because this is an uncontrolled airspace. Also remember G is for ground because, typically, you see Class Golf up against the surface. Class Golf is everything that's not Alpha, Bravo, Charlie, Delta, or Echo and it's the least restrictive of all the airspace classes.

Review Questions

1. Describe the key characteristics and differences between the various categories of aircraft available in Microsoft Flight Simulator 2024.
2. Explain how the different aircraft types are suited for different types of flying.
3. How does the simulation of the various airspaces, such as controlled airspace, uncontrolled airspace, and special use airspace, impact the flight operations and decision-making process for pilots in Microsoft Flight Simulator 2024?

CHAPTER 10

BASIC FLIGHT OPERATIONS

This chapter will cover different flight maneuver techniques such as steep turns, steep spirals, level turns, climbing turns, descending turns, and more.

Cold and dark start

In this section, we are going to look at the cold and dark start and for this illustration, we'll be looking at the India Foxtrot Echo F35 in Microsoft Flight Simulator.

First, we'll start her up on the lower left panel, and turn on the IPP master, the engine inverters, and the batteries. You'll see the displays start to come to life. Initially, you'll see a ton of warnings but don't worry we'll clear those out.

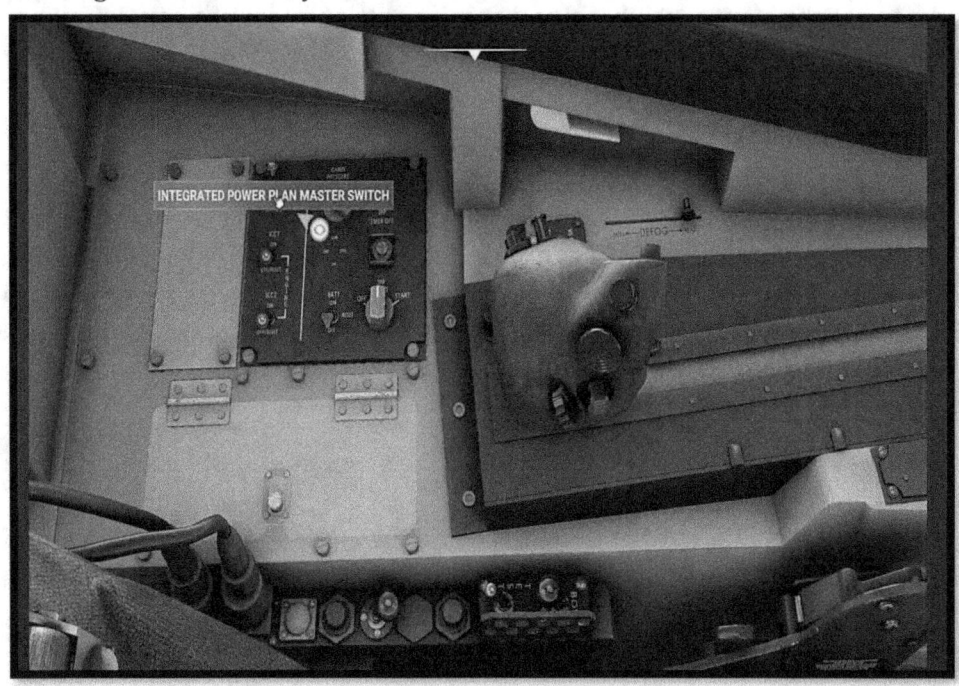

The next step is to open the main fuel shut-off valve which is a touchscreen button on the MFD. With that done, we'll head down to the lower-left panel, turn the IPP switch to start and you'll see the engine start to spool up.

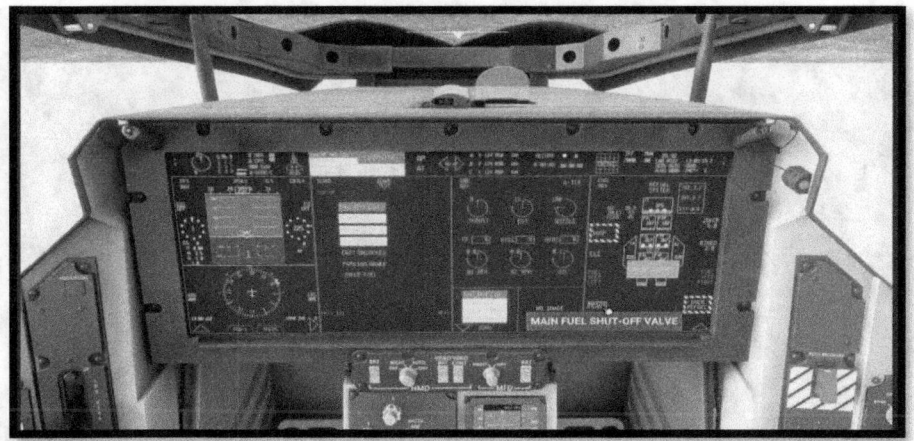

Before we turn on the fuel switch we're going to do a few other bits which don't need to be done in any particular order but we like to do it before we start a plane properly. We'll turn the cabin pressure switch to normal, remove the toggle and arm the ejection seat, remove the toggle on the canopy, and switch on the HMD.

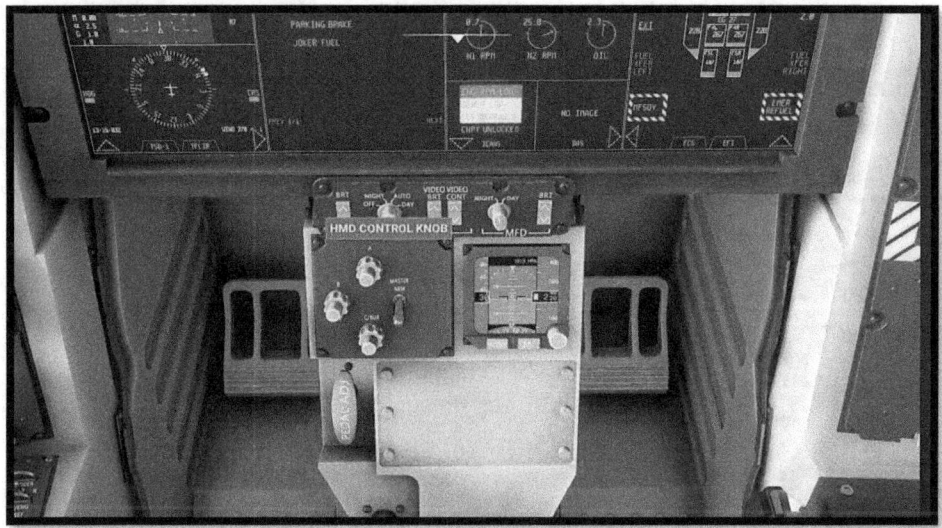

We'll now switch the engine mode to normal and complete engine start. The final warnings will clear as the engine comes to life and the IPP switch has now returned to Auto. You can configure the lights to your taste in the menu but then we're just going to switch on the strobes here and exit the menu to return the displays to a default state.

The final step is to close the canopy which is a lever to the lower left of the seat and that's it, you're good to go from here on out.

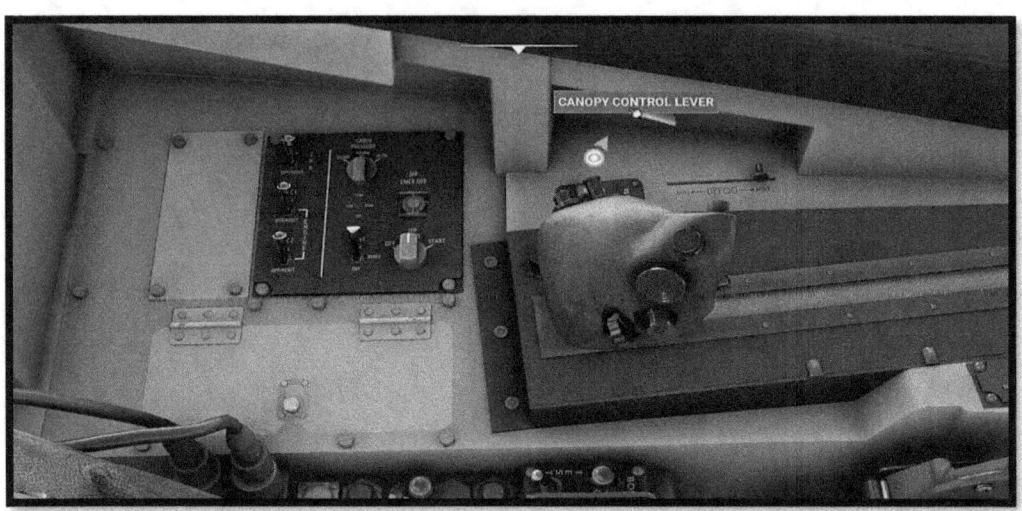

Maintaining weight and balance

In this section, we're going to take a look at weight and balance. Your weight and balance are a combination of how heavy the aircraft is, as well as just how the center of gravity is positioned on the aircraft.

For example, we have a 172S and by default, this aircraft can hold 53 gallons of fuel (required fuel for this bigger flight).

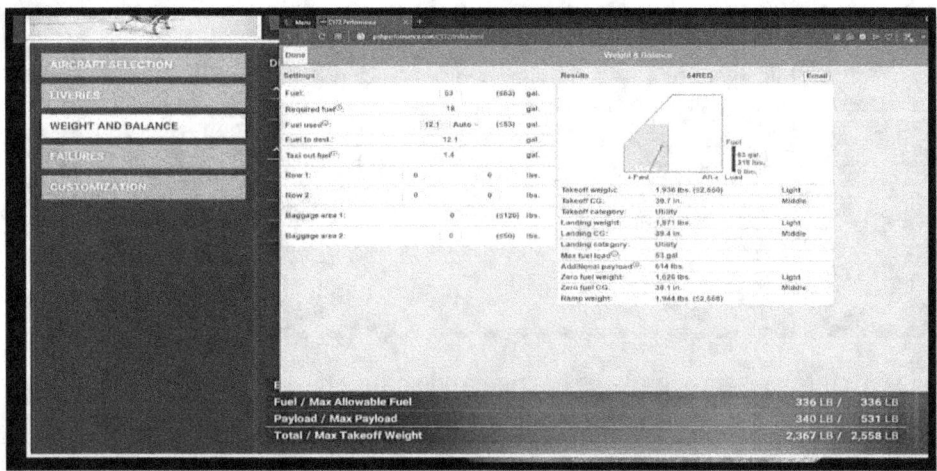

If we increase the weight of the airplane to about 2,100 pounds, for example, this leaves us in the Utility category. A Utility simply means you're allowed to do certain types of aerobatics. Let's say we want to go ahead and toss somebody else in there, so we throw a copy of someone up there in the right seat, things will change a bit. Now there are two people in the front and what it has done to the aircraft is not only has it increased our takeoff weight significantly (we're now at 2200 pounds), but we can also see that we've taken our center of gravity and we've shifted it forward because there's so much extra weight up in the front seat.

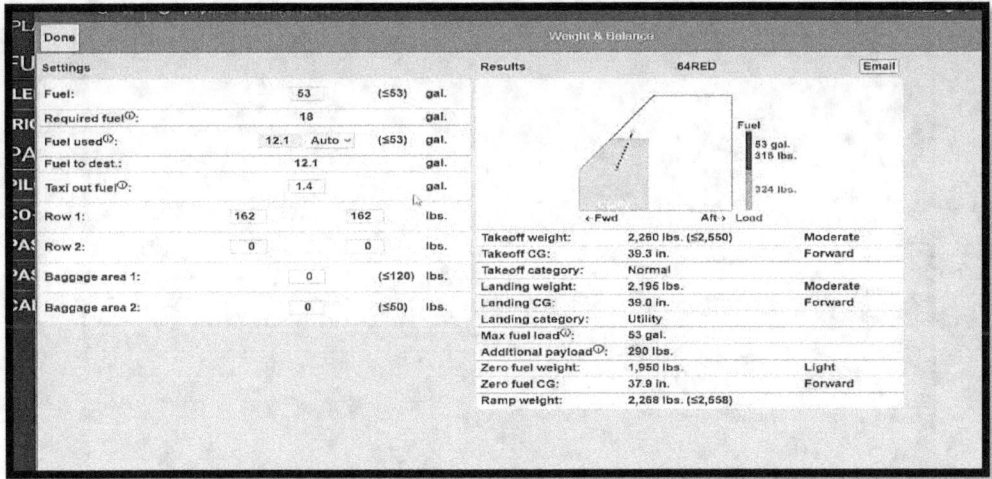

Let's say now we want to throw a copy of someone in the backseat too. Now, we'll notice that the center of gravity of the aircraft has shifted back towards the middle but also that we're dangerously close to the maximum gross weight of our aircraft. What if we go a little bit over? What's going to happen? When you go to land when you're too heavy, guess what happens to the wheels? You can imagine that yourself.

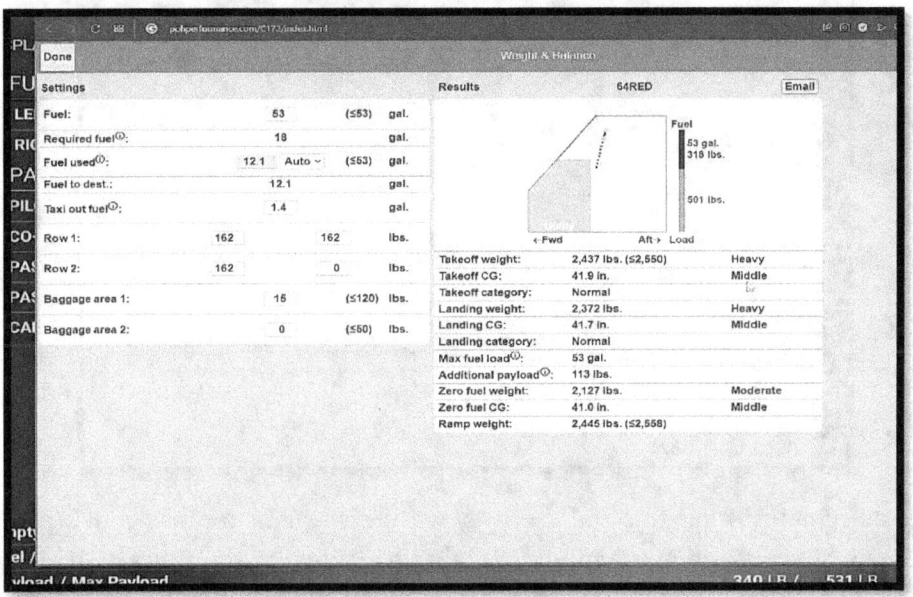

Let's go ahead and throw another copy of someone so there are four people inside this airplane right now. What's happened here is our takeoff weight is now too much; 2,550 is the maximum but we're now at 2599. This means the aircraft is not safe to fly. If you were to crash this plane they'd blame it on you for not doing your weight and balance properly.

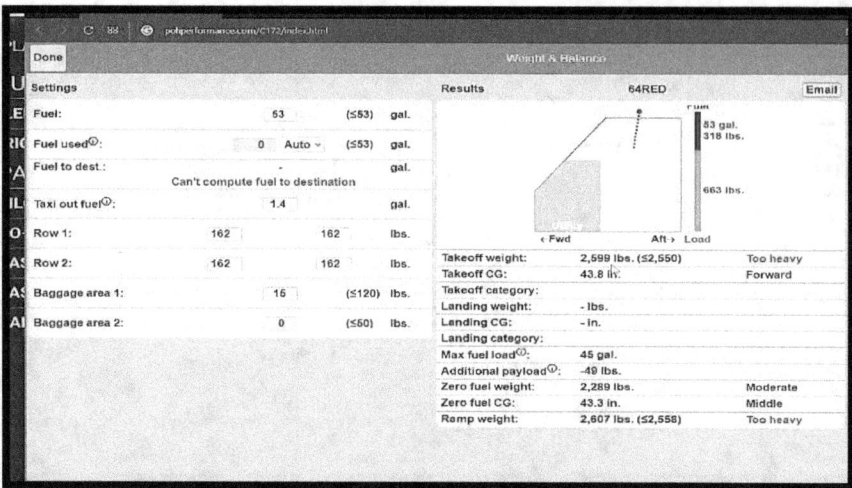

What if you want to do people inside the plane? Well, something will have to go and that's going to be the weight of the fuel. We'll go ahead and drop the fuel counter down a little bit here and pop it to 45 or 44 gallons. Now we can see that by decreasing our range we have increased our capability to carry four people.

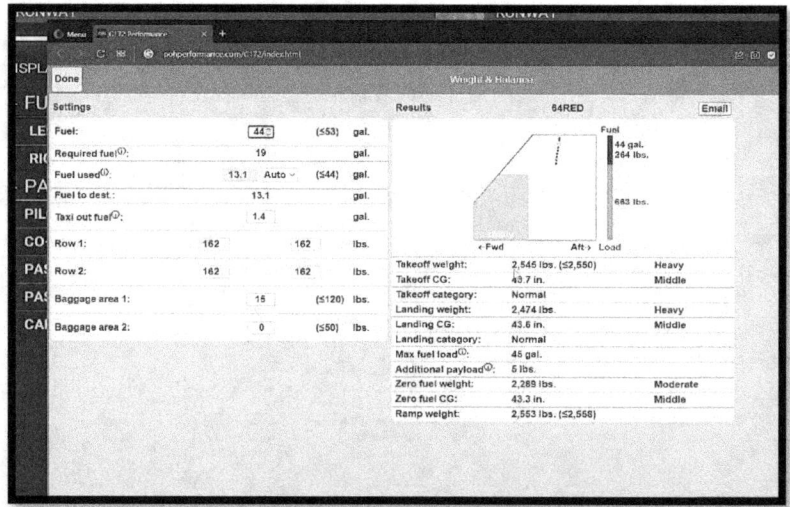

You could do something like this and get away with this legally because your starting fuel is going to be greater than your takeoff fuel. It takes gas to get to the runway so a lot of times you can be 2551 and then you're still legal because you're going to burn off that last pound. If the landing weight is 2400 pounds and the takeoff weight here is 2545, that's pretty substantial. The center of gravity is also perfectly in the middle.

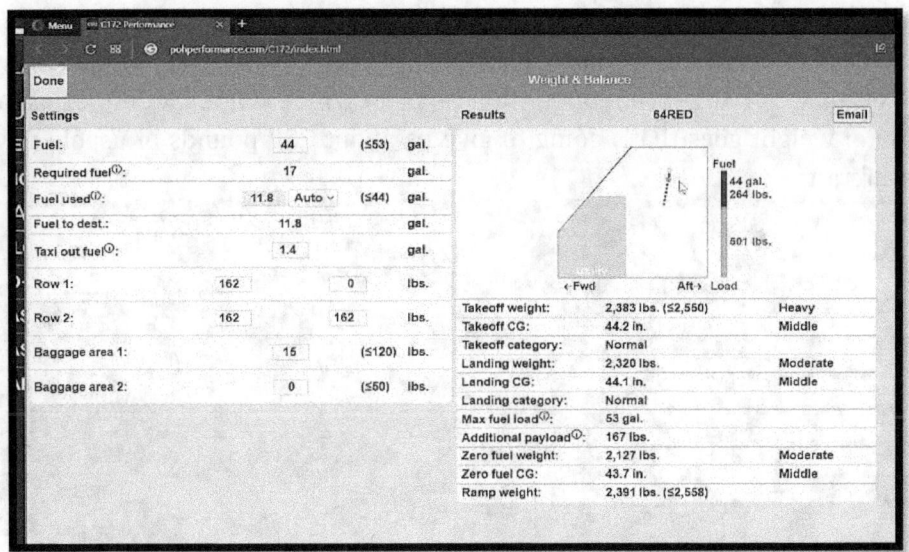

Now here's where things get interesting. Let's say we want to just put people in the backseat. We'll start with one person in the front seat and put two people in the back seat. Now the center of gravity of the aircraft is shifted backward, making landing very interesting.

Let's go a little extreme here and put a lot of people in the back seat then crank up the fuel, of which we can't go past 53 gallons. Now that the center of gravity is still completely within the safe zone. Let's put a middle school person in the front seat and then go ahead to put a hypothetical football player in the back seat. Now the center of gravity is significantly towards the aircraft. Again, you can see that it limits your capability as a pilot.

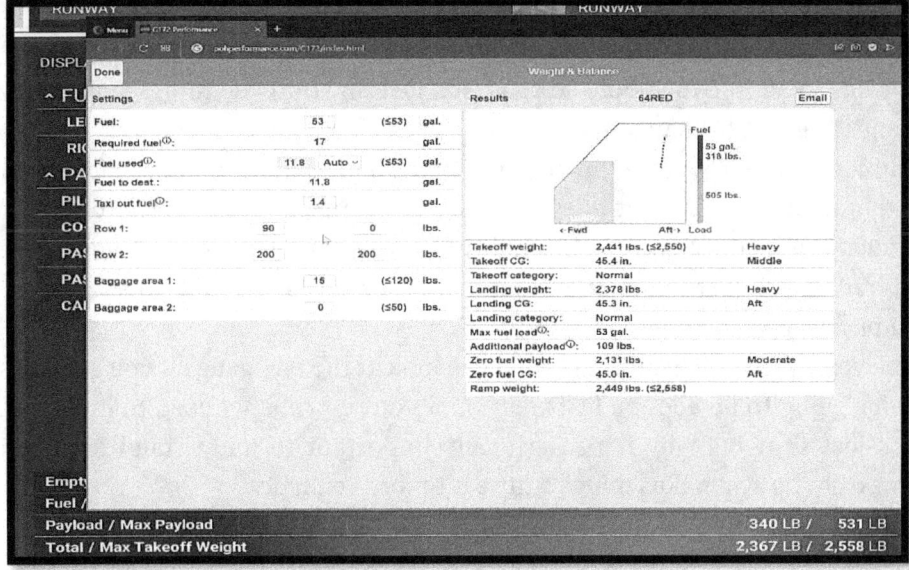

Let's go ahead and reduce our cargo. Now with four people in the airplane, it's looking at about almost half of the maximum fuel capacity. That's not a lot, as a matter of fact, if we were to reduce this to about 50 percent of our fuel capacity which is not a lot of gas, as far as our distribution of weight goes that's going to give us about 700 pounds of usable payload on board the aircraft.

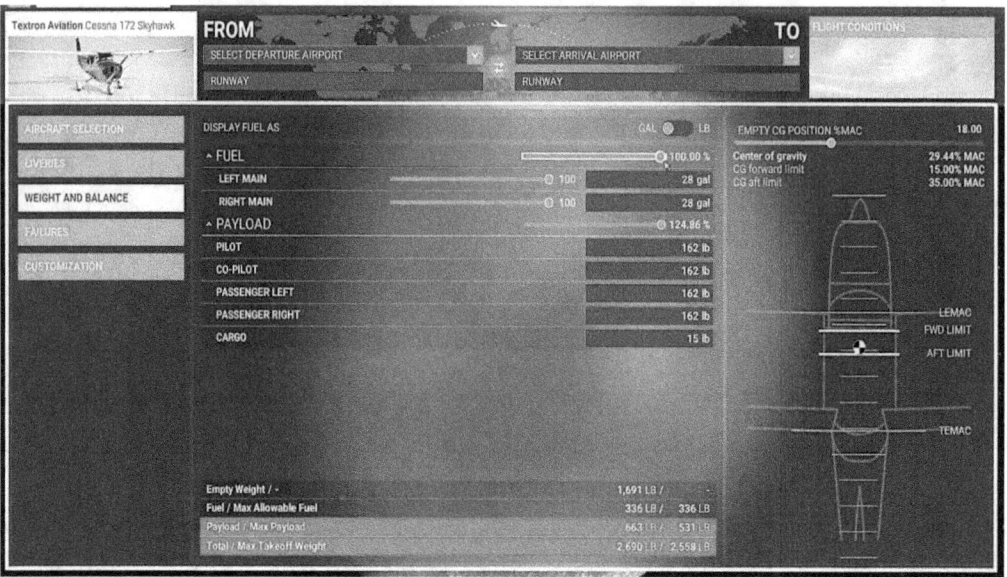

So you're sitting there saying what is the penalty if you decide to simulate bringing a whole family with full tanks? One of the common misconceptions is that just because an airplane has four seats in it means that you can just like a car fill it up with a full tank of gas and go on a long journey with your whole family. That's just not a thing in an airplane. If you know you put two heavy adults in the front seat, you can see you're almost at the limits of your maximum capacity with two people so again it's just one of those things, and depending on your airplane it's going to change.

Another misconception is you get an airplane that's bigger like a Bonanza, for example, and you think that it changes. Well, it doesn't change that much. If you were to carry four 180-pound persons you'll be outside of the center of gravity again even though you have six seats in your aircraft. If you wanted to do six adults in a Bonanza you can carry zero fuel, which means you physically can't do it.

So next time you fly in a small airplane go take a look at the fuel gauge if you get a chance. We guarantee it's going to be about a little less than you're probably used to in Flight Sim and again that's just showing why it's so critically important to understand how weight and balance work and how it makes things a little bit more realistic.

Taxiing, Taking off, and Landing an aircraft on a centerline

In this section, we're talking about the center line with the main focus here being on the perspective of where that line should be. It's going to be your job through rudder and or stick and yoke input to get it there but we want to talk about the wear factor. This goes for taxiing, takeoff, and landing.

With today's Flight Sim culture, a lot of new flights and pilots when they're first starting tend to put a lot of focus on buttering landings before learning this technique but centerline control should be practiced before moving into that or at least simultaneously. It all comes down to perspective and knowing where to aim looking out the window and once you master the centerline technique it will carry over into any aircraft you fly.

Keep in mind that we're talking about a static view on your computer monitor which is different from the 3d view you have in real life. Of course, if you're using VR or a tracker that puts you a little closer to the real view but as a disclaimer this is for flight simulation.

Now whether you're flying a single-seat aircraft or a two-seater aircraft the aim point for the center line is going to be about the same, no matter which side you sit on. Everything we'll explain still applies to demonstrate this.

You can load up your aircraft on a runway or position yourself centered on a taxi line. Loading on a runway will generally center you on the line depending on which sim you're using and if you are a little offset just correct it until you are in the center then have a look from inside the cockpit and this will be the spot you'll want to remember.

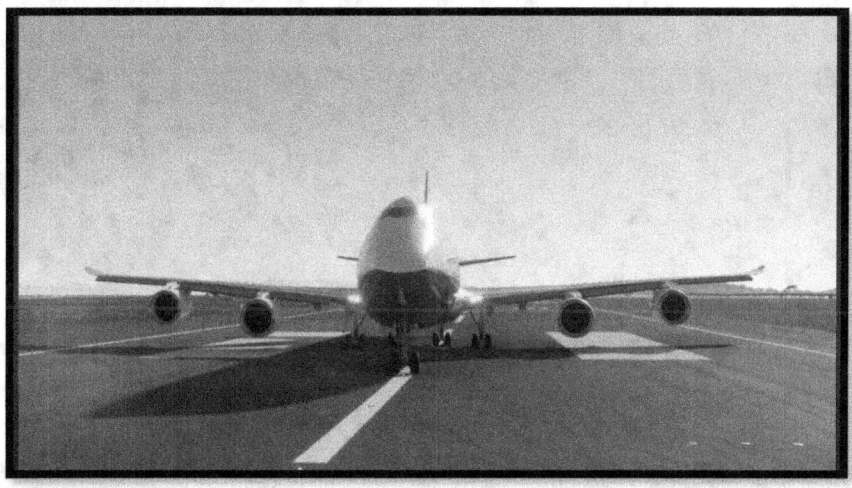

When you first start Flight Simulator you might assume the centerline spot is in line with the center glare shield frame which is from the straight on angle but when seated your aim point is the center of your view.

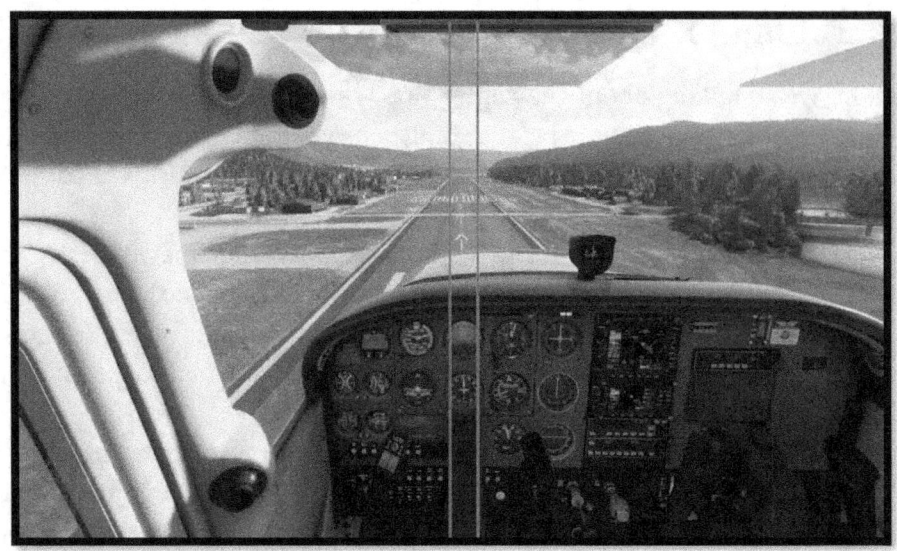

Your primary display or artificial horizon is sometimes a good marker to hold that sight picture in your peripheral view but the exact spot changes depending on aircraft layout. In a 172 you can get away with using the artificial horizon as a place to aim but generally, it's just going to be the center of your view and this is going to carry over naturally the more you do it and see it.

From a Cessna 172 to a 747 to a helicopter, if you're aiming down the center of your seat or yoke you will be in the centerline so always make sure your camera view is centered appropriately with the seat just like your head would be if you're actually to sit in the aircraft.

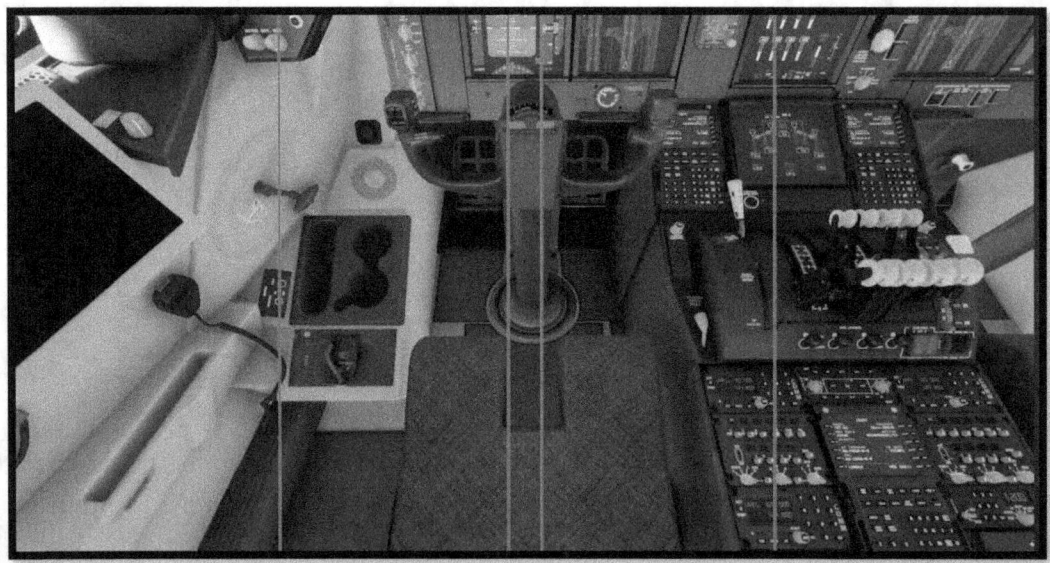

Now once you know all of this it's going to be practicing over and over again; some days the weather is going to fight you on this and if you get caught with a good gust while in ground effect this can blow you off the centerline a little bit but you can quickly correct that once you touch down. The important thing here is to get as close to the center line as possible and hold it there, and knowing where that spot is will be key.

What we're trying to drive home here is where you want to be aiming and where that line is from the cockpit. Good landings also come from good approaches. On a final approach, it's good to keep looking down towards the end of the runway and hold that site in the center. This will help with your approaches.

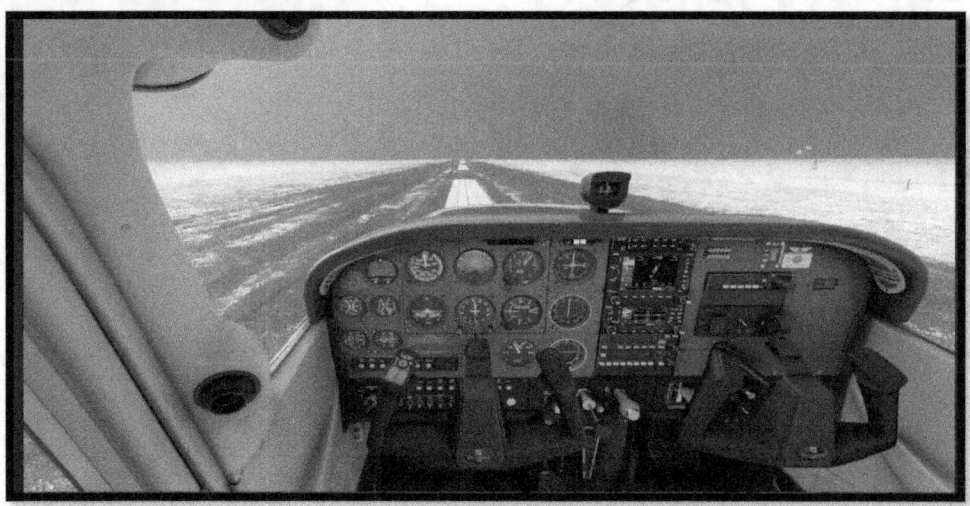

If you're struggling to land a certain aircraft in the center, remember to make sure you are lined up in the seat, center yourself on the line, and pay attention to where that line is from the cockpit then just practice taxiing on that line.

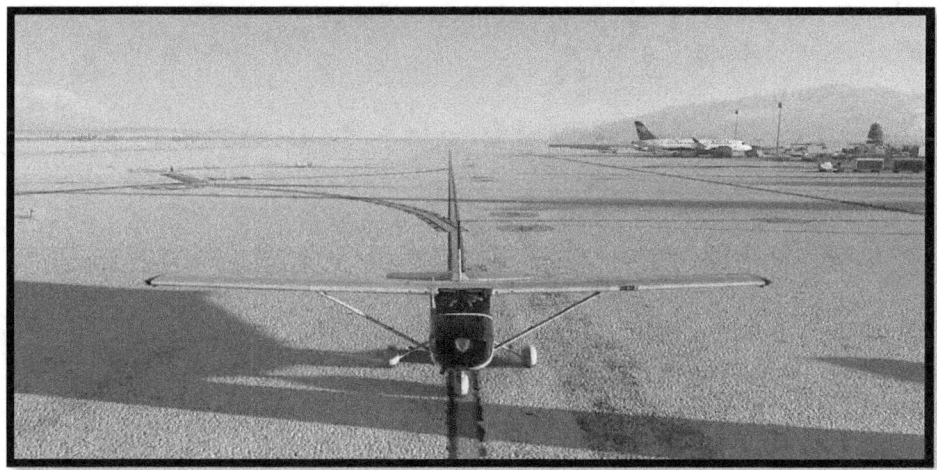

Most sims have replay systems so you can debrief to see how you did and if you're consistently staying on the line then you're ready to land that way too. Through practice, this will all become normal for you.

Stall recovery

A stall occurs when the angle between the wing and the relative airflow or angle of attack exceeds that which will allow smooth enough airflow to produce sufficient lift to maintain controlled flight. While this is an undesired aircraft state it's not unrecoverable as long as timely and correct control inputs are made.

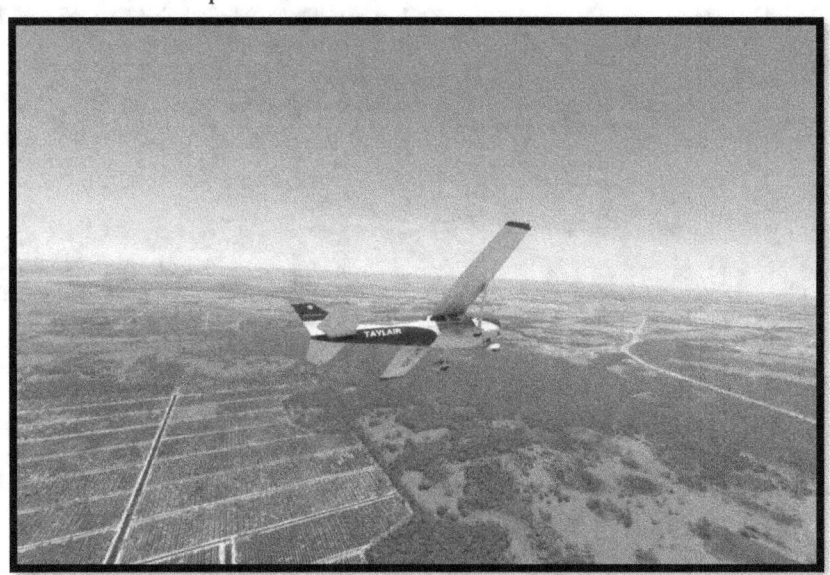

Stall awareness

We can look for these warning signals of an impending stall:

- Increasingly high-nose attitude
- Reducing control effectiveness
- Low and decreasing airspeed
- Onset of buffet

With any of these signs, you can reduce the power to idle and attempt to maintain the altitude. As the altitude is maintained with insufficient power you will start to see these early warning signs:

- Increasingly high-nose attitude
- Reducing control effectiveness
- Low and decreasing airspeed
- The stall warning horn
- Pitching Betty screaming stall

It's important to note that all of the precursors we discussed occur long before the aircraft senses an approaching stall and recovery at the earlier signals is by far the safest technique. If Betty is getting involved you're not having a good day. That being said, what if you do miss all of these warning signs and the aircraft enters a full stall?

- A stall is defined as:
- An uncommanded wind drop,
- Nose drop
- Inability to maintain level flight
- Buffet.

You do not need to wait for more than one symptom; if you experience any one of these symptoms recovery should be initiated immediately.

Again, if we have four elevator back pressures and a descent is being shown on the instruments, we can conclude that we are unable to maintain our altitude however we've not encountered a wind drop but as we said before any one of these symptoms requires a stall recovery.

Stall recovery technique

- Move the control column centrally forward - this unstalls the wings.
- Apply full power - this minimizes height loss.
- Proceed to level the wings.
- Retract gear and flaps according to POH guidance.
- Enter a VY climb.

We have now recovered the aircraft to a safe flying state and we can fly back to base and stop off the stall on the way down.

Remember that an aircraft is more at risk of stalling during takeoff and landing when close to the ground so any stall recovery will require a sacrifice of height to recover. Recognition of the early signs is therefore key to avoiding impact with terrain.

Spin recovery

In this section, we're going up for some spin recovery training using the Cessna 172. The first thing we need to do is make sure the aircraft is set up correctly. Cessna says spins are approved in the 172 when the airplane is operated in the utility category. This means no backseat passengers or baggage and a gross weight of 2,000 pounds. You also don't want any loose objects around your microphone. The seat belt shoulder harnesses should be secured and also restrain you during the spin because there's a possibility you can move forward in your seat.

We don't have to worry about all that as those things are static. For this illustration, we're at 6,000 feet in Fortuna, California and we're going to start doing a few of these.

To enter the spin we're going to leave the power at about 80% so we can get a nice spin going. You can also add the Cub heat and as the stall approaches you're going to apply full back pressure on the elevator and then full left rudder and you're going to hold that. You can hold that as long as you want to get the spin going or you can correct it right away. If we get into a little bit of an agitated spin, just hold that rudder and it's going to give you a nice spin.

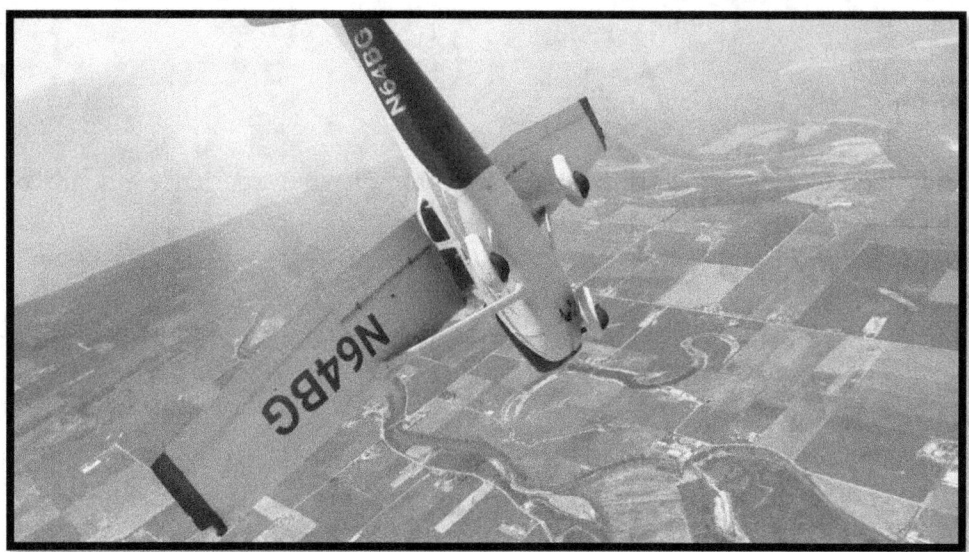

When you're ready to recover, set the throttle to idle, neutral on the ailerons, full opposite rudder, and down on the elevator then bring it back to recover. You can just bleed off the speed before adding the power back. Now you're in a Sim so you don't have to recover right away. Like we said, you can let it spin as long as you're high enough but that's all there is to it.

Since we went up to 6,000 we might lose anywhere from 500 to 1000 feet depending on how quickly we recover it but they're very easy to recover from. Again, we're going to start giving it that back pressure so that speed is going to start bleeding off, and when we start to get that stall horn, we'll apply full back pressure to the left rudder and hold it then we can start to recover just like that. It's pretty easy to accomplish and fun to do especially with VR being out for Microsoft Flight Sim now.

Engine Shutdown

Here's a quick guide to shutting down the engines and we are using the F18 in Microsoft Flight Simulator for this illustration. The first thing we have to do is head down to the right side panel and turn the bleed air off then head over to the left panel and look at the throttle.

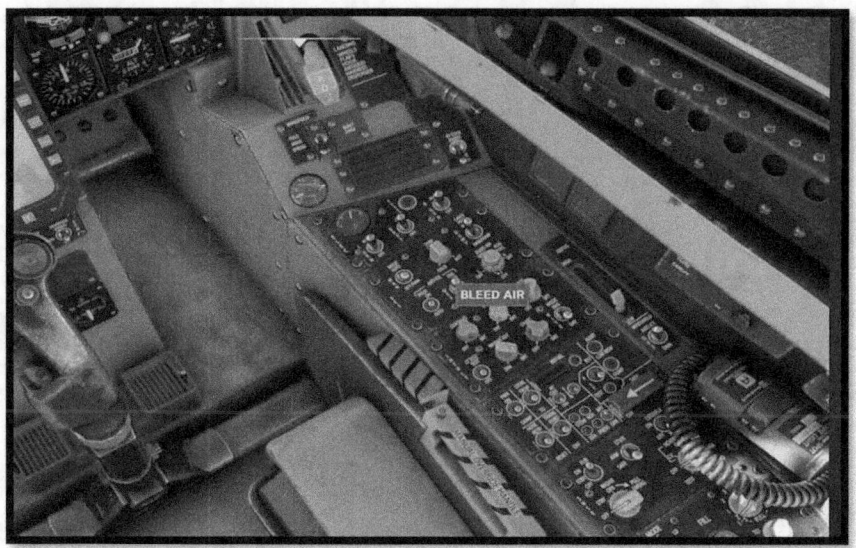

We'll Left-click and hold on to the left throttle and while we're holding the left click we'll right-click once. That will begin the shutdown of engine number one and we can see over here that engine number one shuts down very quickly.

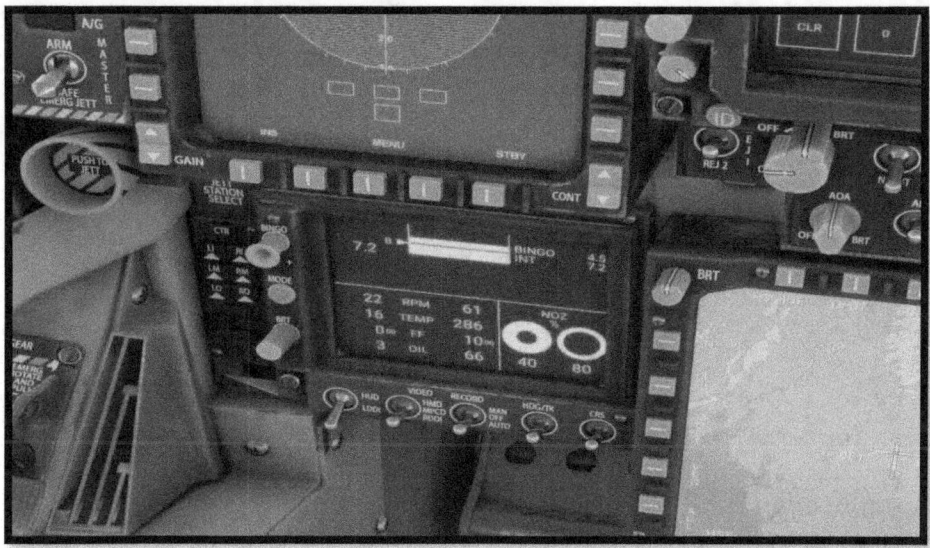

Once the shutdown of engine number one is complete we'll repeat the process on engine number two so we head down to the throttle, left click and hold on the engine number two throttle, and right click once while we're holding the left click. That then starts the shutdown procedure for engine number two.

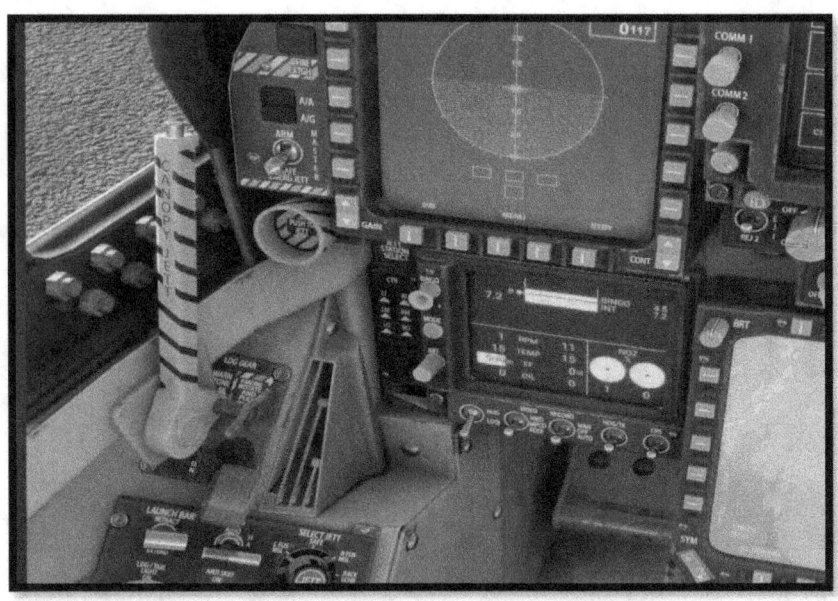

With that procedure complete and once our engines have shut down, all that remains is to switch off the battery in the F18 which can be done on the right-hand side panel and you click the battery off switch.

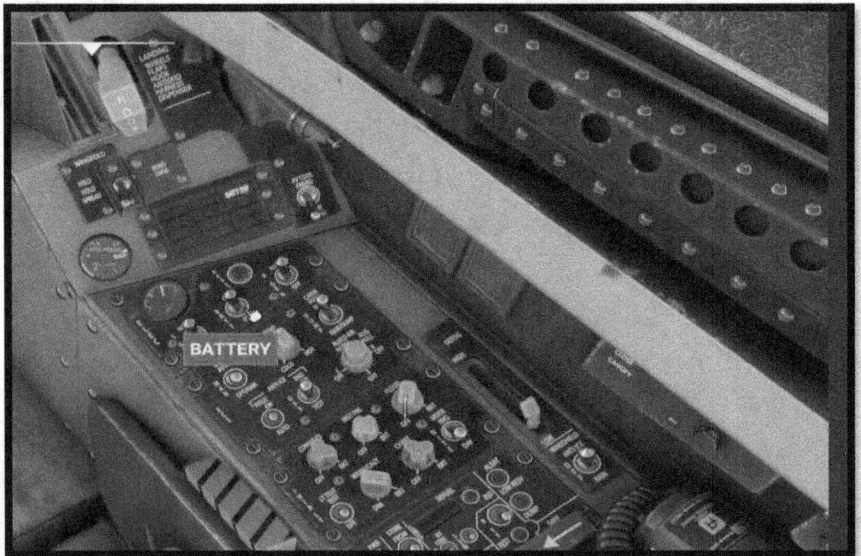

Steep turns

In this section, we're taking you through steep turns. With any of our maneuvers, it's all about getting the airplane ready. For starters, we're at 3,500 feet. We've got the airplane trimmed up. We've got Va, just perfectly maneuvering speed. Everything is locked in. We do need to knock out our clearing turns, though, first. So, we'll look left, and we're heading that way. Always start your clearing and turn to the left. Why is that? Well, in a perfect world, if you are being overtaken, the aircraft that's overtaking you is to pass to your right. You wouldn't want to blindly turn into them, so, you'd want to turn to the left, look for them, and then make your turn back to the right.

Catch any little climbs early and make sure you're truly configured. Get your RPMs set where you want them. Then, trim the airplane. Get the power setting there first. Then, trim the airplane. We're going to show you steep turns where you use trim to do what we call hands-free steep turns. Now, you may think this is cheating, but we call it using all available cockpit resources. Are you ready?

Let's look left one more time. Coming from maneuvering speed and a trimmed airplane, we roll left. Now, when we say we add a roll of trim, we are grabbing from the top of the trim to the bottom. Do it in three rolls. Three rolls that you have access to of the trim. You may have to adjust two and a half, something like that, but every aircraft loves a little bit of trim like that. Are you ready? Verify clear left. Roll left, do your trim, one, two, three. Set the airplane on the horizon, and let it go through. You can make a little adjustment there if you have to and just let it go through, let it work its way on through, slicing across that horizon. There you go. So, for steep turns, you could utilize a trim to help you.

Steep spiral

A steep spiral is a commercial pilot maneuver and the reason we practice this steep spiral is maybe that amazing landing site is right below us and we don't want to lose it or we don't want to drift away if we have an engine failure so we steep spiral down to it.

There are two things to note about a commercial pilot steep spiral: one, you need to choose an altitude high enough to allow you to make three full turns and recover obviously by 1500 feet agl and your bank is up to and not to exceed 60 degrees so if we put it 60 degrees and we try to hold the whole way it's not necessary because you need to compensate for wind drift.

How it's going to work is we'll go in the plane, carburetor heat on, smoothly apply our power back and with a steep spiral, you want your point just below your tire. You should be looking out down just about underneath your tire. Now we're going to bring the power back and roll out. The goal is to maintain the same distance all the way around.

Something else you want to get in the habit of is called a clearing burst because oftentimes you're doing this from a very high altitude so you might want to go like this every 180 degrees with the throttle, get a little power try to kill the engine or you can also shock cool the engine when coming down from a very high altitude.

Level turns

The next on our list is to do turns and the first we'll look at is level turns. For this illustration, we are flying along with somewhere between 2,000 and 2,500 rpm. We're just above 2500 feet, we're about 19 knots traveling North and we're going to execute a right turn.

To turn, we bank the wings over and we want to align the turn coordinator's wing onto the standard rate, one turn marker so we're just going to bank over then watch the vertical speed and balance the vertical speed as well. This is all just about keeping the airplane turning at the same rate and maintaining altitude.

As we rolled into the turn we lost some lift because obviously, the forces are off to one side now. We need to climb ever so gently to get it back to two and a half thousand feet so all we're looking to do is align this marker and keep the vertical speed the same.

We're now coming around to the South and for that, we'll do a 180-degree turn. It's just enough to practice. The next thing is to anticipate the rollout so we roll the airplane back out and we're now traveling south; we've done a 180-degree rate one-level turn.

Climbing turn

Next on the list is a climbing turn. It's the same, but we're going to climb at the same time so we need to use the throttle to maintain our speed Target AirSpeed during the climb. If we begin climbing we're pulling back gently, going a thousand feet a minute and we're going to use the throttle to maintain 80 knots. We probably wouldn't be able to maintain a thousand feet a minute but we'll have a go and then we're going to turn in the same way. Yes, we're not going to be able to maintain the speed so we're now doing three things at once - we're maintaining speed with throttle, we're managing about 70 knots at 70 feet a minute and we're now looking to balance the turn rate, the climb rate and the speed at the same time.

A much more comfortable rate of climb in the Cessna would be about four or five hundred feet a minute. Again, this is us finding out along the way so if we hold 500 feet a minute on the vertical speed and we can happily keep going at about 75 knots and as we're coming around to North we'll roll back in our turn and just keep on climbing for a moment to get to three and a half thousand feet which works out quite nicely for us. We'll level out, holding about 80 knots at 2500 feet, traveling North and we'll level again. This is a climbing turn.

Descending turns

There are several types of descending turns. The first one is a gliding descending turn and what we're going to do is cut the engine or pull the engine back to idle and essentially, the airplane is then gliding. As soon as we do that we'll drop the NOSE to maintain our speed. This means we'll use our attitude to maintain airspeed and try to hold 80 knots.

We're going to cut the engine back so the indicated airspeed is dropping off to 80 knots and we'll begin our turn. Again, we're doing the same trick - we are at the inner glide, using attitude to maintain airspeed. If we're slowing down we drop the NOSE gently and if we're speeding up we pull up the NOSE gently.

One thing you need to be careful of is that the outside wing is going faster than the inside wing so the plane will tend to roll into turns because there's more lift on the outside.

We're rolling around or turning slowly, holding about 80 knots just by using attitude to do that and we'll just make sure we do this until we get around to the South , then we'll increase the throttle, level the plane up and we're back to normal flight.

Powered turning descent

We're going to maintain not as much power but some power and descend. We will increase speed this time, roll, and watch the indicated airspeed. We'll hold about 90 knots at about 300 feet a minute. We don't want to have this accelerate too much during this maneuver so we're running about 2000 RPM again, we're maintaining the rate one turn and the wing is on the marker on the coordinator. You don't have to worry so much about the Cessna 152 as the tail tends to follow the fuselage through the turns.

We're just coming around to North, we'll pull out once we're going North so we're almost down to 2000 feet.

Just to recap, we did a level turn which is a cruise throttle level. We did climbing turns, so again, we set the throttle and then used the attitude to manage speed in the climbing turn. Then we did descending turns and we did gliding descending turns and powered descending turns.

Landing in crosswinds

Have you ever had a nice cross-country flight in your Cessna or Diamond Prop plane in Microsoft Flight Simulator only to have a terrible landing and not know why your nose kept pointing left or right off the runway? Or maybe you know what is going on but you still haven't gotten the landing down in these scenarios? In this section, we're going to take a quick look at landing at crosswind conditions on Microsoft Flight Simulator using the Crab-to-Side slip or Wing low method.

This method will not only get you down safely but also smoothly and with proper directional control when executed properly. We'll go over some examples so that you know what it should look like and the control inputs that will get you on the center line every time. We'll also cover proper crosswind takeoff procedures as well.

How to detect wind direction

Now before we get into the actual crosswind technique for takeoff and landing we want to talk about how to recognize a crosswind if you're on approach or if you're just trying to fly straight. Let's say we're not using any rudder whatsoever and we're flying towards the runway, however, the nose is not aligned with the runway centerline.

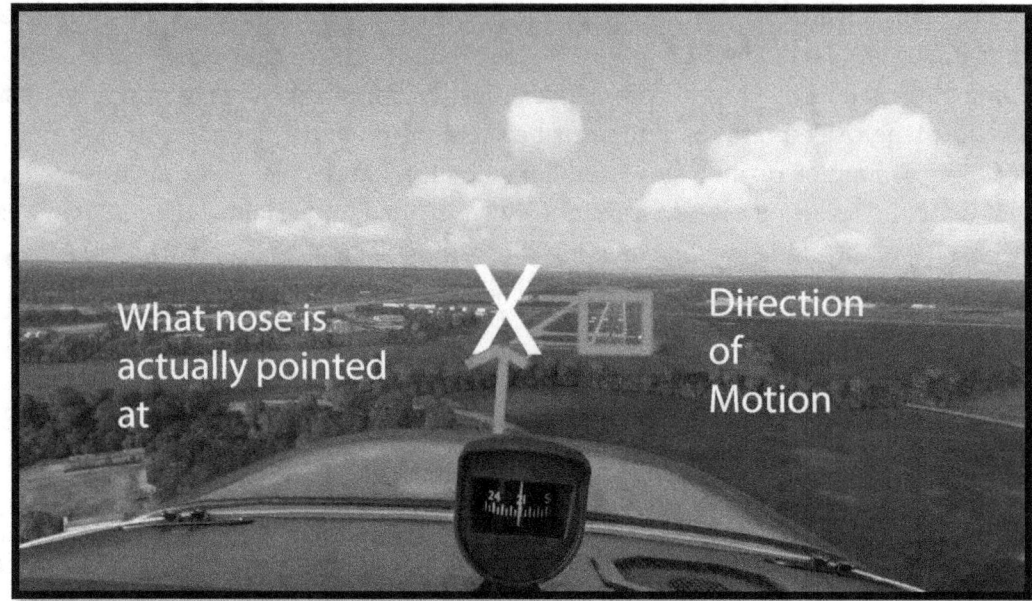

Now that is a key sign of there being a crosswind because when the wind hits the side of the aircraft, the nose wants to point into it. We know that because the nose is pointing left of motion and you can also look at the windsock off to the right it is pointed well to the right so that is a dead giveaway that there's a crosswind and there are certain controls that we have to use namely Aileron and Rudder to combat this.

Now the way that we do that is we use the left aileron as we go down the runway with the right rudder to maintain center line and as we hit rotation speed in this aircraft 55 knots we're going to ease back, let the plane come off the ground. The left wing with the aileron input to the left should be the last to come off the ground so the left main should come off last. For landing it's going to be the opposite. We're going to touch down with the left aileron into the wind because we have a left crosswind in this situation so we're going to touch down on the left main, hit the right main, and then let the nose come down and start to break.

Review Questions

1. Walk through the step-by-step process of performing a landing procedure for an aircraft in Microsoft Flight Simulator 2024.
2. Describe the techniques for maintaining proper weight and balance during all phases of flight, and how this affects the aircraft's handling and performance.
3. Explain the recommended procedures for recovering from a stall or spin, and how these skills can be practiced and refined within the Microsoft Flight Simulator 2024 environment.

CHAPTER 11

FLIGHT PLANNING, GPS, AND ILS

We're going to use the world map to program a routine we're going to spawn an airplane on the runway and then we're going to fly a route using the autopilot and get the autopilot to do as much as we can.

So we're in the simulator, we've just loaded it up, and we're just going to use the most basic controls so all you'll need to have working is the stick, the throttles, and the flap levers for flying the airplane. We'll go in and click on world map then we're going to be flying the Cessna 172 Skyhawk that comes with all versions of the simulator - this is the one with the G1000 (the glass cockpit) so we're going to be using the Cessna 172 Skyhawk.

We are going to be taking off from Petaluma in California but how do you find Petaluma? You can either type the name of it into the search or you can type the code in for it so this gives us a bit of a sideways conversation all of a sudden.

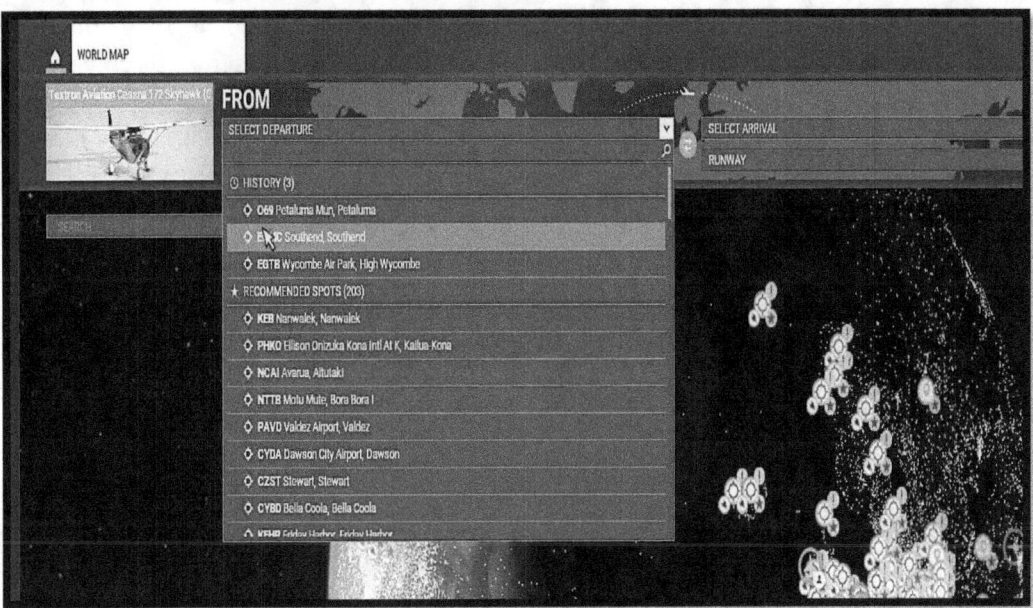

Using a third-party software

Running alongside the simulator, we have another piece of software called Little NavMap - this is a free download off the internet. Simply search for little NavMap in Google then go download, install, and run it alongside the simulator; it won't work if you're running Xbox. What it does is it superimposes all of the data from the simulator onto a map so once you've got the simulator installed with any scenery or anything you can go into the Scenery Library menu in little NavMap, load scenery and it will take a copy for its own purposes.

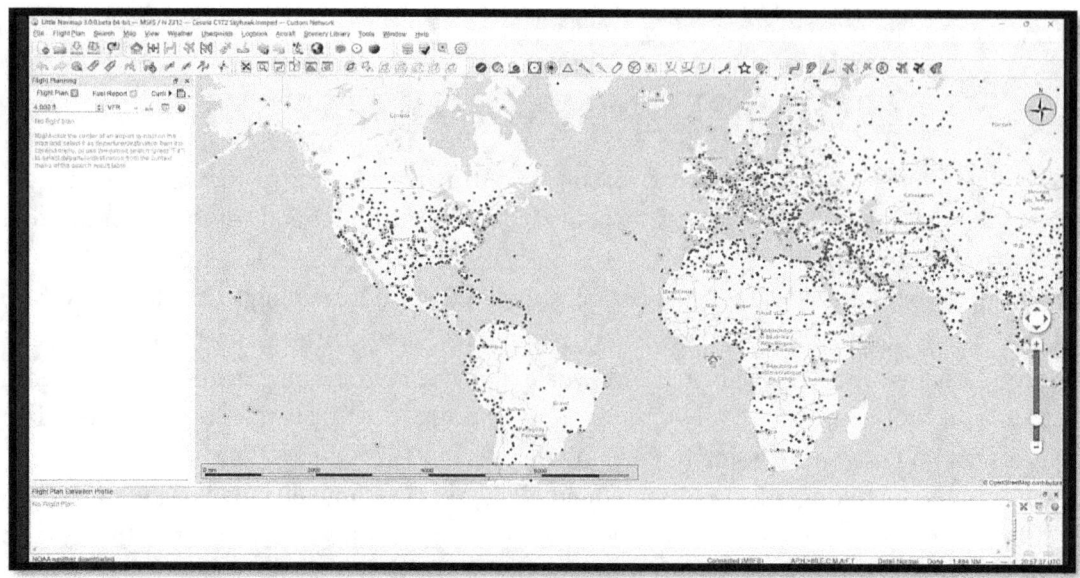

If we go and zoom in over West Coast America, the more we zoom in the more we see waypoints, airfields, ILS, and all sorts of things and we can plot groups in Little NavMap since it will make sense to visualize what the route we're going to do. We are going to pull up the search box in Little NavMap and go from Petaluma which has 069 as its ICAO code. We can click on that and set Petaluma as the departure airport and you can see it's lit up yellow on the map. If we go and look on the map here we're going to take off from Petaluma then fly over and land at Charles M Schulz or Sonoma Airport so we're going to right-click on Sonoma and set that as the destination. That has rubber-banded a basic route across the map so what we would like to do is to get ourselves in line with the ILS before we even get there to keep things simple.

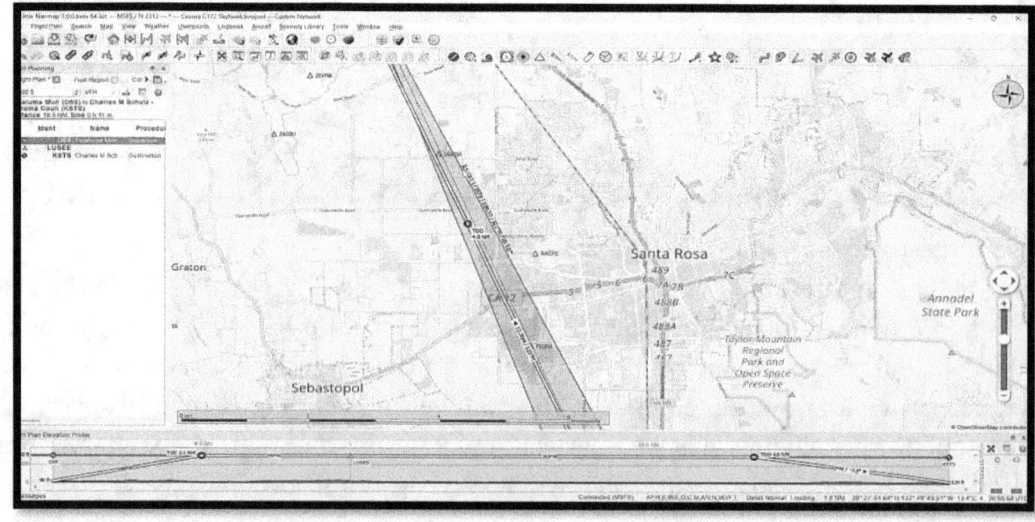

If we right-click on Lusee we can add that waypoint to our flight plan and it goes now from Petaluma via Lusee over to Charles M Schulz and we can see that built up on the list over here as we have 069 o Lusee and then KSTS. We also see this navigation plot down here showing us altitudes so we'll be flying the whole route at about 1500 ft. We can see it's figuring out if there are any Hills along the way but then all we are interested in is just to see what the route might look like and more importantly, we can see the ILS information.

Now going over to the simulator how do we put this into the simulator into the world map screen? We'll select departure, and click in the search box, now we can either type in Petaluma which will bring it up and we can click on it and it zooms the map into it or we can type the code number in. We'll go to Arrival airport now and we can type in KSTS which will bring up Charles Schulz (we could have typed Sonoma as well) then we'll click on that and there's our basic route across the map.

You'll notice in the simulator it's missing all of those waypoint markers. They are here. If you go to the "More" option at the bottom of the screen, open filters, and then scroll down to the bottom you'll see the Fix and RNAV Position Report. Turn that on and you will see that little white dots have appeared all over the map. Close that dialogue again and go back and then if we zoom in a little bit more they'll all light up and you should be able to find there's Lusee.

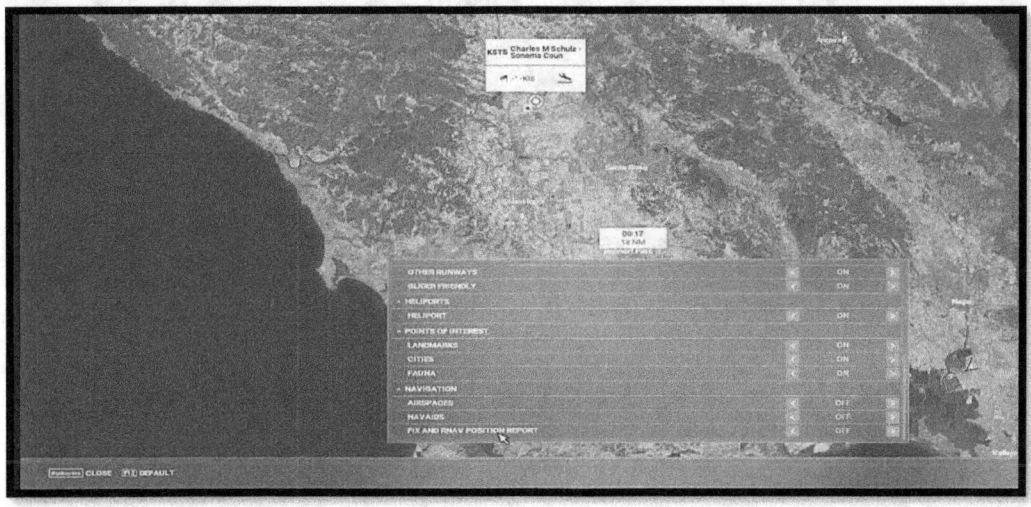

If we click on Lusee with the left Mouse button we can now add it to our flight plan so we've now got a flight plan that leaves Petaluma, goes to Lusee, and then flies straight on to Sonoma. You can see there's an important point here when we chose Petaluma: it put the airplane by default on the runway, we can choose a parking ramp but we're not going to spawn on the runway and the reason we're doing that is the airplane will be ready to go with the engine running. What's more? The airplane will already have this route programmed into its GPS. Now we'll click "Fly" and let that happen so the simulator is now busy loading.

Working with the ILS

The most important thing that little NavMap gives us which isn't so straightforward to get a hold of in the simulator are the details of the ILS. So we're going to be flying into Sonoma and we follow the ILS, and we can find out what the weather's doing and if it says there's hardly any wind today then we don't have to worry about the wind so we can leave the weather on live weather since it won't hurt us.

The simulator shouldn't take too long to load and if we say ready to fly we're going to turn our head tracking off because we want this to look as you will see it. Now we are sitting on the end of the runway, the engine is running, and we're just going to check our recording volumes to ensure they're looking good. If we look across we can see on the navigation display - our route is already programmed in and we can zoom out. We've got a range knob, if we increase the range by rolling it with the mouse wheel we can see the whole route so by default, in this Cessna when you first log into it or when you first fire it up, this map will be North oriented. You can change that so what you can do is press the Menu button on the navigation display and it pulls up a dialogue with map settings flashing.

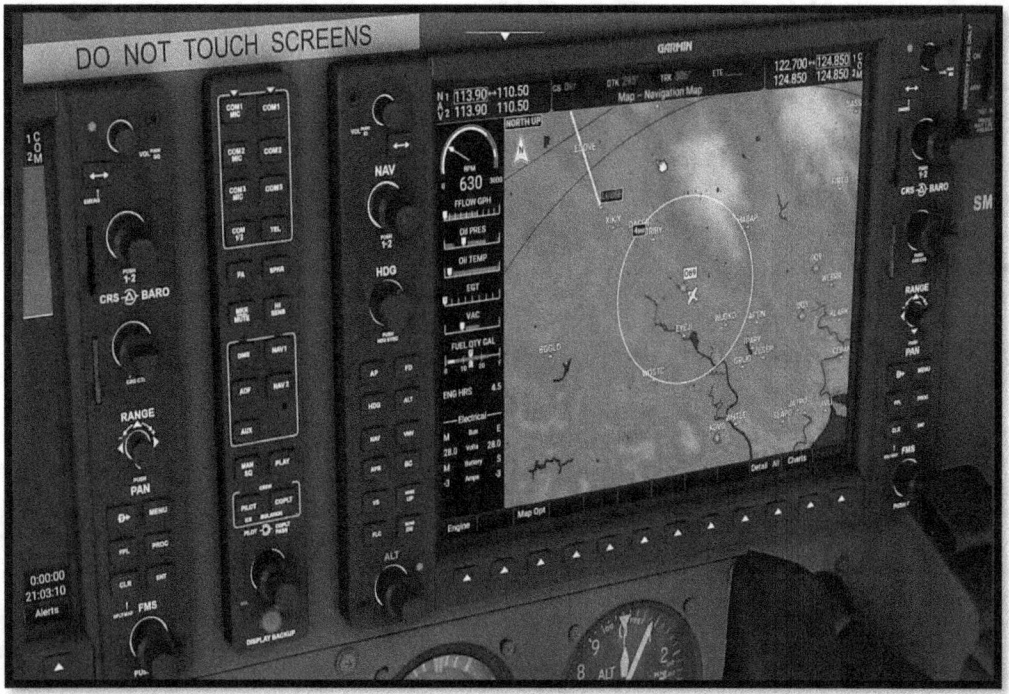

We can get rid of this yoke by clicking on the stalk so we can see all the buttons. We'll click on the stalk of the yolk and make it disappear. What we can do is press enter on map settings and then we can use that outside knob on the FMS knob at the bottom right to scroll down and then when we get to orientation we can roll the inner knob which will change its setting. We could say "track up" or even head up and press enter and the map has now spun around then we can press clear now to get rid of the dialogue so the map is now facing the direction we are going.

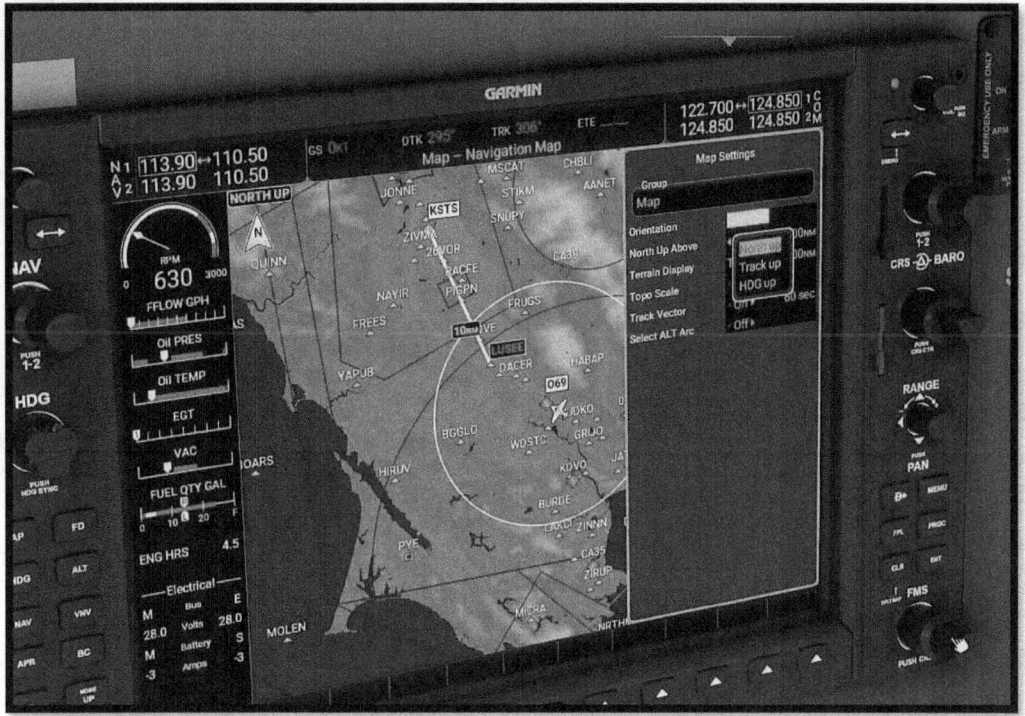

There are the compass rows so we get a much easier way of navigating just by looking at the map but then before we do anything we're going to familiarize ourselves with some of these buttons and what they do and some of the instruments.

On the left side of this screen, we have the indicated airspeed - this is measuring the air rushing past and hitting this pipe so that air pressure tells the airplane how fast it is going through the air and that will be indicated here in the panel.

On the right-hand side, we've got the altitude above sea level. Currently, we're at 240 and now we just pressed B and it suddenly changed so by the same token the altitude is read by the air pressure. When you get into the airplane it may not be calibrated but by pressing B on the keyboard we have calibrated that and we can now see the measurement in inches. We've also calibrated the air pressure for the altimeter so it's accurate to the AirField we're at so currently we are at about 90 ft above sea level.

Down here, that circular instrument with a compass around it is a horizontal situation indicator. It's a clever version of the whiskey compass which you can look at to see which direction you're going. This has a little airplane in the middle meaning the airplane is going the way indicated by that airplane so the direction you're going is always at the top of the compass and is shown by the angle here as well but you'll notice there's a line on this Horizontal Situation Indicator or HSI.

The GPS

If you have a magenta line it's showing the GPS or the lines it's showing represent the track on the GPS and if you look closely, the route on the GPS goes through our airplane and directly out in front of us. You'll notice there's a course knob over here with a triangle. If we try to spin it when we're in GPS mode it doesn't do anything so what's this all about? If we press the CDI button (you may load into the airplane and may find this is in a different mode), the CDI button steps between localizer mode, localizer 2, and GPS so we have localizer 1, localizer 2, and GPS.

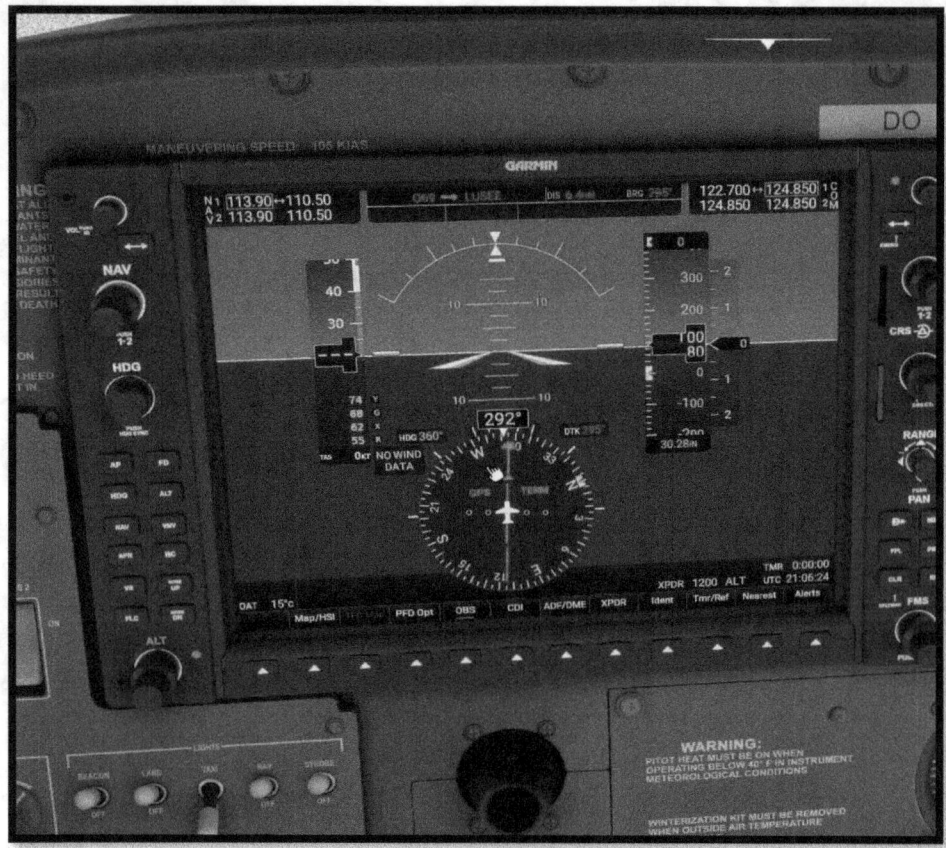

The reason we need to know about that is while we are flying point to point following the route that we programmed in, we will keep this in GPS mode then when we get to the ILS to land on the runway we have to switch to localizer mode so we're switching over to the navigation radios, not the GPS and the navigation radios are up here, there are two of them which is why we have localizer 1 and 2 that corresponds with Nav1 and Nav2.

To tune these in we can go and have a look at the ILS for Sonoma. 109.3 is the frequency, 321° is the magnetic track to the runway so if we press the middle of the Nav knob it will flick the focus between Nav2 and Nav1. Remember, we're doing this all on the ground so we don't have to worry about it when we're in the air. We want this to say 109.3. The big knob does the integers so we'll roll it backward using the mouse wheel and the small knob does the decimals so we can roll it forwards and it will go off through zero and back around to 109.3 but this is a standby frequency, it's not the active frequency, however, we can flick that over to become the active frequency.

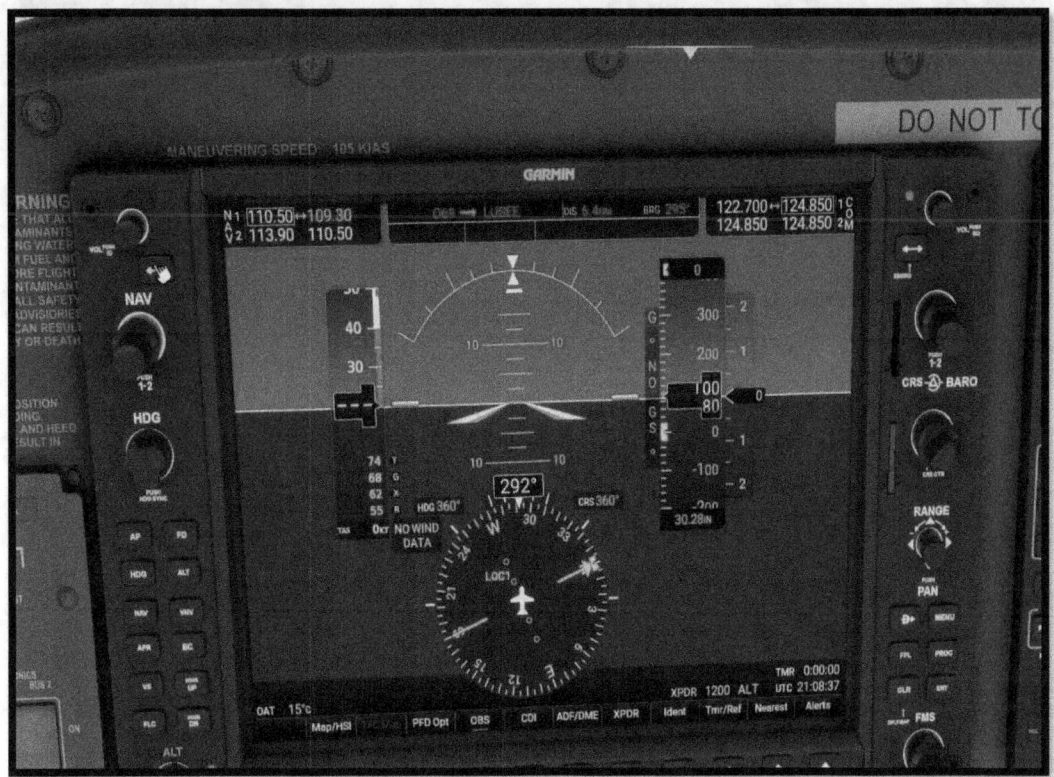

You might not see it change because we're on the ground but this will come to life when we're in the air because it's a radio (the ground interferes with it) and you have to be at some altitude for radio instruments to work properly. We'll press CDI for the moment and just show GPS.

One thing we could do just before we got there, we talked about the heading of the runway as well, didn't we? So we've already tuned the localizer, the Nav1 radio and it would be good if our course knob was ready to go on 321°, remember that triangle one is the course. There's a little diagram there explaining that and we can pull that around and now we've got the instrument here 321°. All we're doing here is doing everything in advance so when we're flying we have nothing left to do.

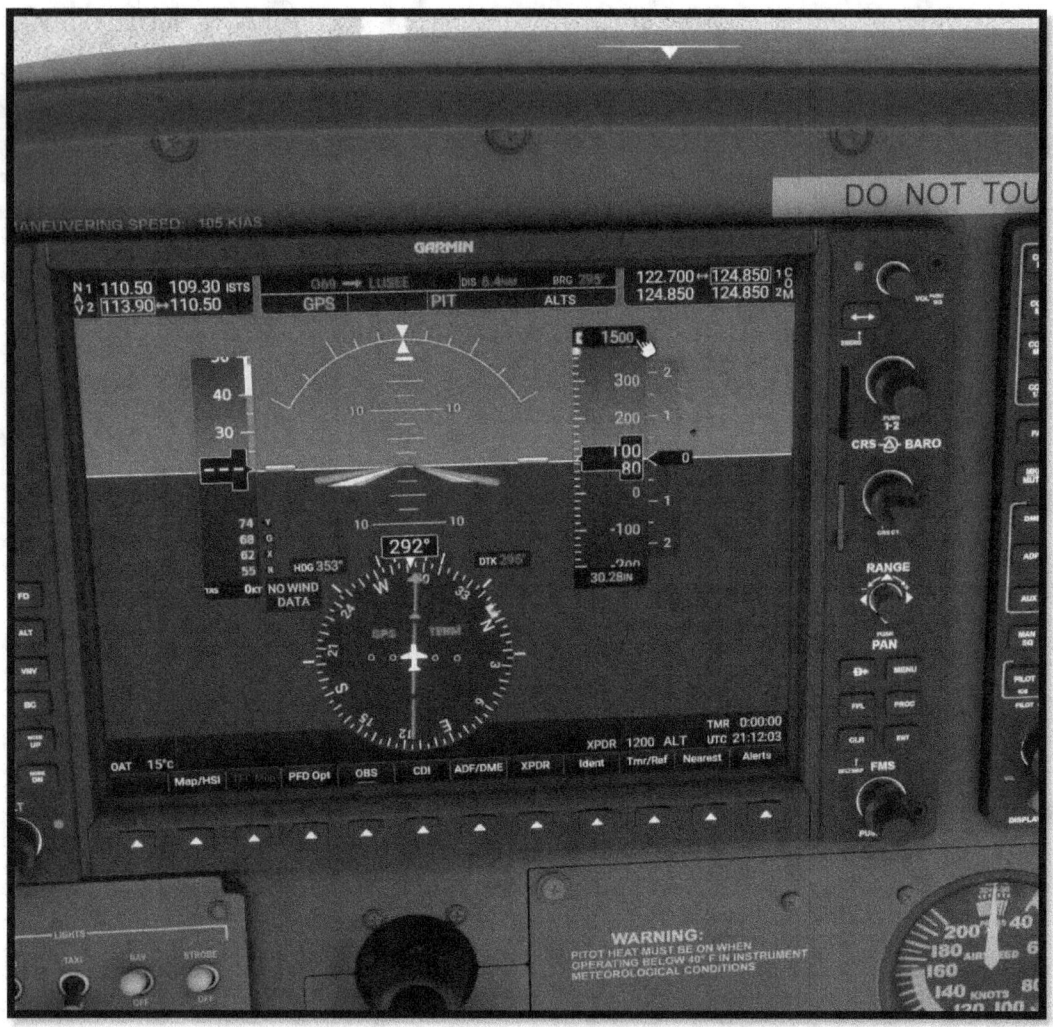

Remember, we're going to be flying GPS to begin with so we change the CDI mode back. When it says CDI what it means is Course Deviation Indicator - that's the line in the middle of the HSI. If we are off to the left or right of the track then you can see on the map how that line will slide to the left and right meaning the line on the map is to the left or the right of us so we can chase the line. We'll see that happen as we fly out.

One thing we haven't covered is heading. As we roll the heading around you'll notice this marker goes. We can fly the autopilot in various modes - there's heading mode, Nav mode, approach mode, vertical navigation mode, altitude hold mode, and vertical speed mode and a lot of these can be used in combination with each other. We've got flight level change mode down at the bottom as well but we're not going to worry about too many of them now. What we are going to focus on is as we switch the autopilot on we would like the airplane to follow the track that we've programmed in so we're going to press Nav and it will show GPS up at the top. This line here will tell us what program the autopilot is on and GPS mode means the airplane will steer left and right to follow the track that we programmed in. If we want the air aircraft to climb or ascend to a given height we have to tell it what heights to climb to.

We have different layouts of these knobs on different airplanes but then at the bottom left of the Cessna you've got the altitude so if you watch the altitude ribbon here you can change the target altitude, let's say we want to fly to 1500. The big knob does thousands while the small knob does hundreds so we can tell it to take us up to 1,500 ft.

The next thing for us to decide after choosing a target altitude is the rate at which we want to get there. This is a huge subject because there are lots of ways you can program this to do it but for now, we are just going to use vertical speed mode. After all, it's the simplest although it's quite dangerous. After all, the airplane will blindly climb at the rate we've told it regardless of speed or power.

We'll say vertical speed and up here, you'll see it say "VS," and then you can press the NOSE UP and NOSE DOWN buttons repeatedly to change the rate in hundreds of feet per minute. We can click NOSE UP about five times and it's going to climb to 1500 ft at 500 ft per minute. You can get away with about 700 ft per minute in good weather in the Cessna 172 at full power so we're going to climb to 1500 ft at 700 ft a minute and this has all been programmed in. The ALTS here means it will capture the altitude when it gets to it so it will stop climbing all on its own.

In terms of steering, we're in GPS mode so as long as we're close to the track, when we switch the Autopilot on it will make sense of it and steer left or right to get us exactly onto the track.

Arriving at our destination

Now as we head down to our destination and the airplane's flying down the track, with the GPS track on this map we can zoom out a little bit so we can see the destination. If you see the green arrow that's the localizer (the magenta arrow is the GPS) and you can switch the modes by pressing the CDI button so in a moment that small diamond you can only see half of will come down the Glide slope meter. What it means is there's an imaginary line through the sky at 3 degrees on this Runway; different runways have different angles but most of them are 3° on flat ground. It's like a standard.

Imagine an invisible line down to the runway that your airplane is supposed to follow to get safely down to the runway. This green diamond represents where we are in position in relation to that invisible line; at the moment we're flying along level at 1500 ft and the line is out in front of us somewhere so we are below the line. When it gets to the middle it means we are on the line and if it goes below the halfway point it means we are above the line so we essentially can chase that diamond but we don't have to - we can get the autopilot to do it or we can use Approach mode so if we press Approach we'll see it's lit up saying GS for Glide slope.

So with that invisible line in front of us, down to the runway, we're getting closer and closer to it. When we hit it the airplane will start descending all on its own so we'll watch both our vertical speed and the altitude when this gets into the middle because we are in Approach mode on the ILS. The ILS is tuned in, the course is set, and Glide Slope is lit up and is descending, there goes the vertical speed and the height's coming off so the airplane is flying itself down to the runway with no flying skills required for this just some knowledge of how the radios work and the autopilot buttons.

We're going to speed up because we're going downhill so what we'll do is cut the throttle back, we need to be going slow enough and as the speed is coming off, that rate of change marker is showing the rate at which the speed is coming off.

We need to get into the white area on the indicated airspeed ribbon which is the area that is safe to deploy the flaps so we can open the engine again and we can start deploying the flaps. Once we deploy flaps the airplane is causing a lot more drag so we'll have to temper that with more throttle. We can go for full flaps so we can look from outside because the airplane's flying itself.

The idea of flaps if you are a complete beginner in Aviation is so the airplane can fly more slowly. With the flaps extended, they allow the wing to generate far more lift but at the expense of drag. Remember, we're now using the throttle to control our speed on the way in so we don't want to get much less than about 55 knots.

Now the altitude is being read out beneath us. If you want to censor your view quickly and easily you just press the F key on the keyboard and then space and then you can use the right mouse button and drag down and use the mouse wheel to zoom in and out just to get a nice view arranged.

The airplane's coming in on its own, we haven't even got my hand on the joystick but just keeping an eye on the airspeed there and using the power. We're on autopilot, on Localizer mode or Landing mode. We're on the Glide slope as well. The localizer is left or right and the Glide slope is up or down and it's coming in completely automatically onto the runway.

We're going to let the airplane fall onto the runway. Normally you would flare but then you can get away with this; it will flare a small amount in landing mode but not as much as if you did it by hand and again, once we get just above the runway we're going to cut the throttle to idle so it's bringing the NOSE UP.

Now we've cut the throttle to idle, we'll just drift into the ground. The autopilot has stayed on so we have to go and press the AP button down here and it starts flashing which means it's been switched off so now we are in control of the airplane we'll get it back onto the center line and we can use the wheel brakes, we can raise the flaps and we can steer off the runway. This is a beginner's guide to flying between two points on the map with the basic Cessna that has a nice autopilot, a nice GPS, and a nice Nav radio system for use with ILS.

The in-built flight planning system

In this section, we'll talk about the in-built flight planning system and the navigation or the air act data within Microsoft Flight Simulator. All we're going to do is show you how to quickly plan a flight and for this illustration, we're going to fly from Manchester to Heathrow, a nice simple routing and we'll show you just how intuitive it is within the menu system on how to do that.

First things first, we'll click the world map option. We like to select the aircraft first for this flight. We would take the Airbus A320 and on your own, you can have a look at all the deliveries, weight, and balance failures. We'll click close on that and as we said, we want to start at Manchester today so we can either move around the map to find where it is or simply type in the airport.

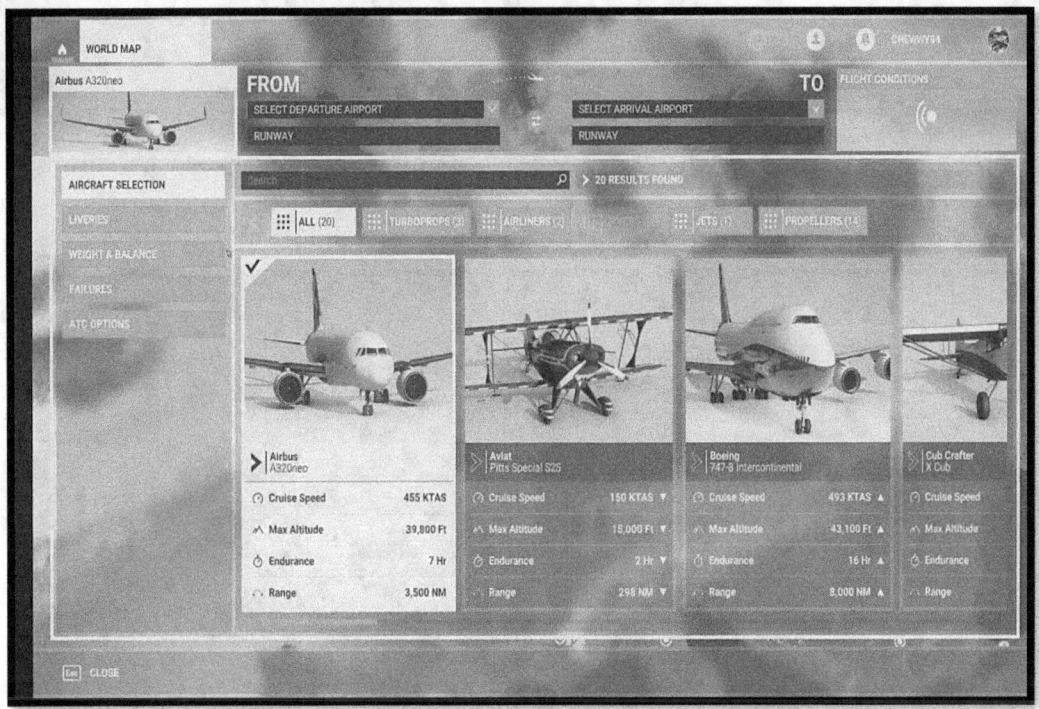

For example, we'll go EGCC for Manchester which is its ICAO code and then we can zoom in, and again, we've got a drop-down menu here to decide where we park or we can zoom the way with our mouse and we'll see all the parking positions today. Let's just say we'll go for ramp four parking and we can click "set as departure."

Then on the opposite side here we can select our arrival airport which in this case is EGLL for London Heathrow today and we can select that we'd like to do a runway 27 right approach.

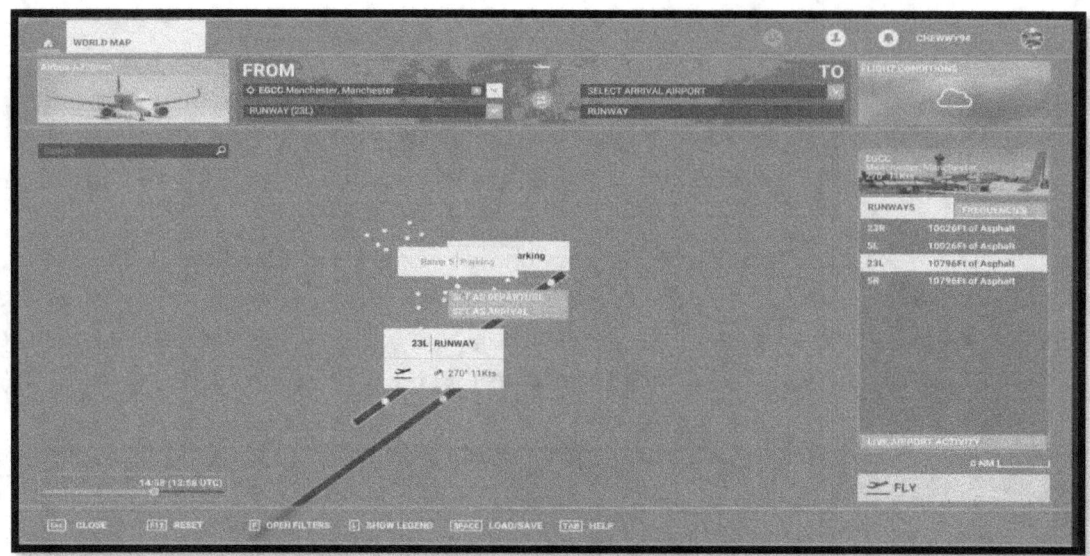

You'll also notice here on the side we can see the current wind data. We've got information about the frequencies and runways and live airport activity which we've turned off at the moment. Now we've got a straight line between Manchester and Heathrow.

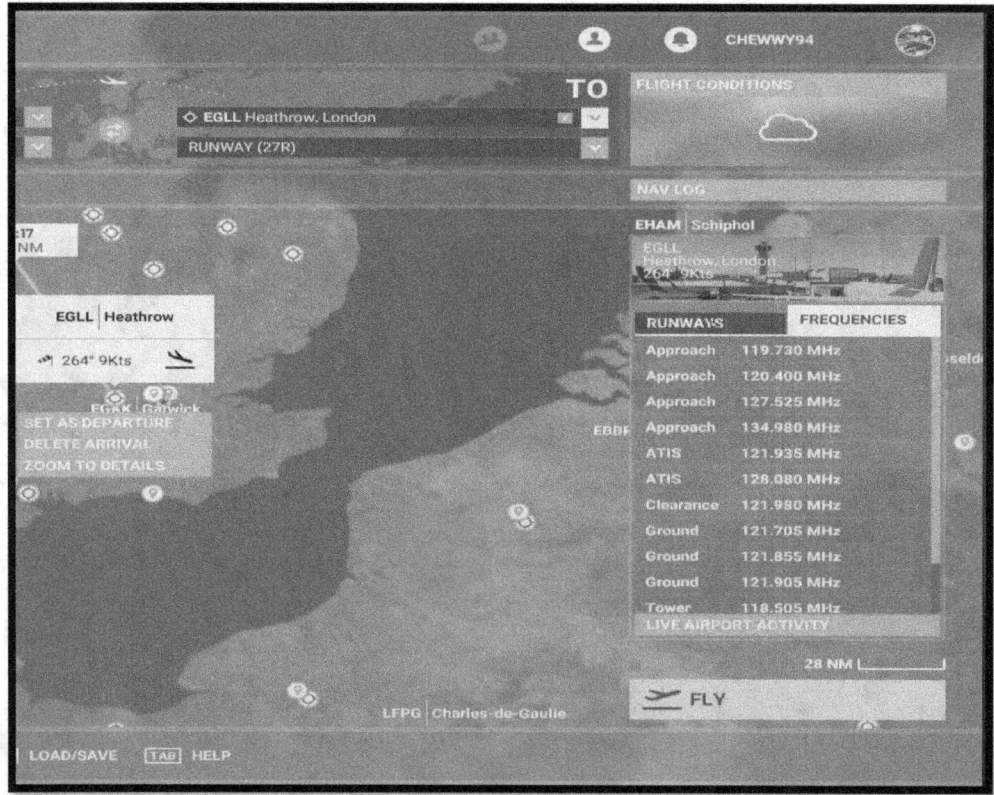

What if we want to do something a little bit more complex than that? In the top left-hand corner here you'll see that we can either do a VFR direct GPS flight or VOR to VOR and then on IFR you've got the low-altitude airways and the high-altitude airways. For this illustration, we're going to select low-altitude airways and you'll see it just takes a few minutes to compute itself. It's given us a flight plan.

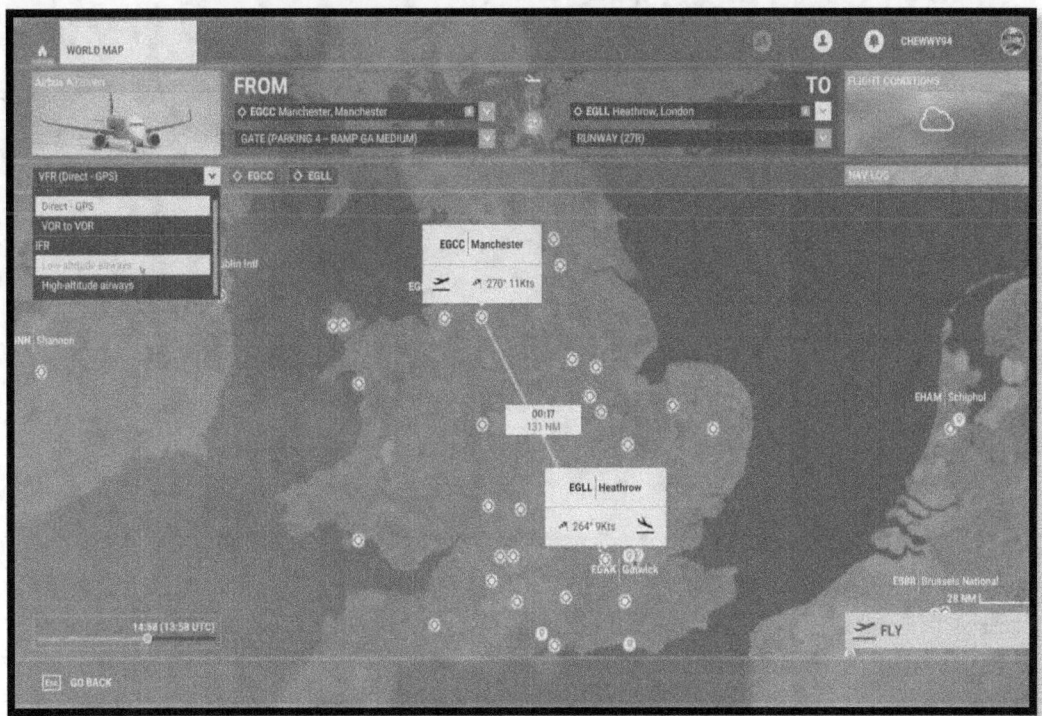

For some of you who might be already regular with flight simulators or aviation, you'll know that Finma isn't exactly a waypoint that we would select landing at London Heathrow and where in the world do we go from Finma to get onto the approach? You could leave it like that or if you want to get a little bit more complex go to the top of the screen, you can see that we've got another drop-down menu for departures and so there is a list of all of these sites here that will work correctly for the Manchester departure.

Now because we fly out of this airport quite often, for this direction we're traveling we would like to go towards the waypoint Sanba so we'll select the SANB1R departure, and as simple as that, it enters the SID in there and differentiates it from the main route by creating it in a nice yellow color.

Again, for arrivals we've got this awkward Finma waypoint that we might not want so, we can go into the arrivals page and select our star which from the direction that we want to travel is going to be the Bobbington 1 Bravo (BNN1B) so we'll select that and as we do that, it selects and pops that into place.

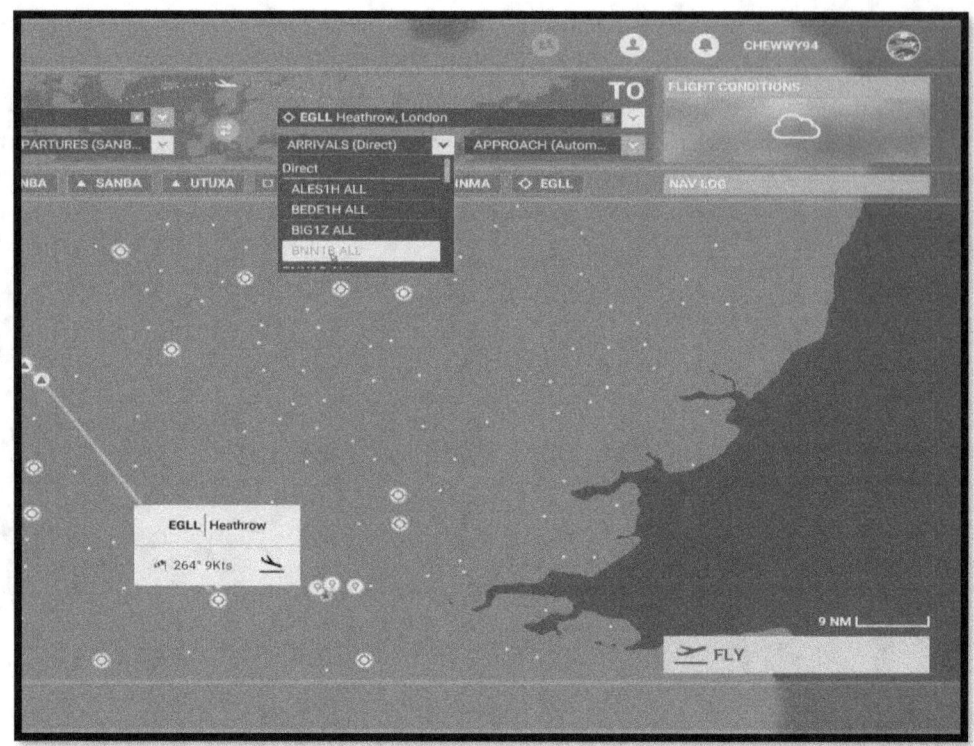

That will take us to BNN or Bobbington but once again, how do we get from Bobbington onto the approach where there's a transition? We'll select the ILS 27, for example, and as if by magic it's created the transition from that Bobbington VOR BNN onto the approach for 27. It is as simple as that.

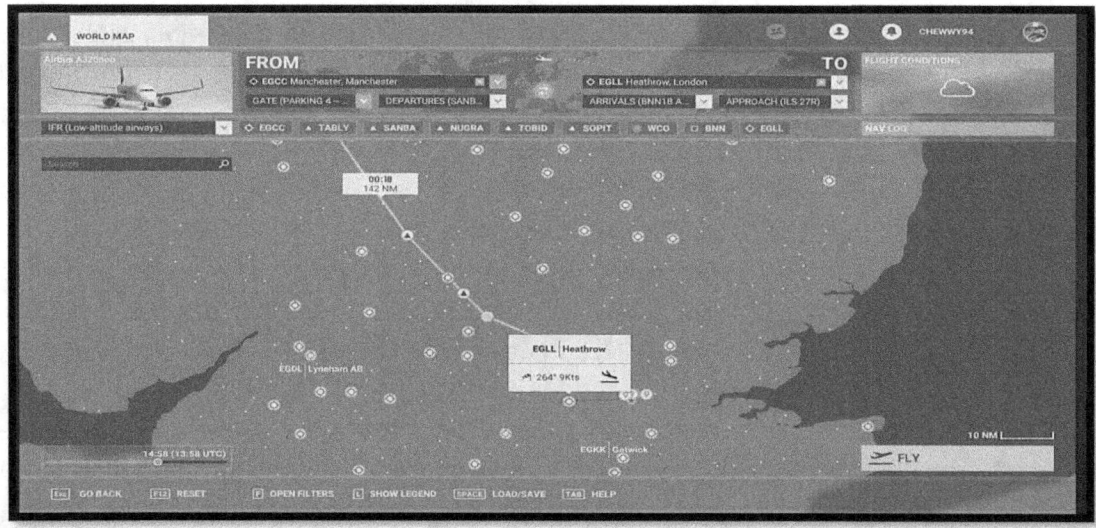

Those of you who are experienced simmers would prefer something else but for a built-in planning area for those people who might be new to flight simulation or those of you just wanting to get in the air nice and quickly without having to play around, this is such a great way to do things and in a matter of minutes we've been able to select our parking, select our SID, our routing, our star, and the approach, all in one area. We can even see how long it's going to take us and what the mileage is as well.

Importing flight plans using third-party software

In this section, we're just going to run through the basics of creating and loading a flight plan into Microsoft Flight Simulator and for this illustration, we're going to focus on using simBrief. The first thing you want to do is go over to the SimBrief website and create your own account. Once you've created the account, you can just move over to the Dispatch Tab and click on Dispatch System.

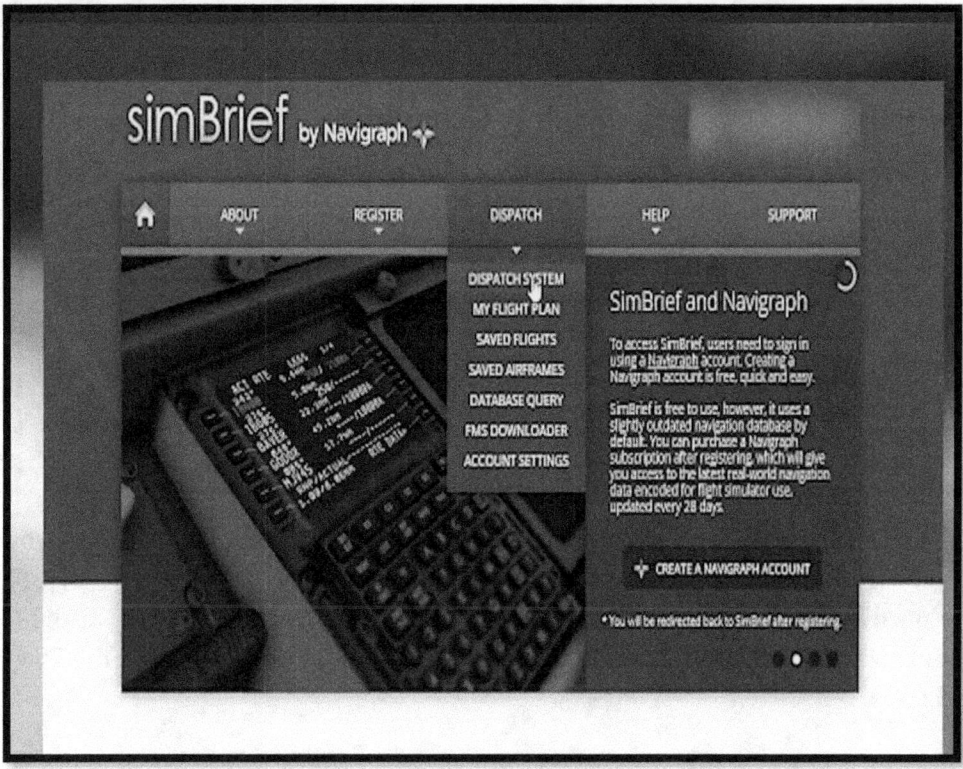

This will bring you to their Dispatch Menu and what we're going to do is create a new flight so we'll click on Create New Flight (this is where we create our flight plan and put in basic information).

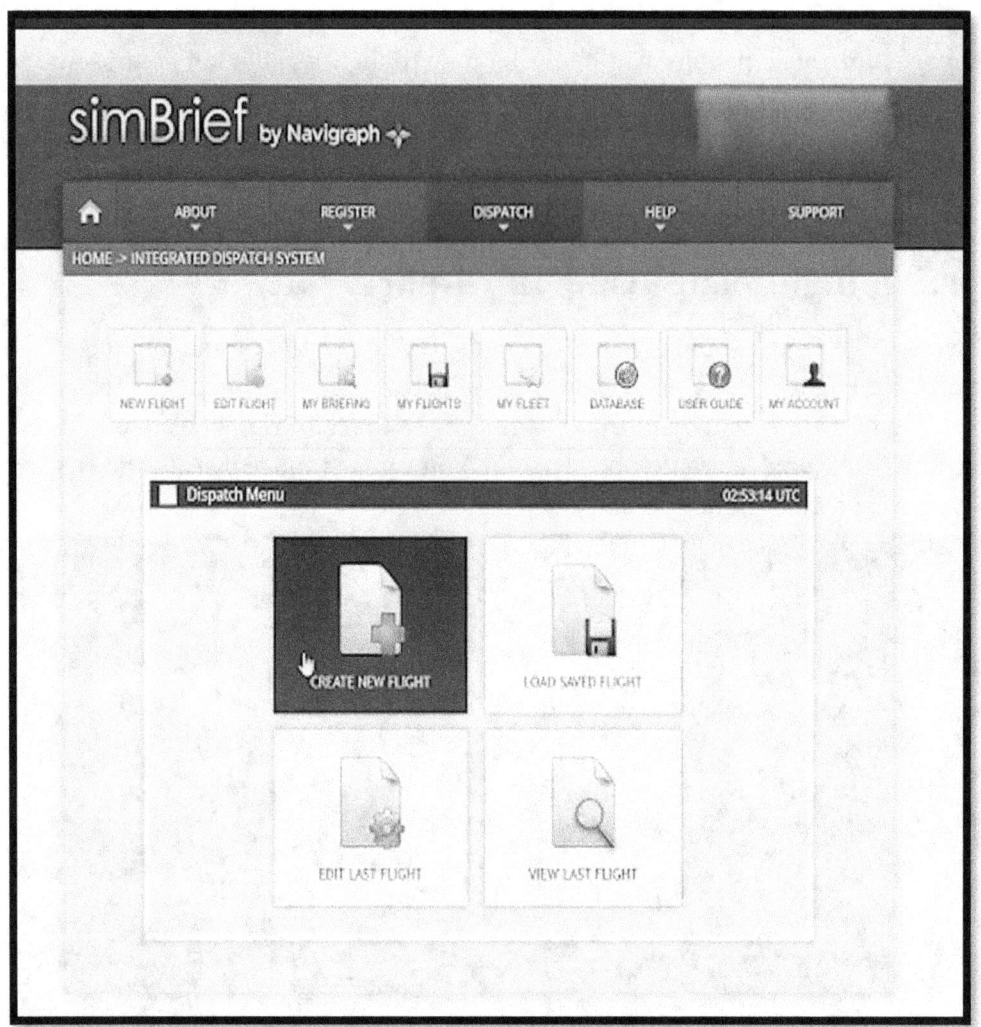

It might seem a little bit challenging to newcomers because there are a lot of spots where you can put information but for this illustration, we're going to keep this super basic. The first thing we need to do is move over to the Flight Information Section which is at the top. We need to put an airliner name there and for this illustration, we're going to put in AFS which is ALT Flight Sim.

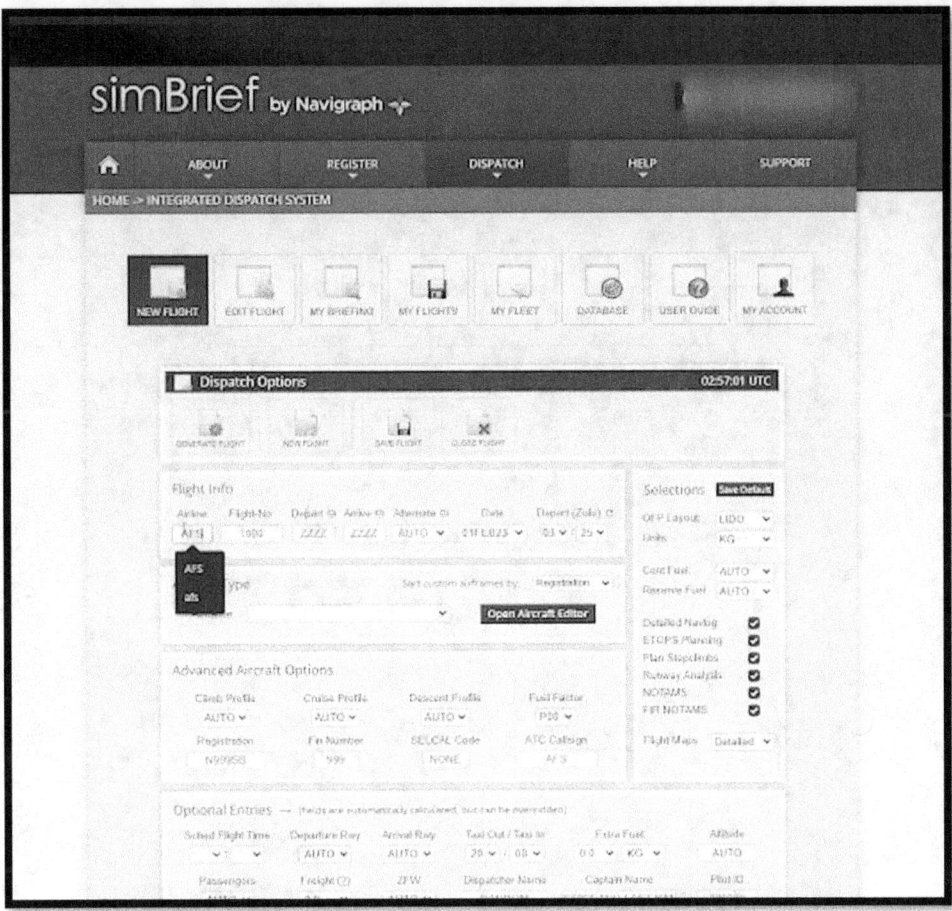

The next thing we need to do is to put in our flight number and for this flight, we're going to call it 1234 just to keep it basic. Now to create every single flight plan we need a departure point which is the airport we're leaving and also an arrival point which is the airport we're arriving at. How airports work here as you already know is that they all have their own codes called ICAO Codes and these are nicknames or short format codes to let the world of Aviation know. We're going to start over at Sydney International Airport which is in Sydney, Australia (the ICAO code is YSSY) and we're going to be flying to Brisbane International Airport so we're going to put in the Brisbane code which is YBBN.

As soon as we've done that, simBrief has already created a flight plan or a suggested route and as we move down to the bottom here, we can see on the map it's created a flight plan from Sydney International Airport up to Brisbane International Airport and the routes in the routing section is there.

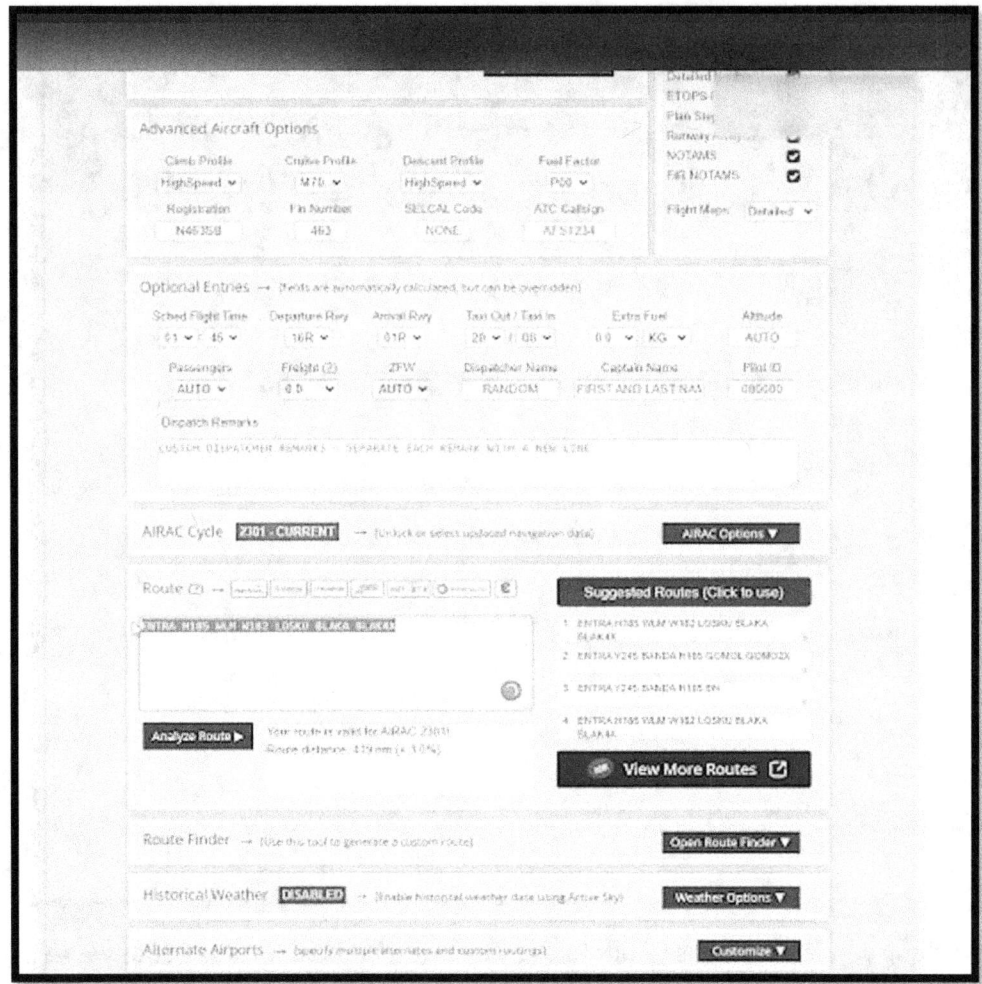

This is the one that's given to us but if we're not happy with that flight plan there are some suggested ones which we can change the flight plan by clicking on these and it will display on the map but for this illustration, we're going to use the one that it's giving us. Now we can scroll up to the top and we're going to generate the flight plan.

SimBrief creates a flight plan by taking into consideration the current weather. You can also change the time to say if you want to set up a flight plan now and you want to change it to fly in maybe six hours, you can change the departure time but we're going to use the current time in this case after which it grabs the real world weather data, combines that with real-world flight plans and that's what it spits out so we're going to generate the flight plan by clicking the "Generate Flight Plan button."

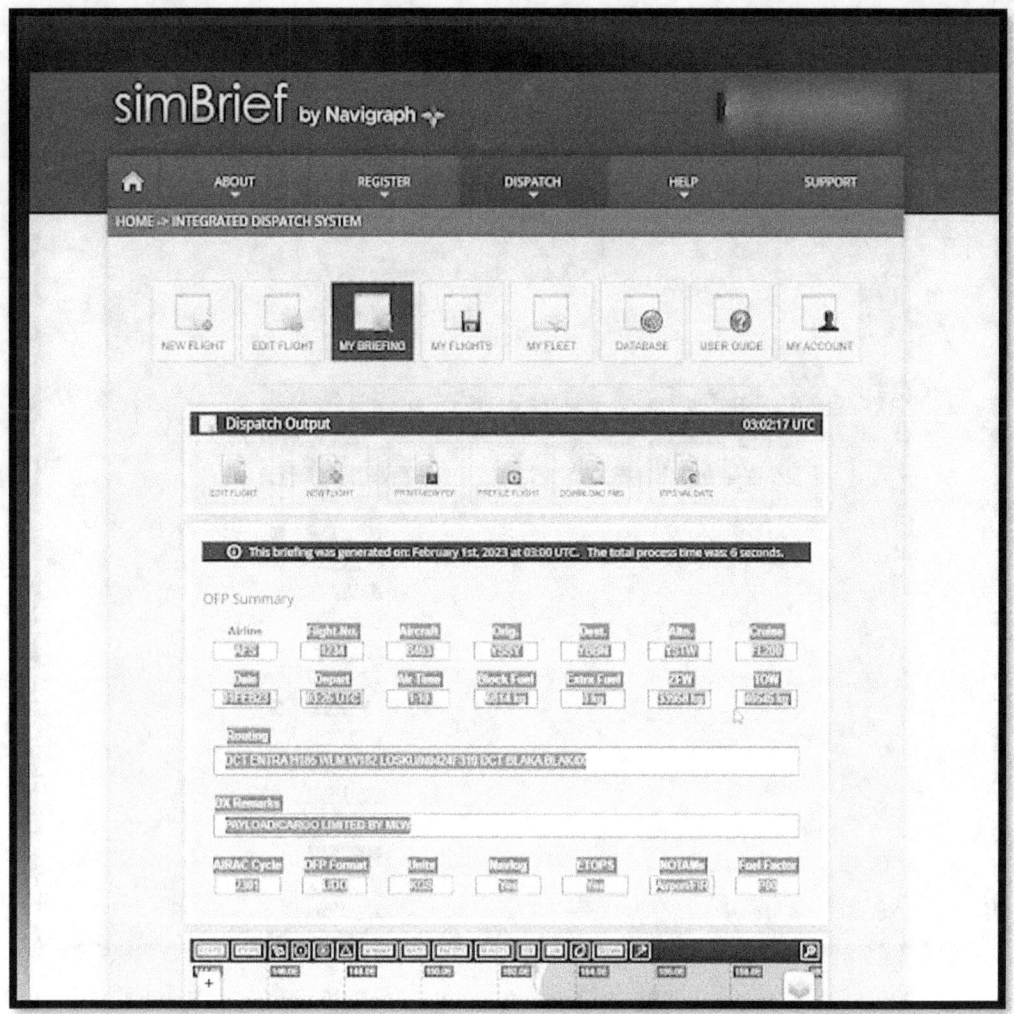

Now the flight plan has been created there are a few different sections here: the first section is the summary of the flight plan information - this will give you basic information about the flight that you can grab straight away. There's also the route map below which we saw on the previous page and then down the bottom, if we were to print out a flight plan we get a preview of what it would look like, this includes the official flight plan and its summary in all the detail. For this illustration, we're not going to go through any of this except for what we want to have a look at, which is the altitude that we're going to be doing for the flight and this is a minimum of 20,000 feet up to 31,000 feet. We're going to choose at 26,000 feet for now but we'll show you where we do that. Now that we're happy with our basic flight plan we'll scroll down the bottom and download the flight plan file.

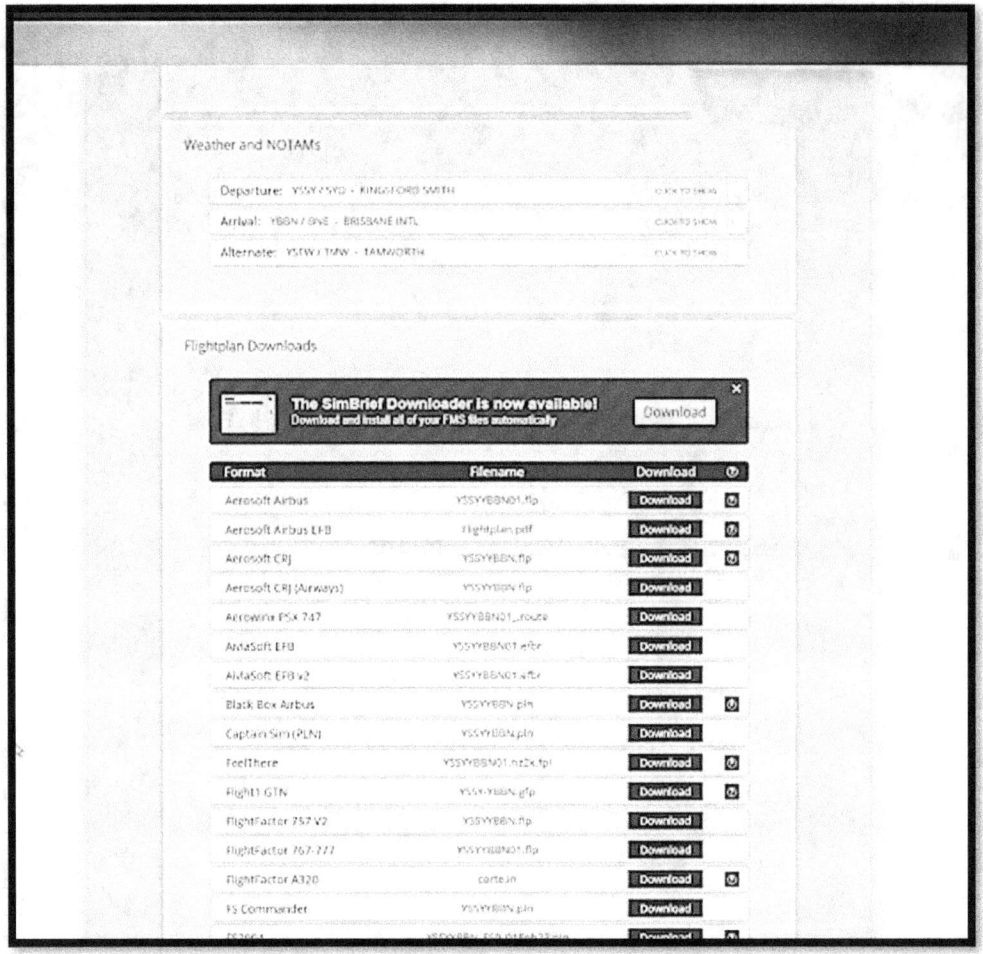

This section has a bunch of different aircraft where you can download the Pacific flight plans for each individual aircraft on many different types of simulators but for this illustration, we're going to keep it basic by adding the flight plan into Microsoft Flight Simulator so we'll scroll down to where it says Microsoft Flight Simulator and hit the Download button. This will download into the folder that we choose or it'll put it in our download folder and once we have done that it is now time to load up Microsoft Flight Simulator.

Now, in the Simulator we'll go over to the world map. The first thing you want to do is pick the aircraft that you want to use for the flight. The next thing you're going to do is hit the spacebar button - this will bring options up to where you can pick your flight plan from so we want to hit "Load from this PC," go to our download section where we have our flight plan saved as YSSY to YBBN. We're going to pick that one, hit Open and it's going to load the flight plan in.

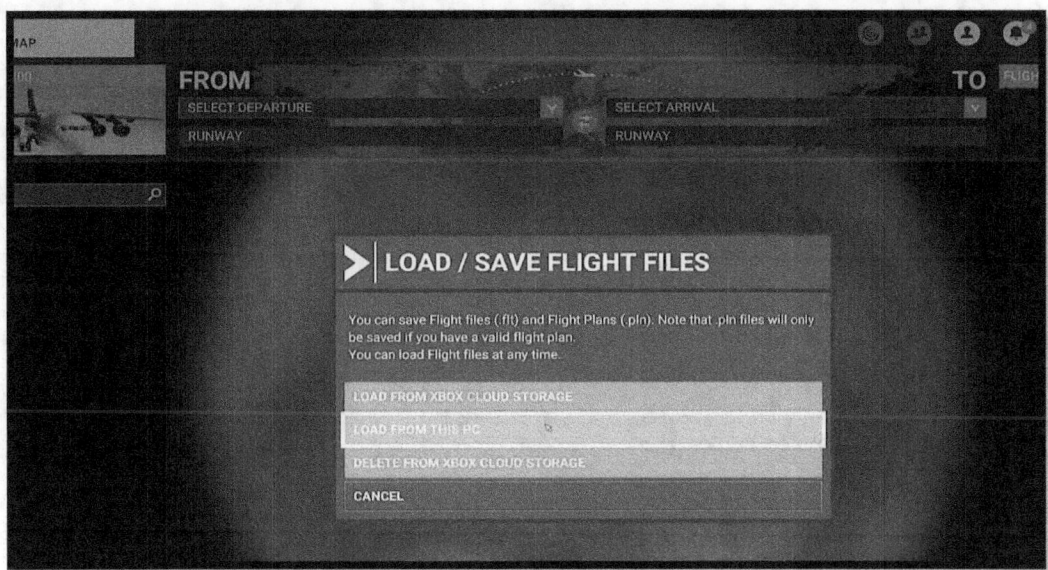

Now we've imported into the Sim, the first thing that you may want to do as we mentioned before is check the cruising altitude for today's flight and it said between 20000 to 31000 feet. We're going to fly at 26,000 feet. To set the cruise altitude we're going to backspace, put 26,000 there, then hit enter and that's going to put that in our flight plan.

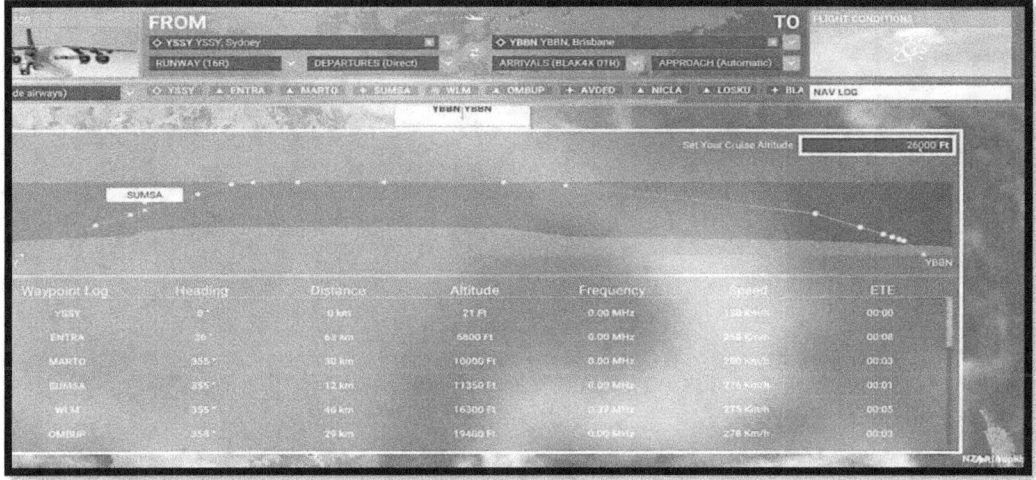

When it comes to the flight plans in simBrief and you import them this way it will automatically put you on the runway so you may want to choose a parking spot to start especially if you want to fly your planes in cold and dark and do everything that's starting up. Now you could zoom into the airport and pick a parking spot by clicking on a blue dot, but we don't want to do this because sometimes when you do this, it will then change the flight plan slightly so your best bet is to go and pick your parking spot by using the drop-down.

We're going to find a Ramp 92 somewhere in the mix and we're going to use that for our parking spot. It's going to start us over there and we need to go and taxi onto Runway 16 for the takeoff.

Once you've done that you may want to include additional information such as departures and approaches. SimBrief has just got us going directly to their first Nav point which is Entra, we're going to add a departure onto this one. We can do that by hitting the departures drop-down box and it's got all the departures outside at the airport.

There are many different ones that you can choose but we're going to keep it simple and we're going to use the SY2 16 Right departure which extends our upwind departure before we make a left-hand turn on the way to go; you can change things here and try putting all the different departures in but for our case, we're going to move up to a Brisbane and we're going to do the same thing.

Now the arrival has been set and the star has been placed here but we want to pick how we want to approach the runway. In this flight, we're going to be landing on Runway 01 Right and we're going to make this an ILS Landing so we're going to choose that in Sim by doing ILS 01 Right and enter that in. That's going to change the flight plan where it will move us over to grab the ILS and when we'll pick up that frequency of the aircraft we'll automatically fly into runway 01 Right. From this point here we would just click the "Fly Now" button and the Sim would place the aircraft over at around a 92 and we'll be ready to do our cold and dark start.

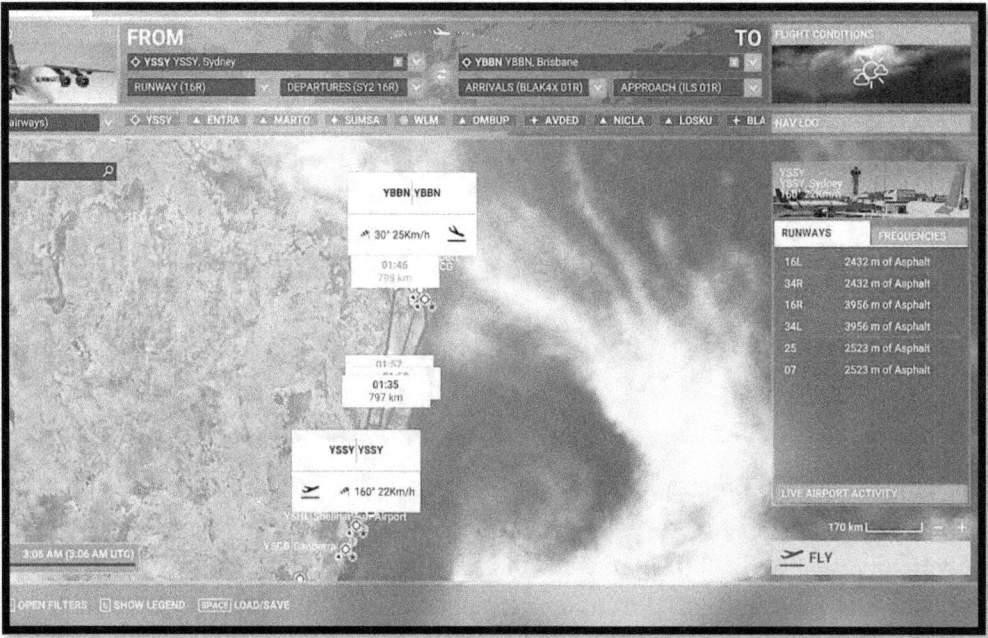

This method of importing a flight plan will work with a bunch of aircraft including all the default aircraft in the flight simulator and some others. When it comes to more complex aircraft such as the Boeing 737 from PMDG this has a few extra steps we would need to import the flight plan into the FMS.

VOR Navigation Basics

In this chapter, we're going to learn about VORs and how to navigate using them in Microsoft Flight Simulator. First of all, what is a VOR? Well, it stands for VHF Omnidirectional Range. This sounds like a lot but the VHF part is just the specific range of frequencies that the VOR transmits. You may have heard that before from things like analog television signals and FM radio signals. VORs just happen to use that same range of radio frequencies.

The O in VOR which stands for omnidirectional means just in all directions so this equipment emits 360 degrees and we can use these radio frequencies to tune into them and the equipment inside our aircraft will let us fly to and from these VORs on a specific heading.

Locating VORs

In the **illustration below**, we have the world VFR map pulled up and the blue compass rose here represents the area around the VOR so whenever you see this blue compass rose you know that a VOR is in the middle of it.

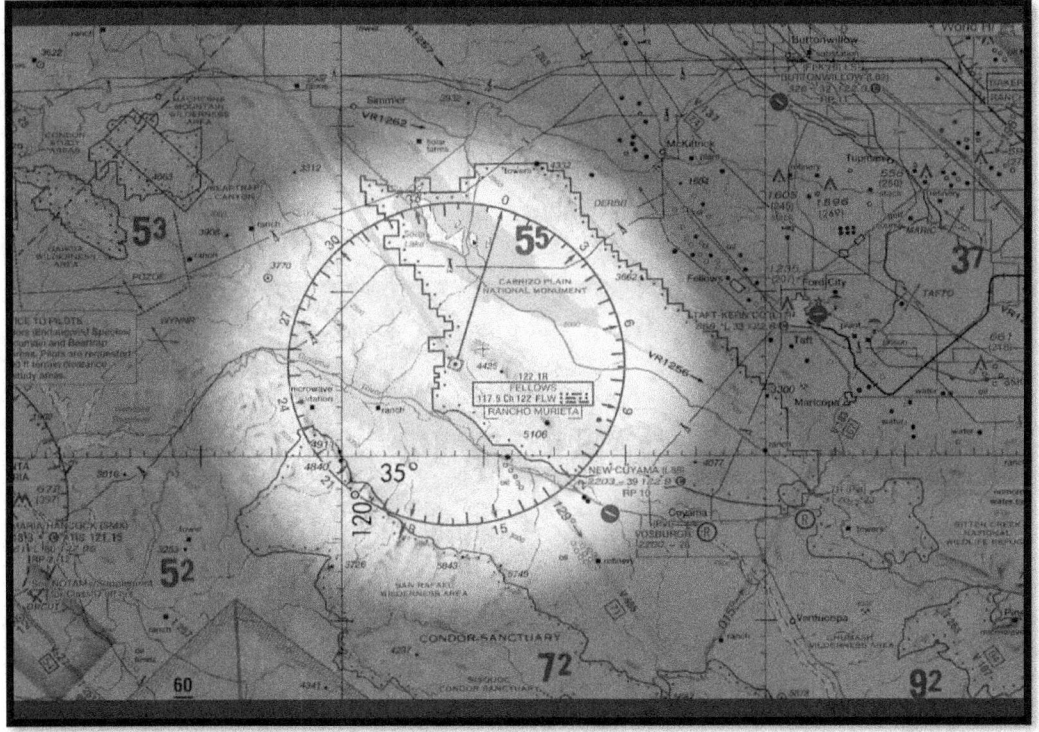

There's one called the San Marcus VOR near Santa Barbara. Over here to the west we have the Morro Bay VOR that's next to the San Luis Obispo airport then we have the Fellows VOR, which is on a mountain range and is not specifically next to any airport.

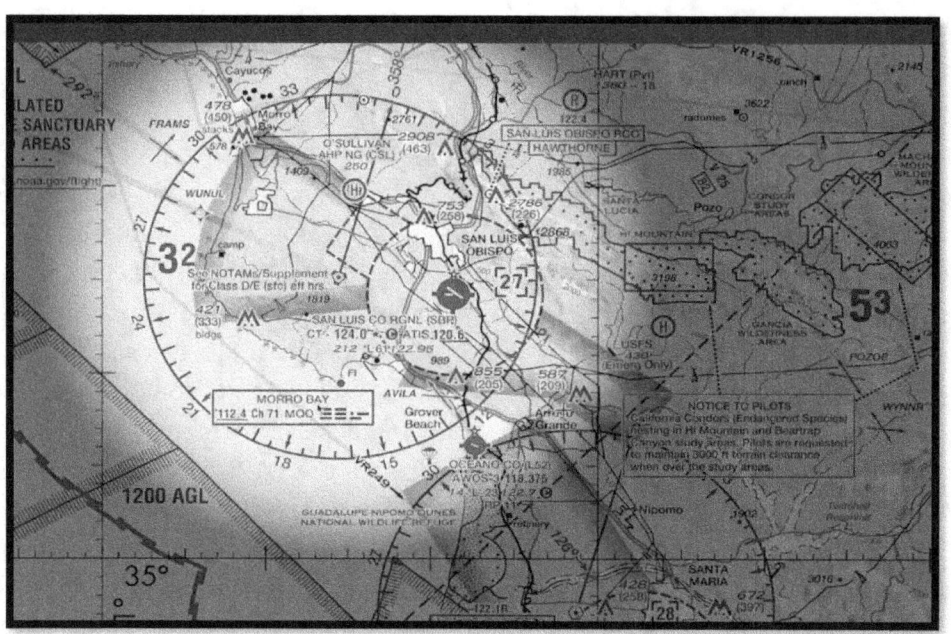

How VOR works

Now let's talk about how a VOR works in terms of navigating. The easiest way to think about VORs is to think about them as a giant wheel and the center of the wheel is the VOR itself, the radio transmissions coming from the wheel are the spokes and there are 360 spokes radiating from the center and we call those each a radial. You can think of each one of these spokes almost like its own highway and you can choose to fly on one of these if you want to from the VOR or to the VOR.

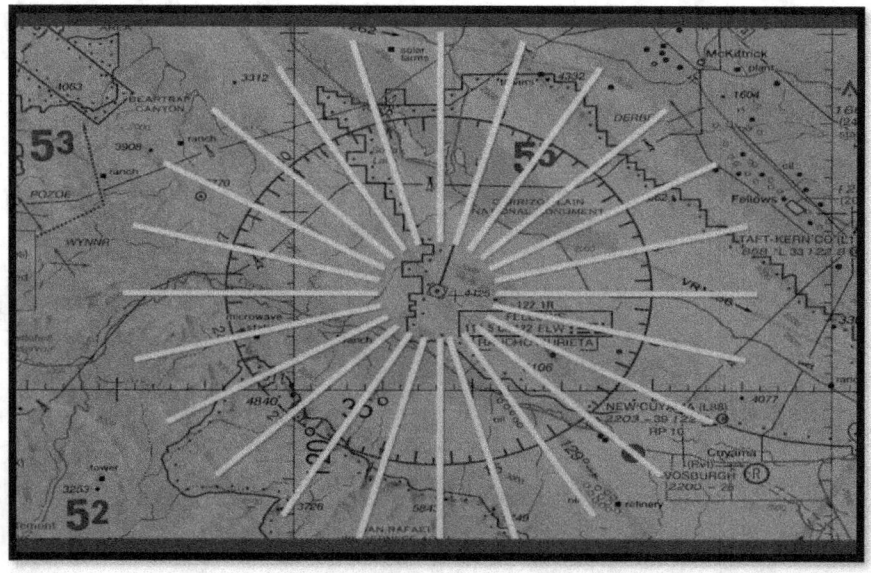

Let's say that we're flying from the exact center of the wheel, the Fellowes VOR on a 090 heading with no wind. We would say that we are tracking the 090 radial outbound which means from the Fellows VOR we could also turn around and fly from the outside straight to the Fellowes VOR tracking the 090 radial inbound.

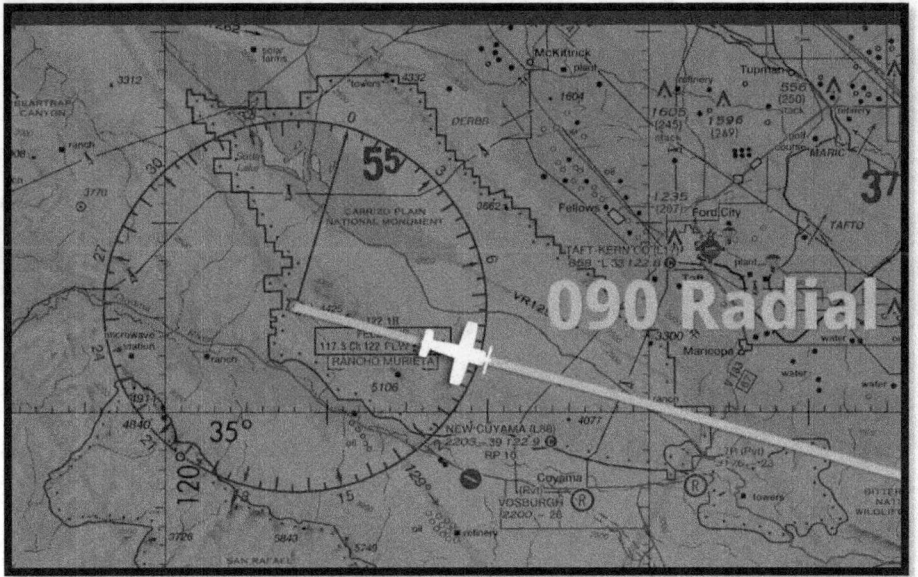

From the **image below** we can see that based on the location of our plane we're on the 030 radial.

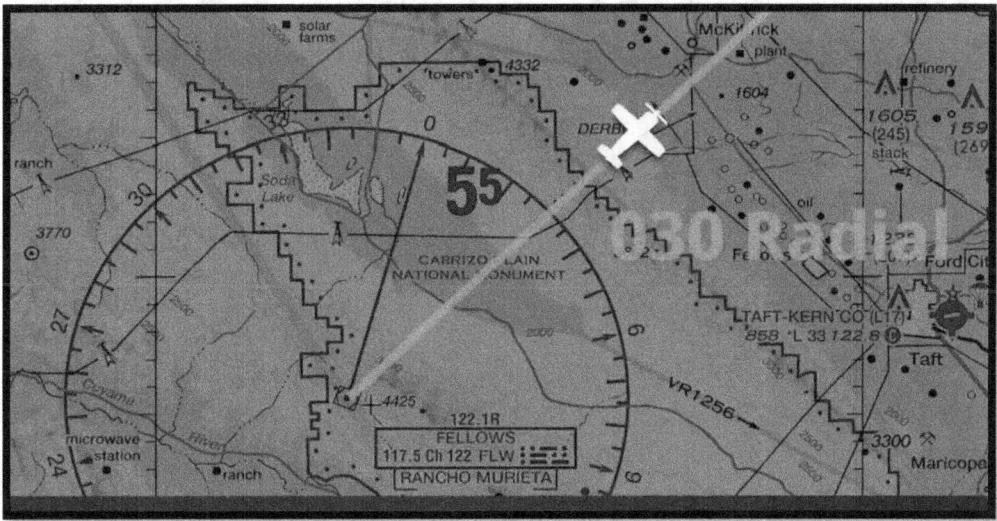

What if our plane is somewhere else but we're heading west, what radial are we on? we're still on the 300 radial, we just happen to be flying to the west.

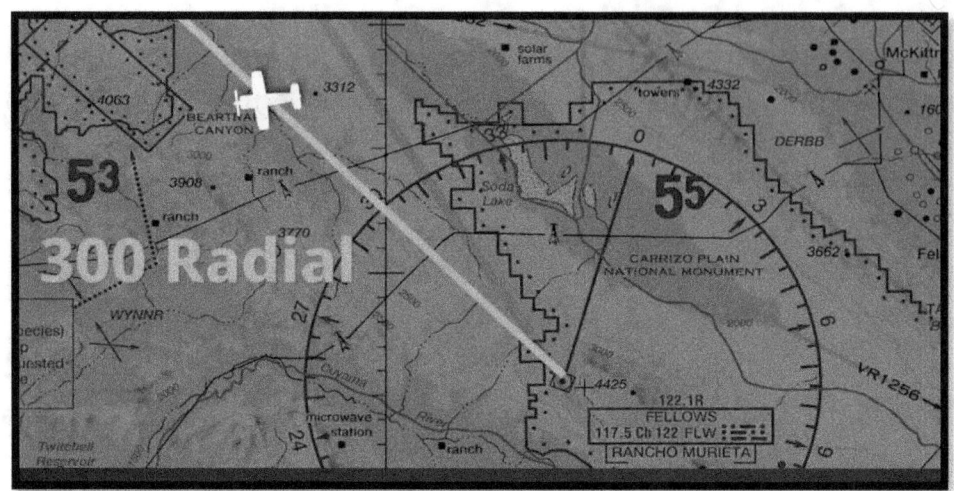

That doesn't mean that we're not on the radial, we may be choosing to not track the radial out or inbound, just fly perfectly on that spoke or highway but at any moment we are on a specific radial as long as we're in range of the VOR and when we're flying a VOR-based flight path we will be choosing which radial we want to fly on inbound or outbound, each leg of our flight.

Instrument Flying

This chapter introduces how to fly in Microsoft Flight Simulator with the instruments instead of flying visually. If you do prefer flying visually in flight sim to enjoy the incredible scenery the game can generate but you've also always been curious as to how to fly precision departures and approaches, the only real way to do that is with instrument flying.

We're going to cover why instrument flying exists, do some very basic IFR flight planning in the game, and wrap up by looking at all of the instruments that you're going to want to understand and know how to operate to be able to do proper IFR flying in flight sim. With all that said, let's start learning about Instrument Flight Rules (IFR).

Why Instrument Flying?

The main reason instrument flying exists in the first place is to allow planes to fly in weather where they can't necessarily see where they're going but they need to be able to get back safely on the ground.

Instrument flight rules allow you to see where you are and where you're going even when you can't see anything out of the windscreen. It's accomplished by detailed flight plans that specify precisely where the airplane has to fly to get to where it's going.

For very basic IFR flights you don't even need to use any external tools or programs to build your flight plan. You have pretty much everything you need here but we will complement it with a few little things that you can find easily on Google.

Planning an IFR flight

For this illustration, we're going to plan a flight from Honolulu to Kahului. We're going to be doing IFR though so what we're going to do is in the drop-down we're going to choose IFR and we're going to choose Low Altitude Airways. Low Altitude Airways has a ceiling of around 18,000 feet and we're going to be staying well below that which is why we chose it. If we are going above 18,000 feet in a jet or an airliner, in that case, we would end up choosing High Altitude Airways.

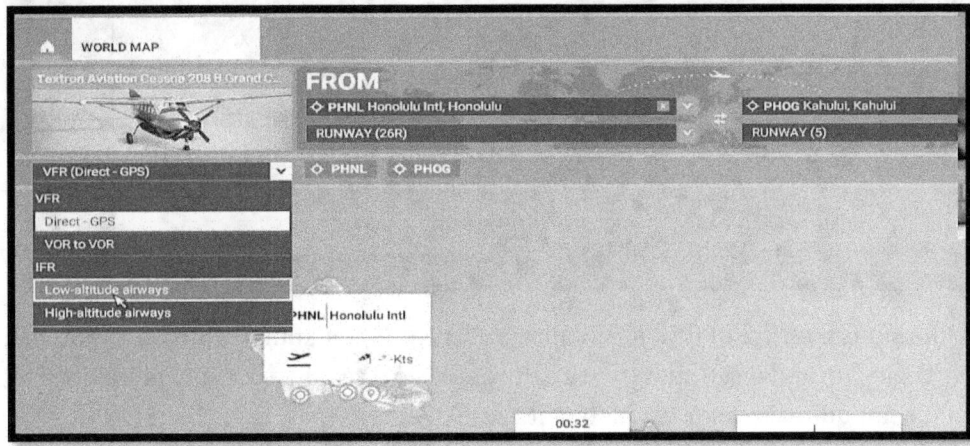

This will create a much more detailed flight plan. There are also a few extra drop-downs that appear once we choose IFR; those are the departure and arrival procedures that you can choose. Flight Sim automatically figures out from our route which departure and arrival procedures to use but we can change those if we want either through the drop-down or we can just click on one of the different arrows which is going to pick a different procedure.

Each departure and arrival is going to be slightly different and depending on the prevailing winds and which runway you're taking off from, you're going to want to pick the most appropriate departure for it. The same thing is true for the arrival. You can pick another arrival if you want but in this case, it makes the most sense to pick the one that lines up the best with your flight plan.

Each one of these procedures has an associated chart that describes the procedure in a lot more detail. It includes altitudes, navigation aids, and a bunch of other details like radio frequencies that you're going to need to safely take off and land when the visibility is near zero. You can get these charts in a few different ways but the easiest solution that is completely free is to just type in the name of the departure or arrival into Google. You'll be able to find charts for all the airports you're looking for just by doing this. Oftentimes it'll come up with something on FlightAware but there are a few other sites that'll tend to have a couple of charts as well. The chart might be a little bit out of date but to fly in flight sim it's going to be more than sufficient.

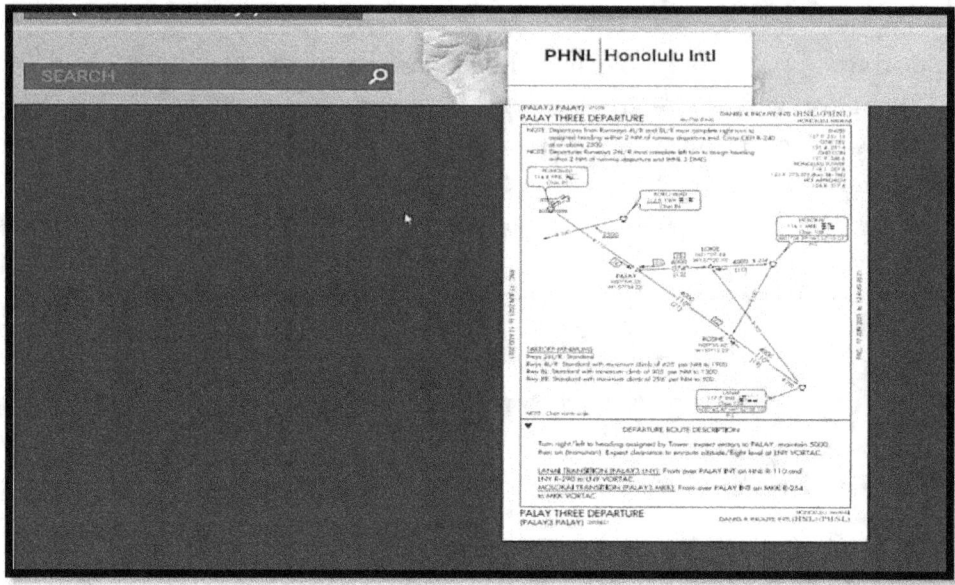

Another option is to install Little NavMap which is an open-source software that reads the data from flight sim and it can show you all the details of the departure and arrival procedure, although It's not quite as clean as looking at the real chart.

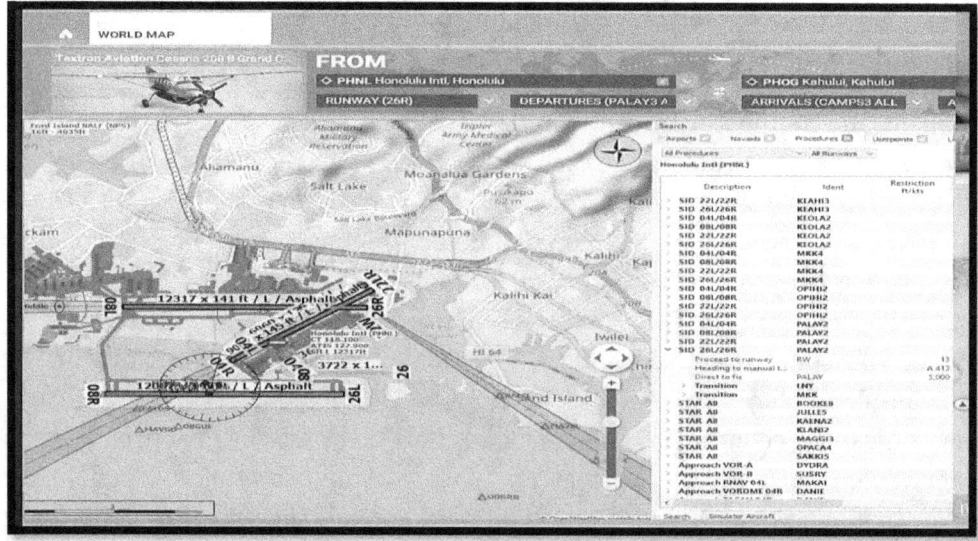

The last option is to get a paying service like Navigraph - which specializes in charts for flight simulation. Once you have found the chart you can either print it out or if you've got a second monitor just have it handy on that second screen so that when you're flying you can reference it very easily. That should be all you need to get started from a flight planning perspective.

Airplane selection

The only airplane you can't use for doing this would be something like the Savage Cub because it doesn't have all the instruments you're going to need but otherwise, you can pretty much use anything you want.

We recommend either the Cessna 208 or a Prop-based plane that has a glass cockpit rather than the traditional steam gauges - it's going to make everything just a little bit easier because you're going to be able to see what you're doing a little bit better than you can with the traditional gauges.

How to use the different instruments in flight

Now we are going to cover all the instruments that you need to be aware of and know how to do instrument flying.

The most important instrument when you're doing IFR flying is the Altitude indicator. If you can't see much out of the cockpit, the attitude indicator will effectively become your eyes and ears, telling you which direction your airplane is pointing. It will tell you if your NOSE is in the air, if it is pointing down, or if you are in a turn. Even in a real airplane, it's quite easy to become disoriented when you're in the clouds but then the attitude indicator is your primary way to know which way your airplane is pointing.

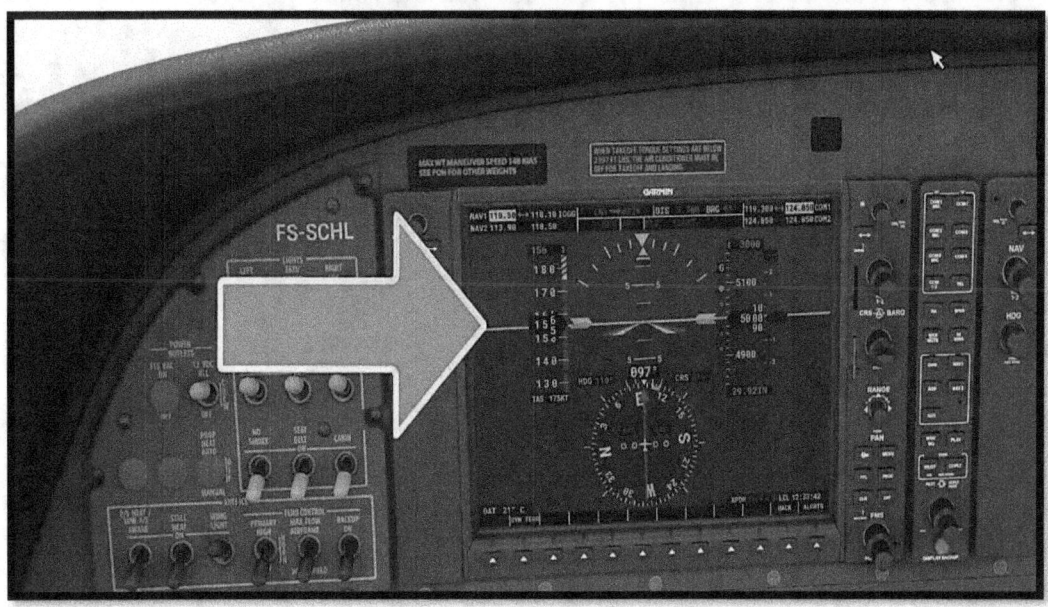

The Altimeter heading and Airspeed indicators are all much more important as well. When you're flying in IFR conditions you're going to be expected to be able to fly the plane precisely according to the procedure that's been prescribed to you. You also need to be able to follow any requests that you might get from air traffic control to either hold a heading altitude or airspeed. That's how ATC achieves spacing between airplanes to keep everybody safe.

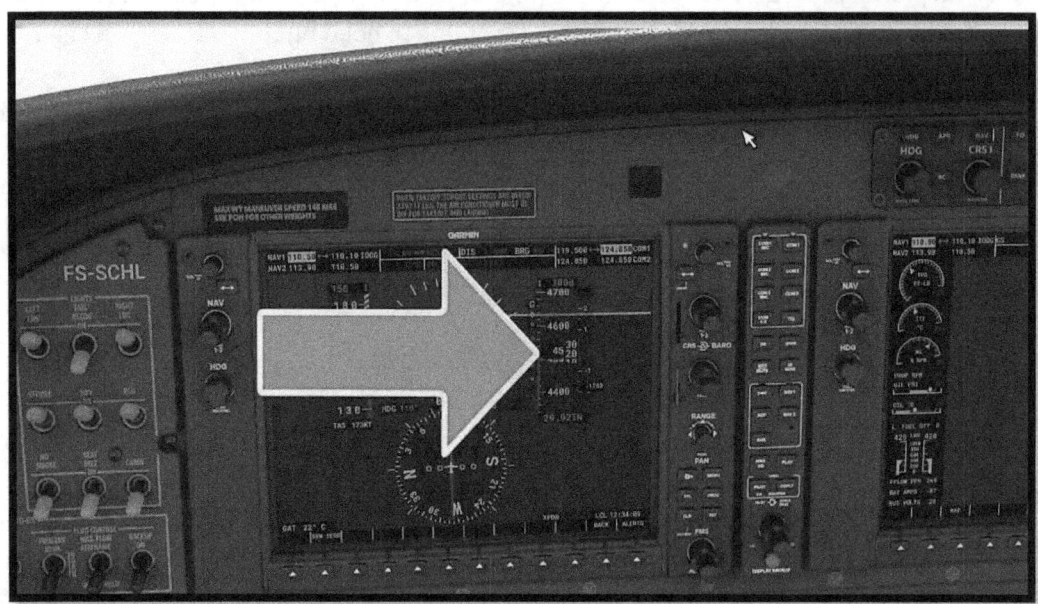

The Vertical Speed indicator is quite important as well and you're expected to use at least 500 feet per minute for your climbs or descents.

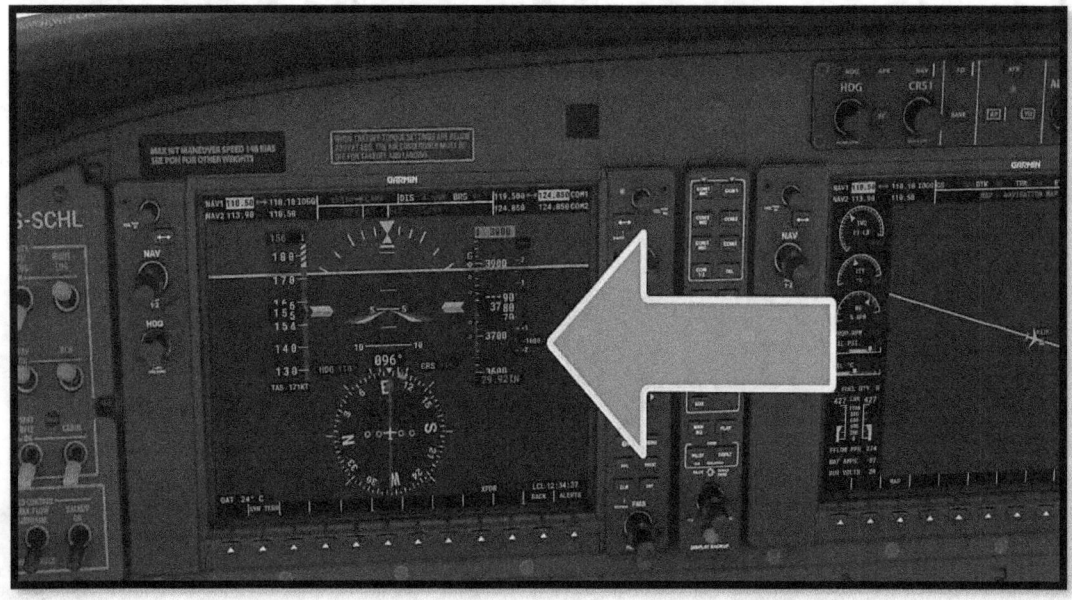

All of those instruments have a digital display in the glass cockpit so it becomes easier to start chasing after a precise number. You only need to be close enough to the actual values though because the slightest little pitch or attitude change can change your altitude or airspeed by one or two knots. You should be trying to keep within 100 feet of your assigned altitude and 10 knots of your assigned airspeed. You'll want to get your heading as precisely as possible, though.

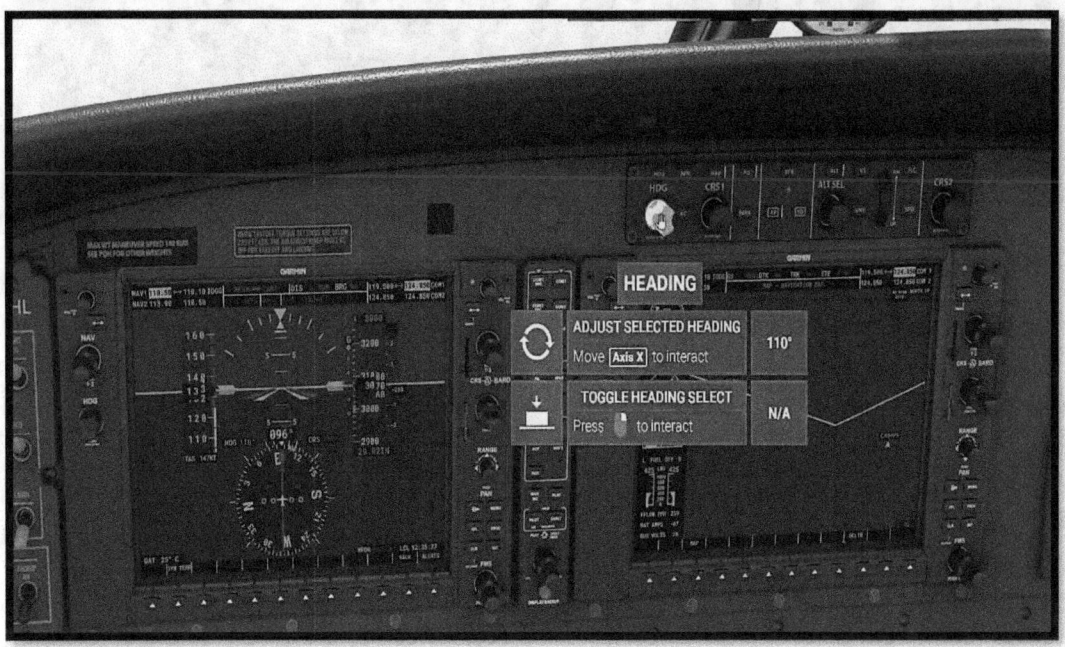

The best way to monitor all of these instruments that we've just talked about is to use something called the Hub and Spoke System.

For illustration, we'll start from our Altitude indicator, head out, and check that our airspeed is correct then we'll come back and make sure the attitude indicator is still right. After that, we'll check our heading, come back to the attitude indicator again, and then check on our altitude. We'll continue that the whole way down to the ground while we're flying the airplane manually and can't see anything out of the cockpit.

One not-so-obvious instrument that you need to be able to read when you're doing IFR flights is the Turn Coordinator which is integrated into the compass. You can see there are two little notches on either side of the current heading of the airplane. When you start a turn, you're going to see a little magenta arrow that appears and it's going to get wider and wider as you increase the bank angle.

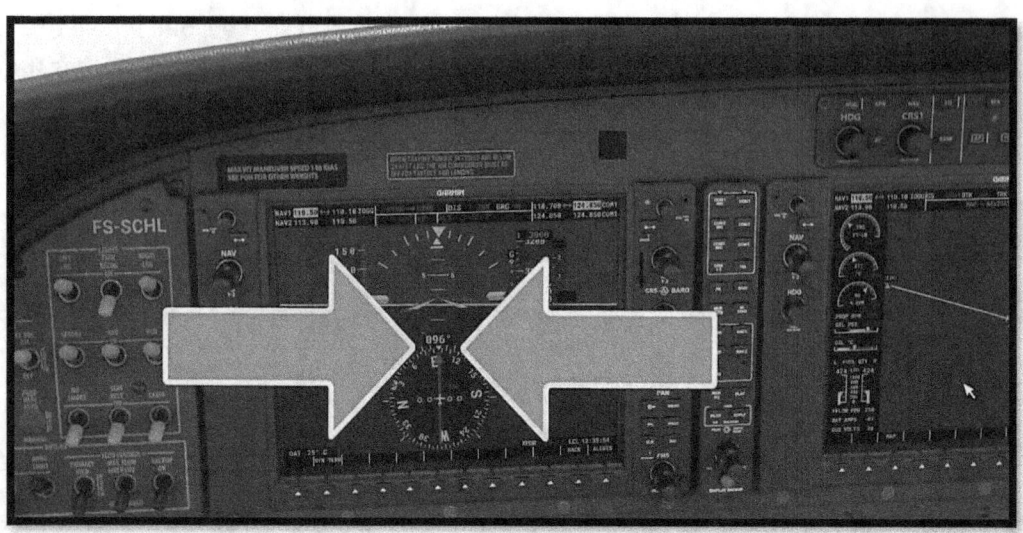

If you line up the arrow that appears with the furthest notch you're going to achieve something that's called a Standard Rate or a Rate One Turn. If you hold that bank angle you're going to end up doing a 360-degree turn in precisely two minutes. That's going to allow ATC to have a better idea of how long it'll take you to perform a maneuver which is going to help them space out the airplanes.

If you're using the autopilot, all the turns that it makes are going to be done at a standard rate, and speaking of the autopilot, you're going to want to be familiar with the 5 most frequently used modes which are ALT, FLC, VS, HDG, and NAV. When you're first learning IFR it's a lot easier to leverage the autopilot to be able to free you up so you can read the procedure and let the airplane fly itself.

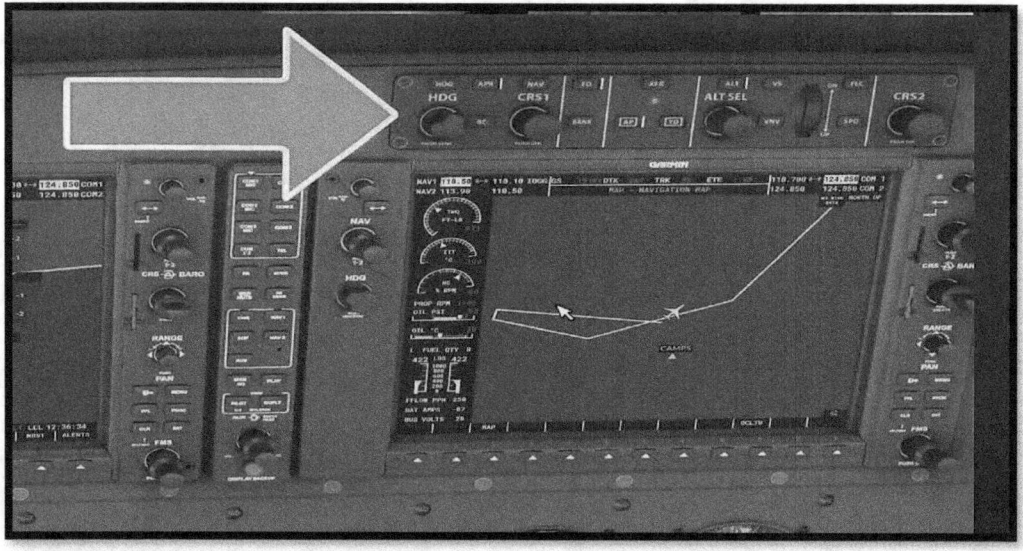

Next, you're going to want to get used to handling the navigation radios. At the top left of the primary flight display, the airplane can tune two Nav radios at any given time and each Nav radio has an Active frequency and a Standby frequency.

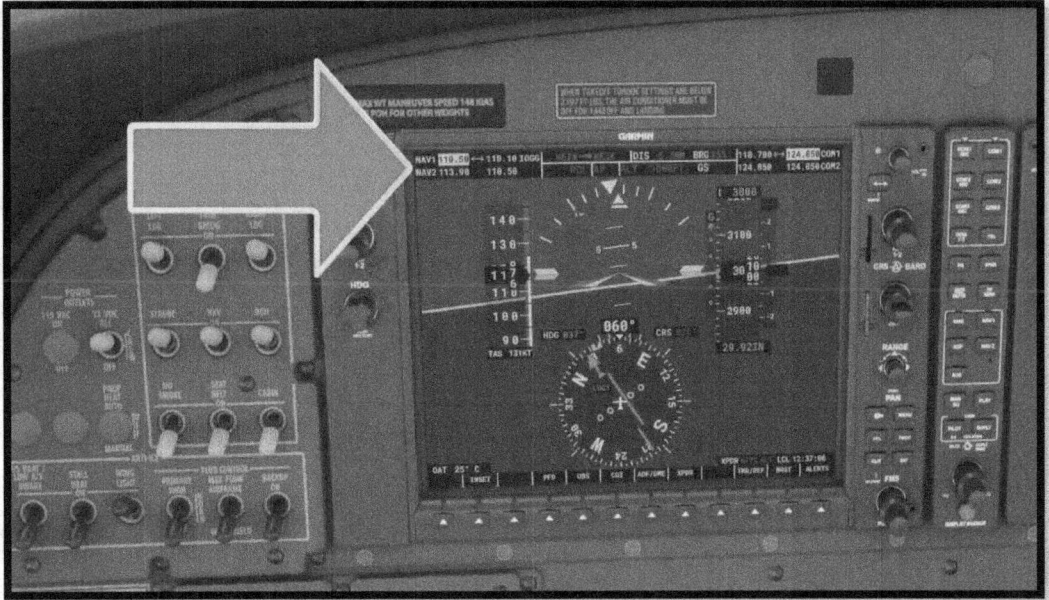

The Standby frequency is on the left and the Active is on the right. You can adjust the Standby frequency using the knob on the left-hand side of the primary flight display. You're always changing the standby frequency though so when you do want to use that frequency that you've just set, what you've got to do is press the little double-sided arrow and it's going to flip the two frequencies to make the Standby frequency the active one.

Let's say we've got the Active frequency tuned to 110.1 which is the inbound ILS runway 2 approach at Maui. You can tell that it's tuned properly because it's got the little IOGG next to it which is the identifier for that approach.

Lastly, we recommend that you get a good feel for the airplane that you're choosing to use to learn IFR first. The last thing you want when you're trying to fly with instruments is to fight the airplane and not know how to fly it in different situations like climbs, descents, and approaches.

Review Questions

1. Discuss the integration of third-party flight planning software and how it can be used to enhance the flight planning and navigation capabilities in Microsoft Flight Simulator 2024.
2. Describe the functionality and use of the GPS and ILS (Instrument Landing System) features in the simulation, and how they assist pilots in navigating to their destinations and executing instrument approaches.

3. Explain the principles of VOR (VHF Omnidirectional Range) navigation and how it is incorporated into the instrument flying experience in Microsoft Flight Simulator 2024.

CHAPTER 12

CONTROLLING WEATHER CONDITIONS

In this chapter, we'll take a look at how to control and change the weather in Microsoft Flight Simulator. There are a lot of different things you can do with the weather in Flight Sim: you can use it to primarily create beautiful flight environments to fly in, you can make changes that will affect your aircraft's performance, you can set up realistic instrument weather for practicing instrument flying or tackling challenging weather scenarios and you can set completely unrealistic weather for just for the fun of it.

There are also a number of different ways to manipulate the weather in Flight Sim and if you're new to the Sim it can be a little overwhelming so in this chapter we'll take a deep dive into the weather controls in Flight Sim and talk about all the ways you can change it to get the most out of your Flight Sim experience.

Settings that affect the weather

First, let's take a look at the option settings that will affect the weather system. From the main menu, we'll go to Options and then we will go to General Options and you can access these menus also from in-flight.

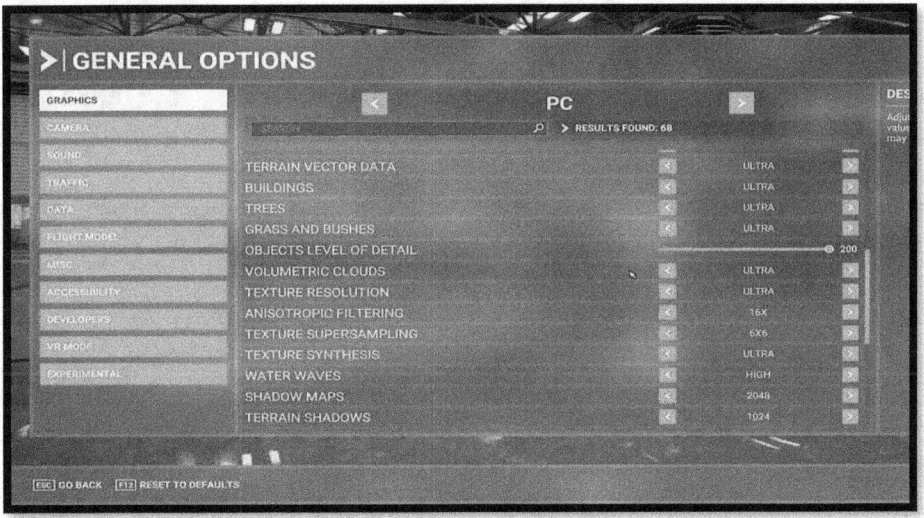

There are a few Graphics options that will affect the weather system. The only one that has a material effect is the volumetric Cloud setting. If you have this set on a higher setting this will adjust the quality of the clouds; they'll look a little better but it will affect your performance. The only other thing in the graphics that is directly weather-related is the water waves and again the higher you set this, the better the water and the waves in the water are going to look and that will be affected by the wind but it does tend to affect your performance. Those are the only two settings in the Graphics that are going to affect the weather system.

The next thing we'll look at is the data options and the only one that affects weather here is the Live Weather data connection option and you can toggle this on and off. This does not turn live weather on or off, what this does is it enables the live weather data stream so you do need to have this on to be able to get live weather but to toggle the weather on and off you do that from the main weather menu either on the World map or in the In-flight weather options menu.

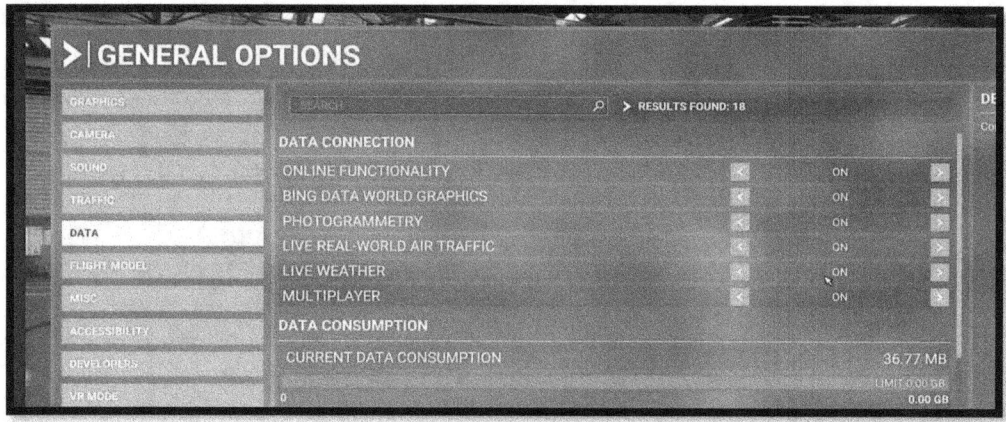

The next setting we'll take a look at is in the Miscellaneous tab and that is the units of measurement. We have three different settings we can choose from here that will determine what values you set for your weather settings. The first is the straight **Metric System**, the second one is the **Hybrid System,** and then the final one is the **U.S. System.** Let's take a look at how those change the way that you set the weather values.

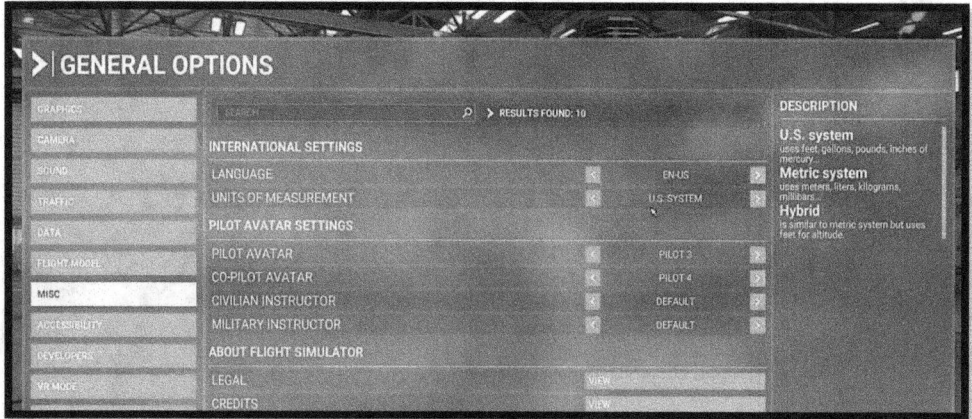

If you have your system set to straight metric, you will have these values set in metric. You'll have precipitation in millimeters/hour. You'll have snow depth set in centimeters, your temperature set in °C or Celsius, your pressure or your altimeter setting set in hectopascals and then you will set your cloud height in meters rather than feet. The straight metric is pretty uncommon in aviation.

Most countries use a hybrid system that we'll talk about here in just a second that has the altitudes in feet, the only countries that use straight metric in aviation are China, Mongolia, North Korea, Russia, and Tajikistan, and the last two only use metric chemistry in their lower airspace areas; they don't use it in the High Altitude airspace so it's fairly uncommon to use a straight metric system in the real world. If you set it to the hybrid system the only difference is that the clouds are now measured in feet rather than meters and this hybrid system is probably the ICAO standard or International Civil Aviation Organization.

Most countries in the world will use this system for reporting weather and setting altimeters so this is the most common system in places like Europe, Asia, South America, and pretty much everywhere in the world except for the United States and a few other countries. This is the standard weather system.

With the U.S. system, the changes are that the precipitation is set in inches an hour, the snow depth is set in inches, the temperature is set in degrees Fahrenheit, the pressure is set in inches of mercury and then the clouds of course are still set in feet. This is slightly off from what we do in the U.S, we do set and read our temperatures in degrees Celsius so that is not standard for what we do in the United States but there's an easy workaround for this if you want to set your temperature in degree Celsius or read it in degrees celsius most of your aircraft has an outside air temperature gauge and so while you're setting your temperature in the weather menu you can just take a look at that outside air temperature gauge if it's set to °C and that will be an easy way to read your Celsius temperature while you're adjusting the temperature. Again, this is the standard for the United States so it's the system you may tend to use but if you're in Europe, you may prefer to use the hybrid system.

Icing Effects

The last option we'll look at is in the Assistance option so we'll go back to the main Option tab, go to the Assistance Options and this will be in Failure and Damage, the Icing Effect option. We have three selections here: on, visual only, or off.

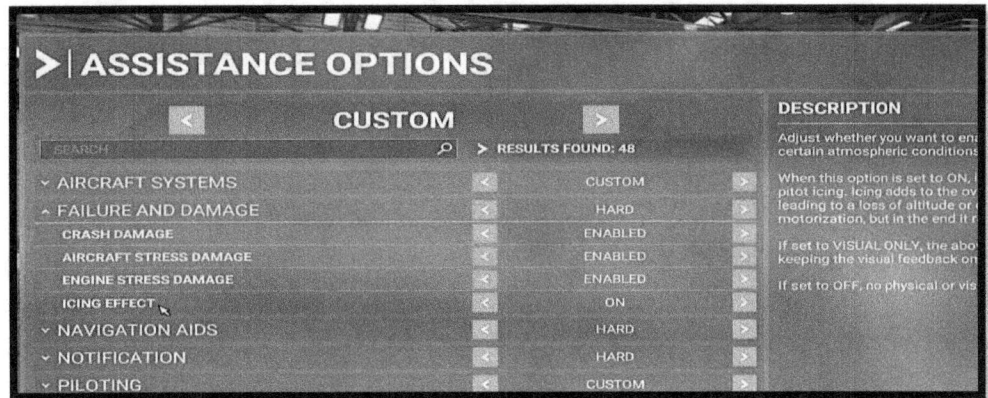

If we have this set to on, anytime we are in Icing conditions we will get icing accumulation, it will be visible and it will affect aircraft performance. What that means is that ice will accumulate on the airframe; it will accumulate in the engine components that are susceptible to icing and on things like the pitot tube, airframe ice will have effects like if it accumulates on the windshield and you don't have windshield anti-icing or de-icing, the windshield will frost over or glaze over and it will become more difficult to see.

For things like the airframe, you'll get ice on places like the wing and the tail and this will do a couple of things: it'll increase the weight of the aircraft and it also disrupts the airflow over the wing the more ice accumulates and so if you don't have de-icing or anti-icing systems on the wing you'll notice that the aircraft will start to perform more poorly, and it may not be able to climb at all. You may see the aircraft slowing down even if you have the normal Cruise power set, you may lose airspeed and eventually, you can get enough icing where your stall speed increases, and you can have trouble maintaining altitude. You can also get it in the engine with carburetor icing and end up losing engine power if you don't have engine anti-ice or your carburetor heat on it does depend on what kind of engine you are flying with but it can result in a loss of power or even an engine failure. So with this set to ON, you'll get those types of effects. You also get the Pitot icing if you don't have pitot heat or don't have the Pitot heat turned on which can block up your pitot tube.

If you have it selected to Visual Only then you will see the ice accumulate just like you will with it on but it won't have any performance effects at all. It'll be more of a decoration and then if you have it set to Off even if you are in conditions that will make icing conditions possible you will get no icing; it'll be like the conditions don't exist. Just a warning here that anytime you are in clouds or precipitation in Flight Simulator and the temperature is at or below freezing at your altitude you will get icing if your icing options are set to On and it will have an effect or if it's set to Visual you will get the visual icing.

In the real world, it's very variable as to where icing conditions occur and it's not always predictable but in Flight Simulator, anytime you're in the clouds or precipitation and the temperature is below freezing you will get icing.

As we mentioned earlier all of these options are available from the main menu through the Options menu but you can also access them from in-flight by hitting the Escape key and that will bring up your General options on the bottom left-hand side and your system Assistance options where the icing options are in the top right.

World Map Weather Menu

One of the ways we can set the weather in Flight Sim is through the world map, although there are some limitations on what we can do with that. If we go into the world map this brings up our flight setup screen that we use to set up our flights.

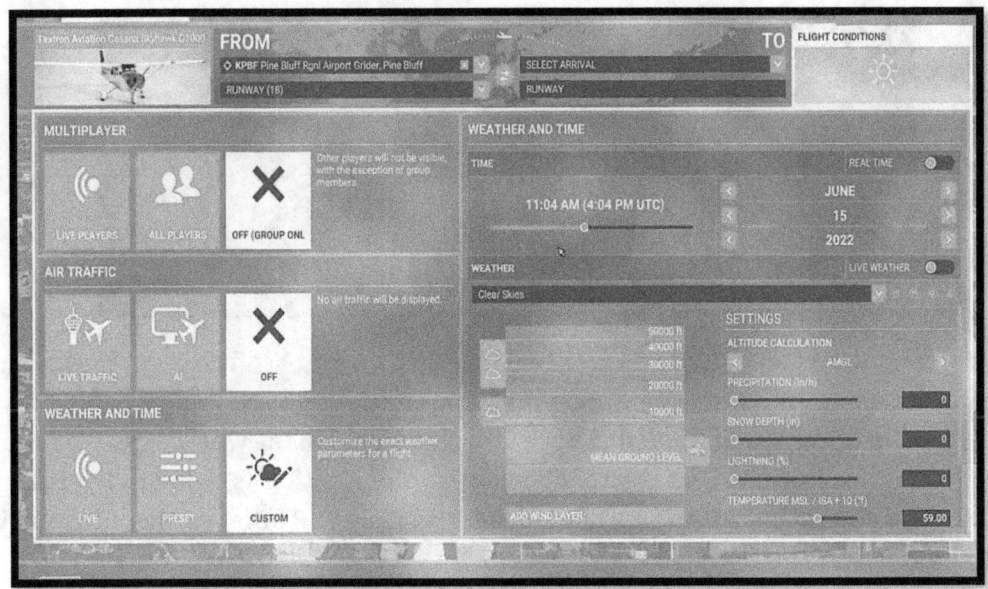

We typically go left to right to get everything set up. You do want to go ahead and enter whatever airport you're going to be departing from because that way, you will be setting the time correctly otherwise it just sets it to Zulu time automatically if you don't have an airport selected. Then to get into the weather menu, we'll go to Flight Conditions and that brings us a menu with a couple of different options here.

The Multiplayer and Air Traffic don't have anything to do with what the weather is doing. The Weather and Time option is a redundant menu that you don't need to use; you've got three options to set live preset or custom but they don't stake and then if you set a preset over here and you toggle live weather on that's what's going to take precedence over this menu so don't worry about these too much because these are redundant and don't do anything.

We can set the time and the date, from here you can also set it to real-time which means setting it to the time and day that it is currently in the real world if you want to do that. There is a little quirk with the time setting here in that you'll notice if we drag this slider, the UTC and the local time show the same. What it's doing here is setting the time in UTC; this is a little bug with this system so we would recommend not setting the time from this menu. Instead, you should set it from the little slider on the bottom left-hand corner of the world map and when you move that it shows a different local time than a Zulu time so it is now setting the time correctly but then you can set the date (the month, day and the year) from this menu.

Using Live Weather

You can also toggle live weather on and off. When you toggle live weather, that will just take the current weather that's in the world and it will put it into the Sim.

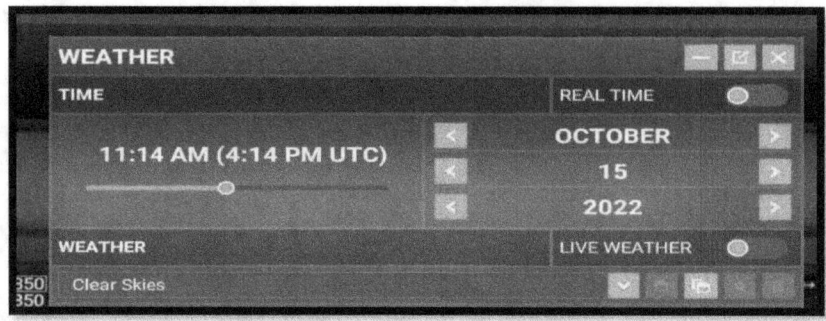

There are advantages and disadvantages to doing this. In the past, it has not been accurate particularly when it comes to sealing and visibility as those are also often quite a bit off from what they are in the real world and there are also large areas in the world between reporting stations where you may not get weather reports so the weather is going to have to guess what's going on there and may or may not fill in accurately what the weather is actually like at those locations.

If you want to fly instrument approaches, the other disadvantage is you're going to have to go somewhere where the weather is IFR at that time and you won't be able to control whether there's icing or not so that's the reason we recommend using custom weather rather than live weather because here, you have control over what you're doing, interns of if you want to practice instrument approaches, set specific ceilings and visibilities and these are things you can't do with live weather.

There are advantages of using live weather: you're going to get a more detailed surface and winds aloft are more accurate. It's going to be hard to set up the winds aloft so that they are accurate over the entire world by using the weather customizations. This is also good if you want to use live traffic or virtual ATC like a vat Sim type service.

If you import the live weather, you know the winds are going to be accurate and you know that you're going to be flying the same ground speed as everybody else, say when you're on approach if you're flying into a busy Class B Air Sport airspace with a jetliner, you know if your weather is different than what's in the real world and what everybody else is using. If everybody else has a 30 knot headwind on Final and you have a calm wind you're going to be overtaking everybody by 30 knots so those are places where you'd want to consider using live weather.

The other option that works from this weather menu is the weather presets and we will talk about those here in a little bit but those are the only two options that work from this weather menu; you can set the time and date, you can set to live weather, you can set weather presets but if you try to customize your ceiling, visibility, precipitation (whether there's snow on the ground) from this menu it will not import into your session. You have to do that from the weather menu in your flight session and that's another little bug that's in this main weather menu.

In-flight Weather Menu

Now let's take a look at the in-session or in-flight weather menu and how those settings work. To access this menu, we'll go up to the top quick menu, then click on the little icon that looks like a cloud, and that brings up our in-session weather menu.

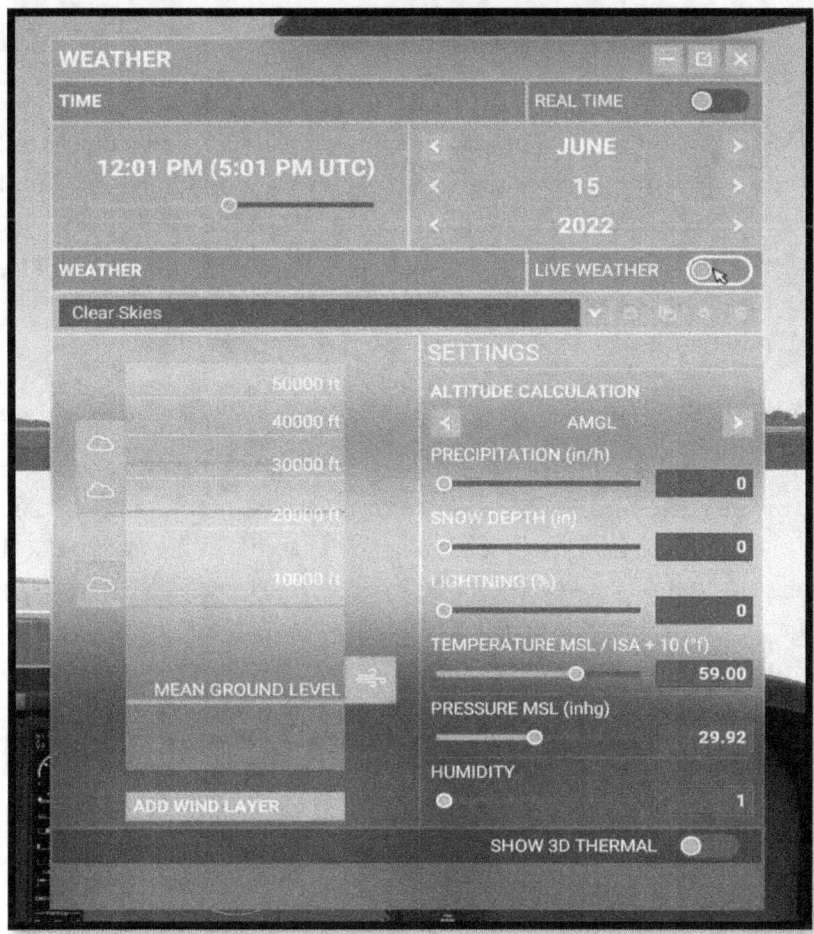

You can see it looks pretty much the same as the weather menu we had on the world map, it has the same fields, we have a panel up here for adjusting the time, we have a toggle for turning live weather on and off, we have our weather presets, we can select from and then everything below this now works correctly. It will change the weather now. We have an area here for setting clouds, setting the height and coverage, and all that sort of thing. If you click on a cloud layer it will take you into a separate Cloud layer menu for that particular Cloud layer and we'll go into detail on this here in a little bit. We also can add or change wind layers and if we click on the Wind layer that will bring up a separate Wind menu for us to adjust the wind. Then over on the right side, we have an altitude calculation and again, we'll go into detail on all this as we go but Altitude calculation is where you want to set your weather.

We also have a precipitation slider, a snow depth slider, a lightning slider that allows you to adjust the frequency of lightning, a temperature slider, a pressure slider (this is an altimeter setting slider), and then a humidity slider. We have a toggle down here at the very bottom that says "Show 3D thermal." What this does is it will allow you to see the winds and the wind currents and that also allows you to see where the wind is flowing upwards, in other words, where the thermals are if you want to do some glider flying. We'll go through all of these in detail and talk about how to adjust all of them.

With the sliders, you can slide things back and forth and adjust the values there but you'll notice it does skip over a lot of numbers and it's not very precise but a nice little feature that was added is if you mouse over and highlight that cursor now and then use your mouse wheel, you can make fine adjustments. For example, you can adjust the time by just one minute and if you go down here to the precipitation and highlight that you can adjust that in hundredths of an inch an hour so it makes for nice fine adjustments except for the cloud heights that don't work quite correctly just yet but that's a nice feature that they added.

Setting the Time and Date

The time menu is pretty straightforward and works just like it did in the world map weather menu. You can toggle real time which will set your clock and set the time in the simulator to whatever the time and date is at that location in the real world. Be aware that if you toggle this on you can't toggle it off and to get it off you have to go over to the date and adjust the date or the time then it will remove the real-time and you'll have to decide to set your date and time from there. It will still have the time and date that the real time was set to so you have to readjust it back to whatever you want.

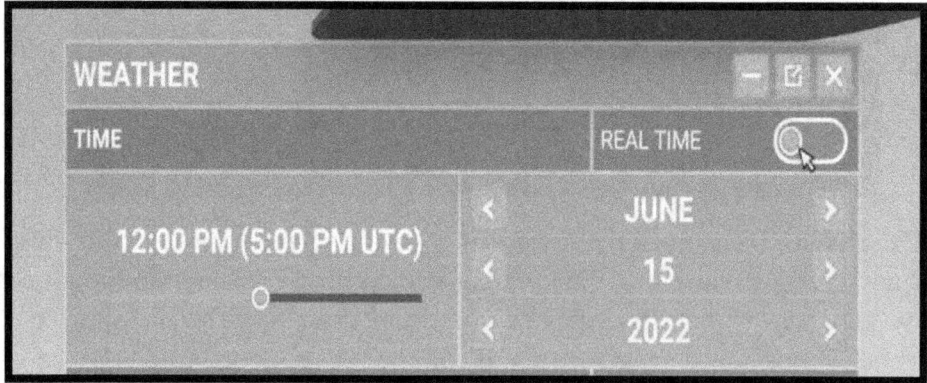

You also have the toggle for live weather. If you turn this on then it will automatically change the weather everywhere in the world to what it is in the real world as it's getting that live data weather stream. When you toggle this off, it will just go back to whatever the weather preset is that you had set before you turned the live weather on.

Using Weather Presets

Moving over to the weather presets tab, if you click on that it will bring up a bunch of different options for what you can use as presets here. Live weather is one of them. Clear skies just give you completely clear skies, no clouds, no humidity, and light winds.

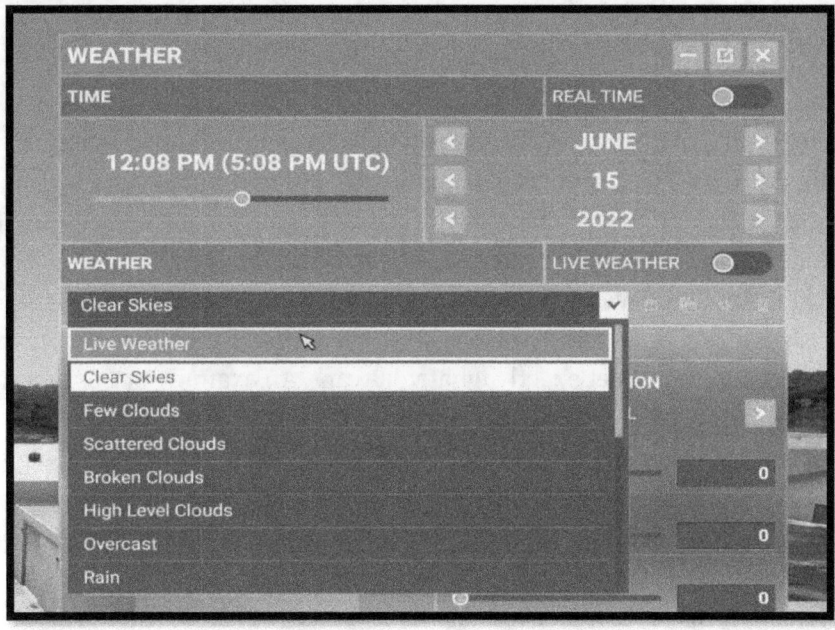

A few clouds will give you a lower layer of fair weather, cumulus clouds and then a mid-level layer of altocumulus, and then a highly scattered layer of cirrus clouds. This is a good setting for a fair-weather VFR sort of day.

Scattered clouds will give you a little more coverage on the clouds; this looks a little closer to broken than scattered but it's the same sort of setting just with a little more coverage.

Then a broken Cloud setting will give you a little more coverage so that you know you've got a broken layer that you're going to have to find some holes to climb through if you're a VFR pilot.

High-level clouds give you a high serous layer and this is good for effects, especially at sunset and things like that.

Overcast will give you a lower overcast cover.

Rain is going to give you rainy conditions.

Snow will give you snowy conditions with some snow depth on the ground.

Storms will give you thunderstorms going on in the area.

Then you have conditions for soaring as well and if we put these conditions in it will trigger the 3D thermals of which we can see the wind currents so we can see over here to the southeast of the field we do have a good updraft going that a glider could take advantage of.

Clear Skies is one that you can use to set up for basic beginner-level VFR flying. The few clouds set up for a nice fair weather cumulus sort of VFR day although you can raise the cloud heights a little bit and we'll talk about that as we proceed.

Scattered and broken cloud cover works to set up those two more coverage sorts of things. The high level is good for a nice aesthetic day, especially for doing sunsets. You may not use the overcast or the rain often, you can set that sort of weather on your own, same thing with the snow.

The storm is a good setting and it's probably one of the most frequently used to get stormy weather because it puts in all the clouds that you need (precipitation, lightning temperatures, and wind settings) to give you that kind of thunderstorm turbulence and setting that all up on your own is a cumbersome Endeavor so you can use that storm setting to set up a stormy weather if I want to navigate through that.

Another neat thing about the weather presets is that once you've set them you can manipulate them. You can use a preset to get you close to the weather conditions you want and then manipulate them a little bit to get exactly what you want. An example of this would be a cloud setting that sets you up with a nice fair-weather cumulus environment.

The cloud layer may be set pretty low such as 1600 feet which is low for VFR flying and you're going to have to dodge through a lot of those clouds so you can go through these options to adjust this and you'll pull the bases of the clouds up to about 5500 feet. This gives you a good room for a VFR flying.

You can also pull the tops up to about the thickness that they were earlier. About 14,000 feet would be about as much thickness and this still has the same sort of effect with the clouds but now the bases are quite a bit higher. With this, you can fly VFR under the clouds rather than having to dodge around them.

Saving a Weather Preset

Another neat thing that you can do with these tabs over here is if you have a weather setting that you would like to keep for later, just click on this folder option here, it brings up a thing for naming it then can save that to your computer.

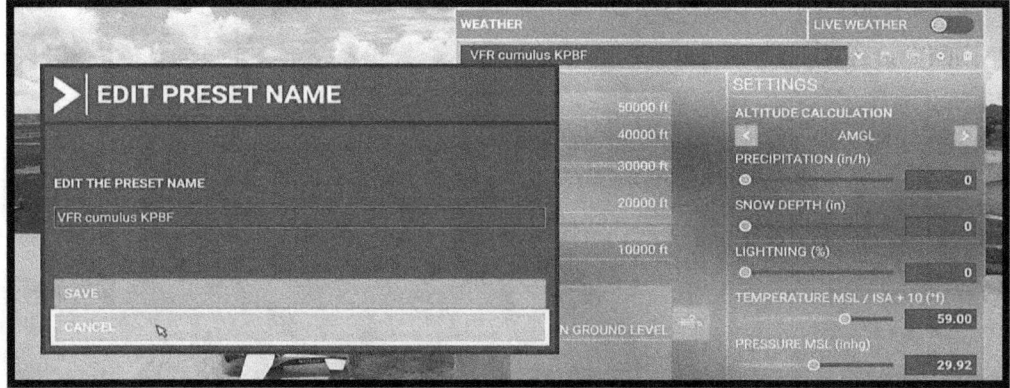

If you want to pull up the setting in the future it will be down at the bottom of the menu here and with that, you can pull up that setting where you have a custom setting that you have built. You can go in and get these other menu options to pop up here where you can have the trash can to delete it or you can go into settings and it gives you the option to edit the name as well.

Calculating the altitude

Let's go into the details of how we can customize our weather using the main body of this weather options menu. The first setting we'll look at is Altitude calculation and this has two settings: AMGL (Above Mean Ground Level) or AMSL which is (Above Mean Sea Level).

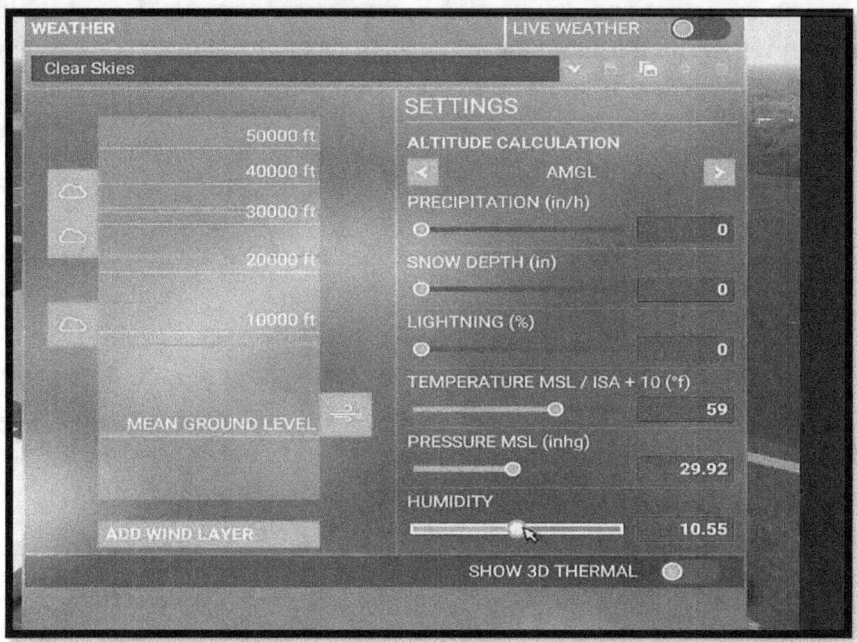

If you set this to AMGL this is particularly important for things like cloud heights, wind heights, and temperatures. This will set those settings so that whatever the elevation of the land that you're flying is, that's where those weather settings will be set. An example of this would be if you're flying over land that is at sea level or flying over the ocean which is also at sea level and you set the temperature to 59°F or 15°C then that temperature will be 59°F or 15°C at sea level.

If you set this the same way and you're at Denver which is at 5500 feet roughly, it will set the temperature so it's 59°F or 15°C at Denver at 5500 feet. If you're over the top of Mount Albert which is 14,400 feet and you have the temperature setting set like this, the temperature over the top of Mount Albert will be 59°F or 15°C at the top of Mount Albert at 14400 feet and this is not realistic to the way the atmosphere works.

Typically, the atmosphere will cool as you go higher but if you have it set to this mean ground level your cloud heights, wind levels, and your temperatures will contour to the terrain. In other words, as the terrain goes up, that temperature that you set Will follow that terrain up. The same thing is true with the cloud setting - if you set your cloud base say at a thousand feet, it will set a cloud base at a thousand feet above the ground which means over sea level it's going to be at a thousand feet above mean sea level or on your altimeter, but as you go over higher terrain that cloud base is going to lift.

For this reason, we recommend using the AMSL setting; it's a little more realistic, you do have to do some math with where your cloud bases are going to be in relation to the terrain and things like that but it makes for a more realistic environment where the temperature is going to decrease as you go higher and you won't be flying over the top of Mount Whitney and it being a temperature way higher than normal. So set this to above mean sea level and then do my math to figure out where the clouds and temperatures and things like that need to be from there.

Exploring the weather options

Looking at our weather options in this main weather panel here we'll start at the bottom and work our way up.

Humidity

The first slider that we have is for humidity. This increases the amount of moisture you have in the air. You can set the slider between 1 and 20. If you increase this slider and bring the humidity level up, you can see it provides this sort of a hazy effect for you and this is true to life. When you have humid air in real life it is going to be a little hazier and the visibility is going to be a little lower. Another thing that is realistic about a flight simulator is if you are looking through the haze into the sun like you would if you're flying into sunrise or sunset, you can see that it decreases visibility even more versus if it's over your head or you're not looking directly into the sun, the visibility is not quite as bad so that is accurate to real life and replicated in Flight Simulator.

The other thing that high humidity will do in real life is it affects aircraft performance. It affects the amount of power that piston engines put out. It does not affect turboprop or turbojet engines but it does affect piston engines so just be aware that if you increase your relative humidity up to a relatively high level you may be getting less horsepower out of your engine. It may not be as dramatic as the effects you'll have with high altitude and high temperatures but in the real world, it does affect aircraft performance.

Atmospheric pressure

The next slider up is our slider for adjusting atmospheric pressure and we read the atmospheric pressure as an altimeter setting. The altimeter setting is the barometric pressure at a given station adjusted to read what it would read if the station was located at sea level.

That way you can set your altimeter to that setting and it should read the correct altitude regardless of what elevation you're located at.

You can adjust it. The low point is about 27.99 or 28 inches and the high point is about 32 inches. What's considered the standard barometric pressure is 29.92 on the inches; anything lower than that is considered lower than standard and anything higher than that is considered higher than standard. When you adjust the pressure up and down that makes the altitude change on the altimeter. When you lower the pressure, since it's a pressure-sensitive instrument that makes it think it's at a higher altitude. That's why we have our altimeter set at the bottom of the altimeter there or on the side of an analog altimeter and we can change whatever we have in here to the current altimeter reading and it will read the correct altitude. Another effect that the pressure has on aircraft is performance. If you have a very low barometric pressure, that air is going to be quite a bit thinner, the same as it would be at high elevations and high temperatures so your aircraft is going to perform more poorly in low pressure and if you have a very high barometric pressure the air is going to be quite a bit thicker with more oxygen molecules packed in the same amount of air so the aircraft is going to perform better. If you want to artificially enhance your aircraft's performance, one way to do it is to crank up the barometric pressure as high as it will go and your aircraft will perform well, just don't forget to adjust your altimeter setting.

Temperature

The next slider up is the temperature slider. You can do two things with the slider and it's dependent on what your altitude calculation is set to. If you have this set to AMGL it will set your temperature at the elevation that you're currently at if you're on the ground or the elevation of the land you're flying over if you're in the air if you set it to MSL it will set the temperature that you've selected at sea level.

Let's take a look at an example of how this works. Let's say we're currently sitting on the Ramp at Denver International Airport. The elevation of the field here is 5,420 feet plus or minus. If we set AMGL in here and we set our temperature to 15°C that sets the temperature here at Denver at 5420 feet to 15°C. It's important to know that the atmosphere gets colder as you climb higher and in Flight Simulator it gets colder at a rate of 2°C per thousand feet so for every thousand feet you go up, your temperature decreases by 2°C. When you have this set to AMGL. That means that this temperature is going to contour to the elevation, in other words, if you take off from Denver and you fly to the East and the terrain drops down to 4000 feet the temperature will be 15° at 4000 feet.

If you head to the west and fly over a field that has an elevation of 8000 feet, the temperature at that airport at 8000 feet will again be 15°C and because of the way, the atmosphere cools as it goes higher, as you fly over high elevations this means that you're flying through higher temperatures and that's quite an unrealistic atmospheric profile. The temperature is going to be a lot warmer aloft than it probably should be and that is going to affect your aircraft performance.

If you set this to AMSL, again, it sets whatever value you've selected here to that temperature at sea level and again, the atmosphere in Flight Simulator cools at 2°C per 1000 feet so at 5000 feet it's roughly 10 degrees colder. Our recommendation here is to set this to AMSL and then if we have an aircraft that has an outside air temperature gauge which is common in flight simulators we can just take a look at what the temperature is on that temperature gauge and adjust it accordingly to get the temperature that we want at that station but to still have a nice realistic profile as we climb, that the air is going to get cooler and be a realistic temperature at altitude.

Lapse rate

As we mentioned earlier, as altitude increases in the atmosphere, the temperature decreases and the rate at which it decreases is called the Lapse Rate. In the real world, the lapse rate can vary. It's not always the same and the temperature can even increase with altitude to a certain extent which is called a temperature inversion. The standard lapse rate or what we use as a standard lapse rate is what they call the international standard atmosphere or ISA and this is 2°C or 3½°F per 1000 feet. This means for every 1000 feet you climb, the temperature is going to decrease by 2°C.

In a Microsoft Flight Simulator, when you're not using live weather the lapse rate will always be standard. There's no way to change the temperatures aloft or to change the lapse rate. You say the temperature either at sea level or at the elevation of the land that you're either on or flying over and then it automatically decreases 2°C per thousand feet from there.

Determining the freezing level

In Microsoft Flight Simulator you can use the temperature and the lapse rate to determine where the freezing level is and the freezing level is just the altitude where the temperature is going to be at or below freezing or below 0°C. To do this you divide the temperature at your elevation or altitude by two and then multiply by a thousand to figure out where the freeze level is relative to your current elevation or altitude.

Here are a couple of examples of that. Let's assume that we're at sea level and that the temperature is 15°C at sea level or standard. Since we are at zero feet, the MSL temperature is 15. Dividing that by two equals 7.5. We then multiply that times a thousand which is 7500. Next, we'll add that to zero feet MSL and that means that the freeze level in our current location is going to be 7500 feet on the altimeter or 7500 feet MSL.

Looking at a departure from Denver which has an elevation of roughly 5400 feet MSL, let's assume that the temperature is 10°C. 10 divided by 2 is 5 multiplied by a thousand gives us 5000 so the freezing level is going to be 5000 feet higher than where we currently are. If we take Denver's elevation of 5,400 feet and add five thousand feet to that we come up with a freeze level of 10,400 feet MSL.

Let's take a look at the last example. If we are sitting in Leadville and the temperature is -4°C, this divided by 2 is going to be -2. Multiplying that by a thousand is going to be -2000 so the freeze level is going to be 2,000 feet lower than we're currently located. Leadville is, we'll say for simplicity's sake, at 10,000 feet so we know that we have to reach an elevation or an altitude and that's at least eight thousand feet MSL to be at or below the freezing level. Ao if we take off from Leadville we know that we're going to be dealing with icing or airframe icing until we can get to a point where we can descend below 8000 feet MSL.

It's important to remember that in Microsoft Flight Simulator, if you have icing enabled you will always get icing when you are at or above the freezing level and you are in clouds or precipitation. The temperature slider has quite a wide range. It can go down to -90°C which is -130°F and it can go up to 60° above zero Celsius which is about 140°F.

Another important consideration with temperature is that if you have lower than standard temperatures that's going to make the air thicker so the aircraft is going to perform better if you set your temperatures way colder than normal and if you set your temperatures way above normal, particularly if you set it to AMGL.

Lightning

The next slide setting we have is the lightning setting and to have lightning you need to have clouds. If we ramp this setting up to 100 it doesn't do anything right now because we don't have any clouds. You can generate it from any layer of cloud that you want. You can generate three layers of clouds but it looks most effective if you have to do it from the lowest level of clouds so we'll just make a quick overcast layer to generate our lightning from and then it's pretty straightforward from there.

You have a slider that's zero percent to a hundred percent. Zero percent is no lightning and a hundred percent means you get a nice lightning show. This is only a visual effect, it does not produce a thunderstorm but to produce a thunderstorm manually, you need to generate tall clouds; you need to generate the precipitation you need to turn on the lightning and then if you want turbulence you have to adjust the winds.

It's kind of a cumbersome process but then if you want to fly in stormy weather you can use the storm setting on the presets and that will automatically generate areas of thunderstorms and then you can control how thick it is or how clustered it is using the cloud tool. However, if you just want an effect you can sprinkle in some rain here and you've got a nice thunderstorm-looking effect.

Snow depth

The next slider up here is the snow depth. It allows you to set the snow depth in inches. Like the lightning, this is just a visual effects slider. As you move the slider to the right some surfaces start to get snow quite early and as you continue to increase the slider, you'll start to get a frosty appearance on some of the taxiways. It's interesting to note that different types of pavement will get snow covered at a different rate and some not at all.

It's important to note that there are some very large airports that are made out of concrete and if you're shooting an instrument approach in snowy conditions and you have some snow depth set or the live weather has some snow depth set, you'll break out and you won't see many of the runway markings. You'll only be able to see the runway lights so that is something to be aware of if you're operating in winter conditions.

As we said earlier this snow will not melt. It's not going anywhere so even if we sit here for an hour, the snow is not going to melt or decrease in coverage. It's just like a spray-on decorative type of snow that you're using to give yourself some ambiance to your winter flying. Another thing to mention about the snow cover is you can have a snow cover regardless of where you are in the world and what temperature you have set.

Precipitation

The next slider up is the precipitation slider. You can go between zero and 1.18 inches per hour or the metric equivalent precipitation to decide how heavy you want to make the rain or snowfall but you'll notice that when you don't have any clouds you don't get any precipitation.

Precipitation is generated from the lowest layer of clouds so we'll go ahead and pop the lowest layer of cloud by picking the bottom layer there to have some coverage and then we can vary that coverage and it will spread out the precipitation. Then all we need to do to get the precipitation is to roll the slider and the further right you roll it the heavier the precipitation gets which will also drop visibility.

The other thing that you need to know about precipitation is that it will automatically generate rain or snow depending on the temperature at the altitude you're located at so if you want to generate snow you'll just drop the temperature down to below freezing and you'll have some snowfall. Again, you can change the intensity of that snowfall but also know that it will affect the visibility when you do that. The snowfall will not accumulate. If you just leave it here and let it go for hours it won't accumulate. You do need to use the snow depth tool to get any visible indication of accumulation.

Another unique thing about precipitation in Flight Simulator is it generates an even precipitation field. You'll notice as you bring the precipitation up it creates these clumps and clusters with areas of no precipitation so it's not a uniform shield of precipitation that you're flying through.

This has more to do with the visibility too because whether it's raining and how hard it's raining will determine what the visibility is and because of that, the visibility will go up and down when you have precipitation. It won't remain steady so for that reason, we don't recommend setting visibility using precipitation but this will show even though you get areas of heavy rain and no matter how hard you pull the slider to the right there are still going to be areas that don't have any rain.

Review Questions

1. Explain the various settings and options available in Microsoft Flight Simulator 2024 that allow users to customize and control the weather conditions.
2. Describe how the simulation models the effects of different weather conditions, such as icing, on the aircraft's performance and handling, and how pilots can learn to recognize and respond to these challenges.
3. Discuss how to use the live weather data feature.

CHAPTER 13

MULTIPLAYER AND GROUP FLIGHTS

In this chapter, we're going to show you how to get started with flying online with other people (Multiplayer flights) in Microsoft Flight Simulator and this is quite straightforward. We are also going to share some tips and tricks you can use when meeting up with friends in the virtual skies. Sometimes things can go wrong but we've managed to use workarounds that often solve some issues whether you're new to online multiplayer or have already used it. There are quite a lot of options and by the end of this chapter, you'll be able to set your own sim up for the best online flying experience possible.

How Multiplayer Works

If we click on the World Map screen in the simulator, you see we have Kern Valley here in the US so we'll go and choose a location. This is the real key to it - you just put yourself in the place where you know the rest of your friends or group are going to be, pick an airplane, go to flight conditions, and make sure you are on "All Players" in the Multiplayer section. Air traffic doesn't matter, you can have whatever you want and also for that of weather and time. The only reason weather and time come into it is if you click Live players you will only see people that have got live weather and you'll notice it grays out "All Players." This means anybody on the server can have whatever settings they like.

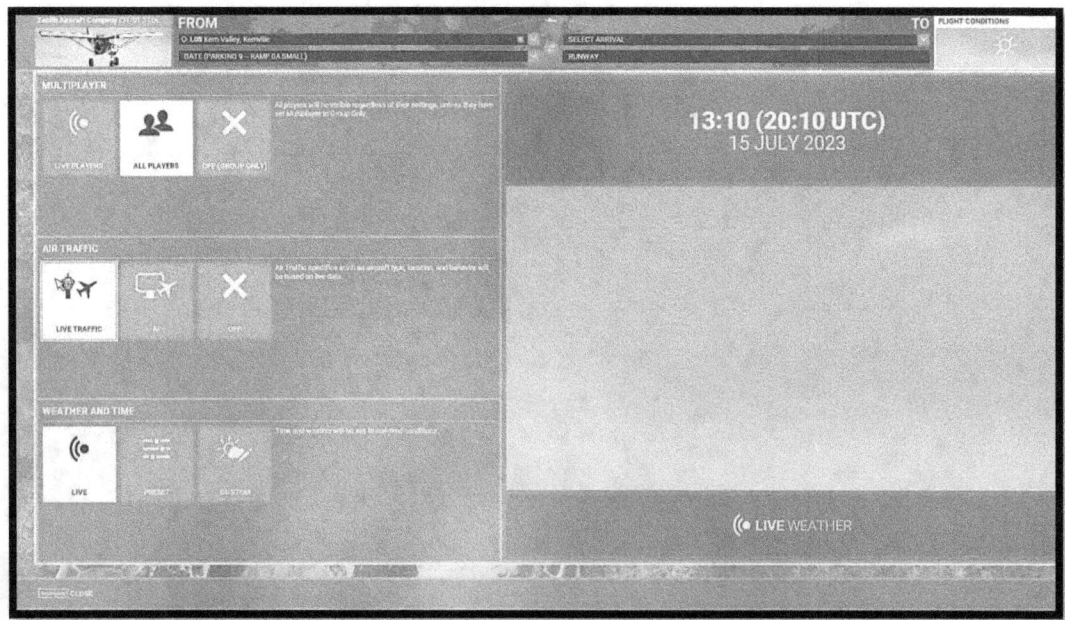

When we say on the server, if you go and click on our name at the top right of Flight Simulator you will see there is a Multiplayer Server option. By default, it will be set to automatic and it will pick up whichever is the most logical server to choose that's the fastest and nearest but you can drop down the list and choose whichever server you want. Keep in mind that you can't see people unless they are on the same server as you.

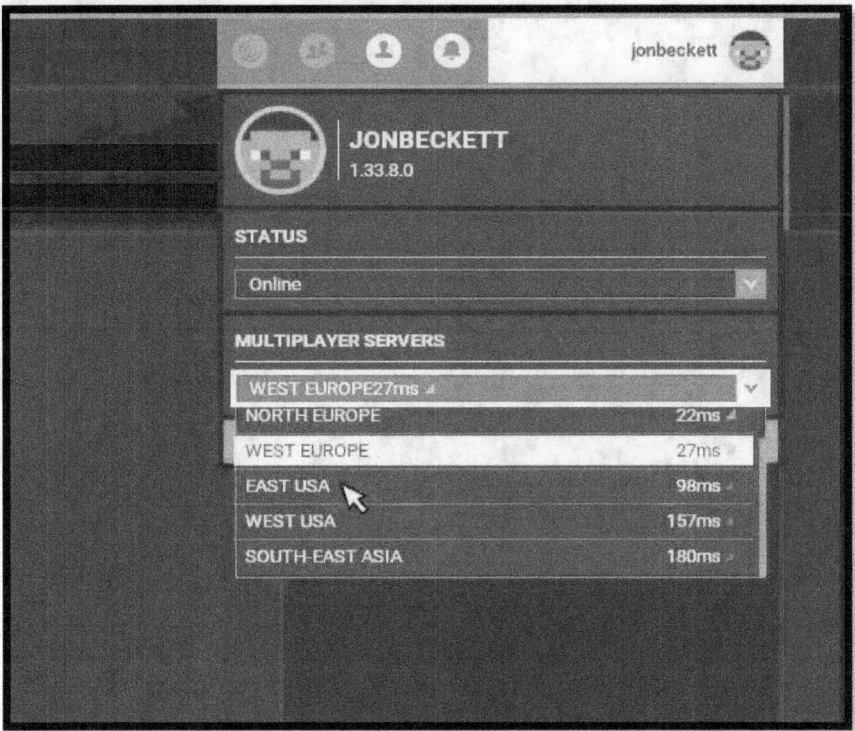

This is where you need to arrange in advance if you're doing a group flight, for example, that you're going to all start from a given airport and you'll all be on the same server as each other. Usually, in the notes of the flight, somebody will have written using capital letters to join a server so if we go and say West USA for our example, here we don't have to sign out. We just click the server, click away from it, and click on flight and the simulator is going to load us in. While it's loading, how do we arrange to be at the same place as each other? You can launch an online community to organize group flights because it's much more fun to be flying together than to just be flying on your own all the time.

Once you land in the server you'll see all the channels down the side and at the top you will see events that members of the community have organized. You can see a little number at the top which indicates how many people are interested in doing that event. If you click on one, you will see some text about it. For example, one saying to take off from a particular Airport on a particular day and time. If there is more information to write about an event there is an events channel.

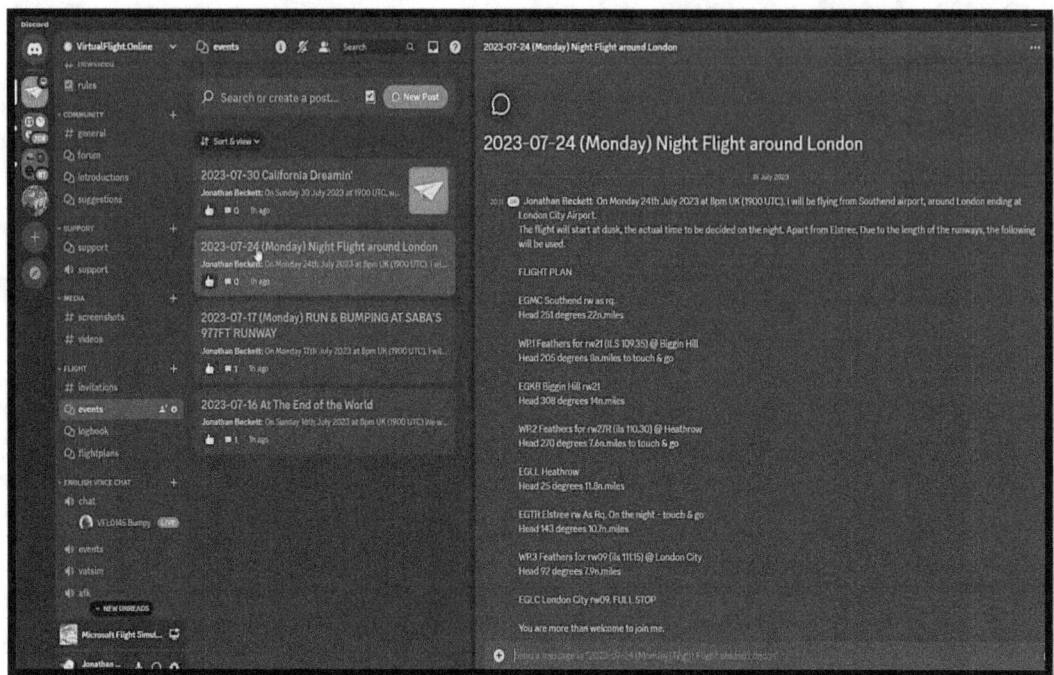

If we scroll down there's an events channel here and you can see some of the recent events here with all of the information you might need to know to take part in the event. So you might see it several days in advance because it doesn't happen until that day. You can see lots of information by clicking on each event. So all you need to do in the simulator is turn up in the right place and on the right server.

To illustrate this, we'll press Escape in the simulator, go to General options and Traffic and Nameplates is on. If we go back and resume, if we press and go to the drone camera we're just going to take off and have a look around. If we jump into the air there are people around. The higher the camera gets the more of them we're seeing over the top of the hills. They're nearby; we've turned the name plates on so we can see people in the distance.

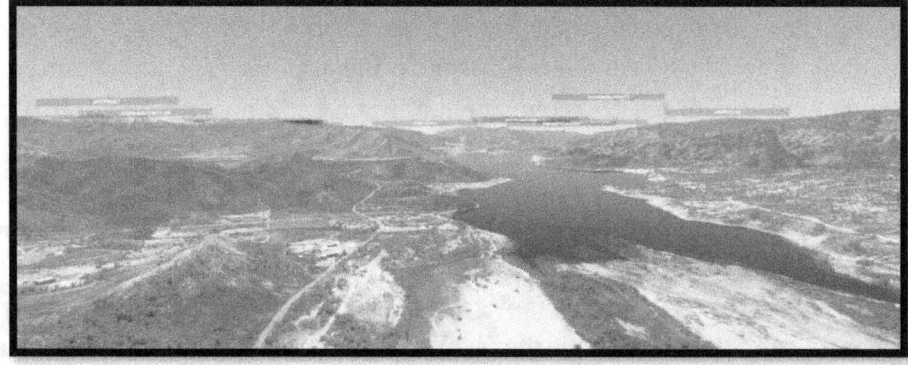

What we can do now is press Escape, go, and click on our name again while we're running in the simulator then we'll change servers and see what happens. We'll choose the East USA instead, close that, and resume. Now everyone's vanished but if you watch for a few seconds, you'll see it takes a few seconds to start loading people back in again and you'll see nameplates start arriving but different ones. These are the people that are nearby that are joined to the east USA server. They're slowly appearing in the sky so it takes a few seconds for it to happen and you will know if a group flight is happening given the concentration of them.

You can accelerate together quickly and land yourself in the middle of the group. The key here is don't be too impatient when you're waiting for the multiplayer to catch up with you.

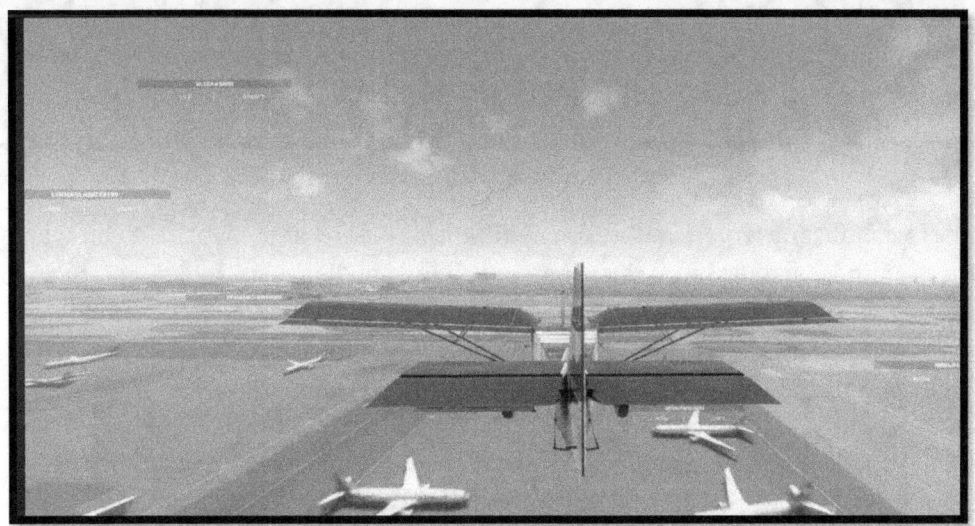

That's how multiplayer flight works. You just need to put yourself in the right location, on the right server as your friends, at the right time and the great way to do that is to come and join a community, and then you can see when the events are coming up and you can jump in.

Setting up Multiplayer in Microsoft Flight Simulator

In this section, we'll be showing you how to get the most out of the online multiplayer mode in Microsoft Flight Simulator and flying with friends in no time.

Sessions

When it comes to setting up flights, it is also very useful when setting up multiplayer sessions. To see who's online you can see the green playing icons on the main map - these indicate who is online and the location. If you hover over the icon a gamertag will appear above the plane. You can easily spawn into players' locations by simply clicking on that person's MSFS gamertag and you'll appear with them in the sim.

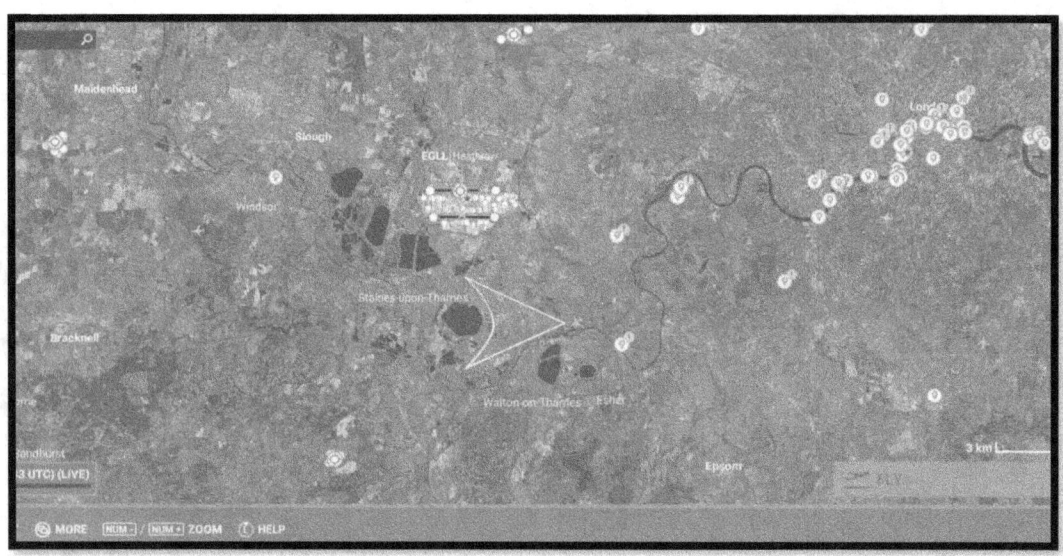

Servers

There are five different servers in the Sim in different regions of the world. If you want to fire with others online you must be on the same server and you'll need to set your status to online. You do have the option of setting it to busy or away.

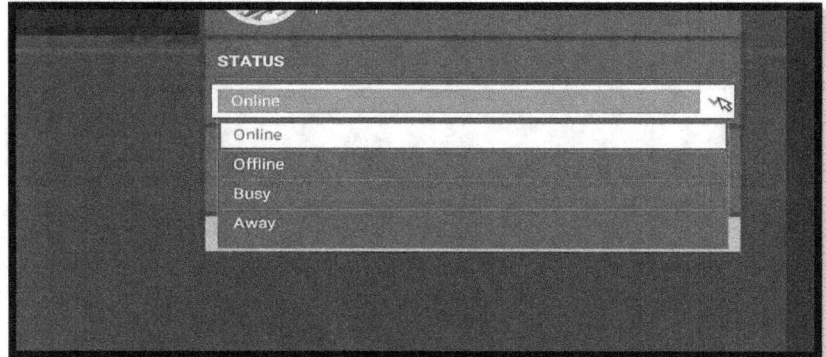

The servers are West USA, East USA, Southeast Asia, West Europe, and North Europe. Pings are constantly updating so try whichever server is closest to your location and go from there to start with.

The objective here is to get the lowest ping possible. Please note that if you have it set to automatic it will constantly look for the best ping, however, this is not helpful in this instance because you want to be on the same server as other people and you want to stay on that server. Automatic will move you in and out so whenever you want to fire with people you always decide on the server first and you simply go to that server. You'll notice that it isn't only related to where you're located as servers do change speeds regularly so don't be afraid to try the servers different from where you're located.

175

Flight Conditions

Next, let's take a look at the flight conditions menu. Here, you can select between multiplayer, air traffic, and weather in time. If we look at the first option "Live Players," this means that only those with live players enabled are visible and restricts the world to Live Weather and Live Time. "All Players" are visible and weather and time are variable. The last option is "Off Group Only" and with this option, only people in that group can see each other.

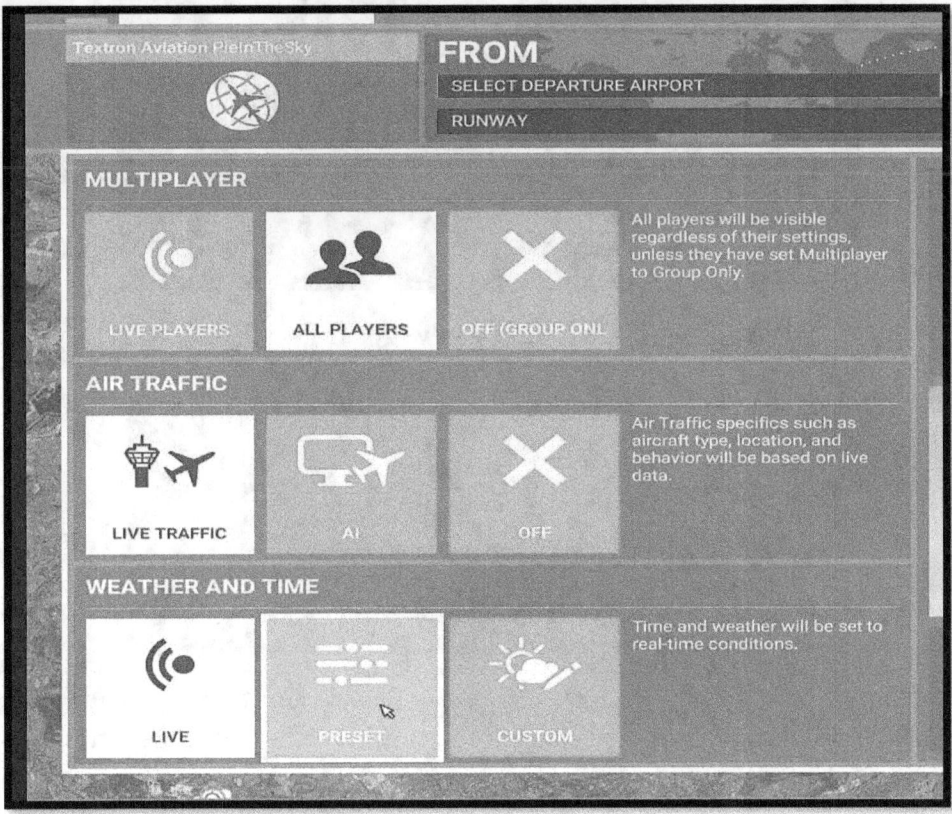

We have the choice of Air Traffic either being real-time or AI and you can also switch this off. Lastly, we have the Weather and Time so you can select live weather in live time or you can go ahead and choose in different presets, the choice is yours between the presets and the live weather.

Find a friend

If you want to find a friend you can add a friend's gamertag by entering it in the search bar. This will send a notification to that person and they can then accept the invite. You'll then see them in the menu under your friends list.

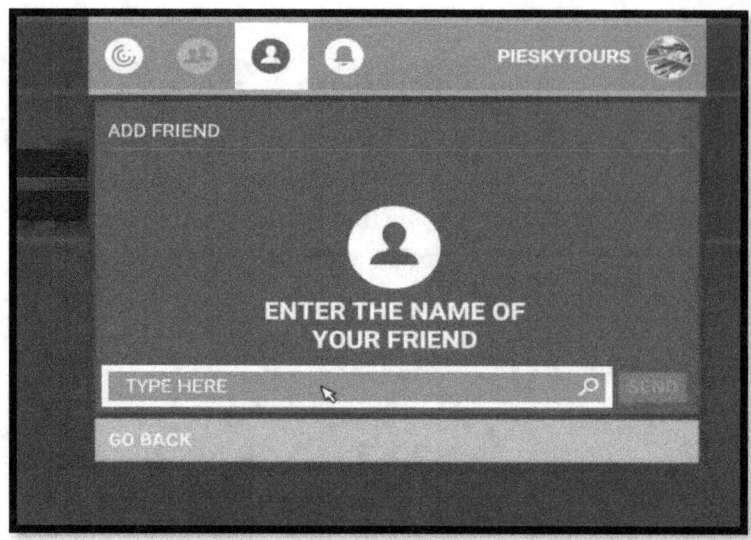

There are different icons at the top. On the left, you've got an icon that shows you who's online in your local area so you can meet people who are physically near you in the real world.

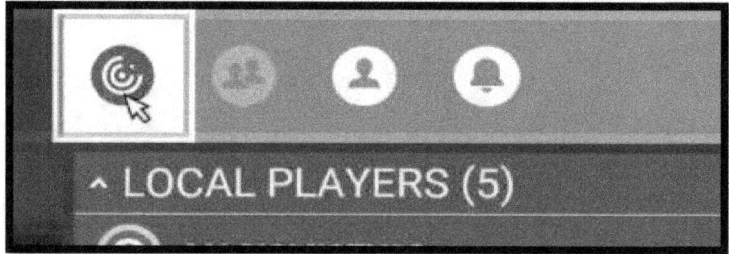

The next icon is a group flight. Here, you can send out invitations to your friends to join your group. Whoever leads that group is in charge of all these weather and time settings.

Join a group flight

A good way to join a group flight is to decide on the actual airport and runway and just proceed there as planned. You'll spawn in and everyone else should be there too. If you miss the start of a flight or lose the group, a good tip when trying to locate a group flight who are actually in the air is to look for a group of green icons on the map and make sure you are on the correct server. Once you locate the group, just click on one of the members and it will spawn you into that area. Remember that you must be visible on the map.

Another approach is to use a flight plan. It's the best way to do it because if you've got a flight plan you can't get lost. To load the flight plan simply click on More > Load/Save and here, you can load the plan by clicking on the "Load" option and it loads up. All you need to do now is to double-check you're on the right server and you should see people on the runway waiting to go.

Multiplayer Tips and Tricks

As you probably know it's not as smooth sailing as you might think and we've got some really good tips and tricks that you can use all the time when you're flying online.

Spawning into the Sim

Now if you lose connection with the sim or crash during a group flight or want to join a group flight that has already started, you can simply click on a user's name and spawn into them. You'll always be spawned at a higher altitude but this helps to locate that person, allowing you to meet up with them in the sim faster. You can always use this option if something goes wrong in flight to quickly navigate the other player or players.

Finding your friends

Sometimes you'll notice that your friend disappears, you simply can't see each other or maybe one of you can see and one of you can't. What you'll do is simply change servers and then from there you reset the flight. It usually works so if that does happen just change the server and then go back to the main menu and restart the flight and more often than not this does the trick.

Name tags

Name tags can be really useful but you may find that they break immersion whenever you're flying in a group or with a friend and you've got the name tags off you may lose them. With the name tags being off you can lose people quickly so what you'll do is go into the Traffic menu under General Options and enable name tags. This takes a few seconds so you have to pause it as you'll usually get further away than you were before.

What you'll do is use this great mod that allows you to program a shortcut to a hotkey so you can toggle it on and off. If you're flying and you lose track of someone, you'll simply click on your hotkey and you can see their label instantly. Some mod offers other options too in terms of labels and POI markers.

Crossplay

The great news about this Sim is that it's cross-play, meaning that PC and Xbox users can fly together.

Voice chat

When you're taking part in a group flight, voice chat is really important. You can chat with friends while flying and you can also use voice channels for all group flights.

Liveries

It's worth noting that selected Liveries will only appear on other aircraft when both have the same livery.

Plane selection

Make sure to choose the non-generic models of planes if you want to see what aircraft other people are flying.

Server Selection

Another tip is to choose a server that's furthest away from where you're flying in the sim and you should see less traffic. It sometimes helps to do this but again it's a bit hit-and-miss.

Installing Community Mods

In this section, we're going to learn how to install community mods in Microsoft Flight Simulator. This is for PC users only because you can't install community mods on Xbox.

What is a community mod?

A community mod is a mod created by the flight sim community so these mods do not have to go through the approval process that the ones that you see in the actual in-sim marketplace do so it's more of a wild west area where you can install whatever you want.

Finding your community folder

To do so we just need to find what's called our community folder first. Just go to the Options menu at the top of the sim and then go into General Options on the left. In the sidebar on the left choose Developers and then in the middle turn Developer mode to ON.

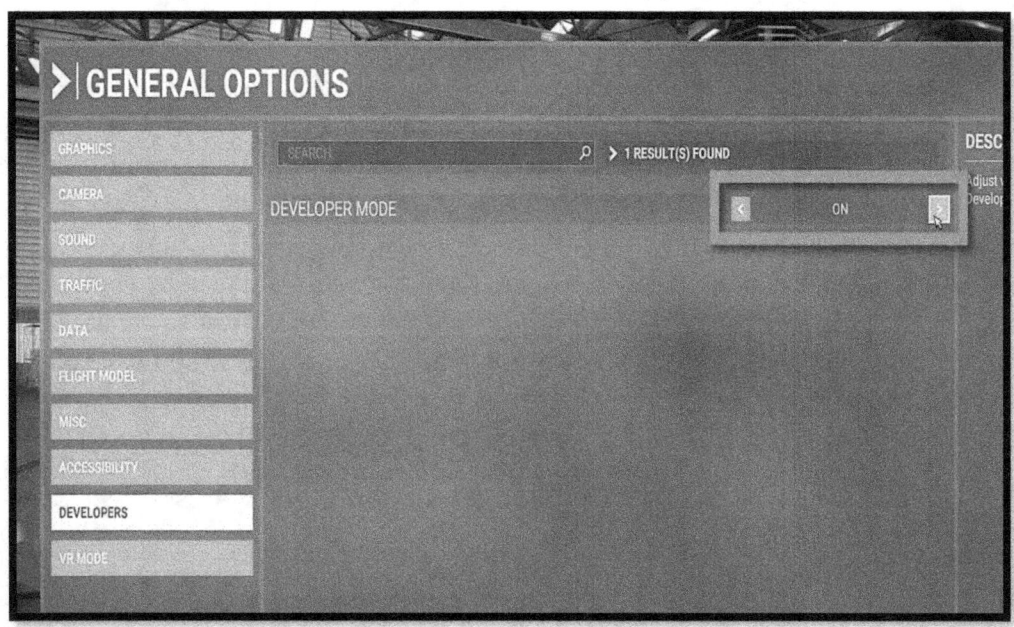

As soon as you do that it'll reveal a small menu bar at the very top of the Sim and click on Tools and then Virtual File System.

This will open a new little floating window. Click the second option, Packages Folders. This will open up and reveal two buttons: the first one says "Open Official Folder" and the second one is "Open Community Folder."

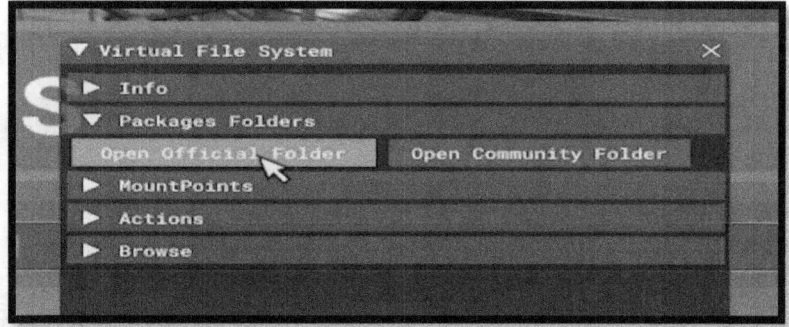

The official folder holds anything that you install from the in-sim marketplace or content manager that even includes things like world updates. The community folder is where you can install anything you want from third-party developers' websites like flightsim.to and GitHub so we're just going to click on "Open Community Folder" and now you should see a Windows Explorer screen come up showing your community folder.

Getting easy access to your community folder

The first thing you should do is go to the address bar at the top and click on Packages then right-click on the community folder in the middle area here and then click "Pin to Quick Access." This puts it on the left sidebar here in Windows Explorer so you can easily get back to the folder in the future without having to go through all these steps again.

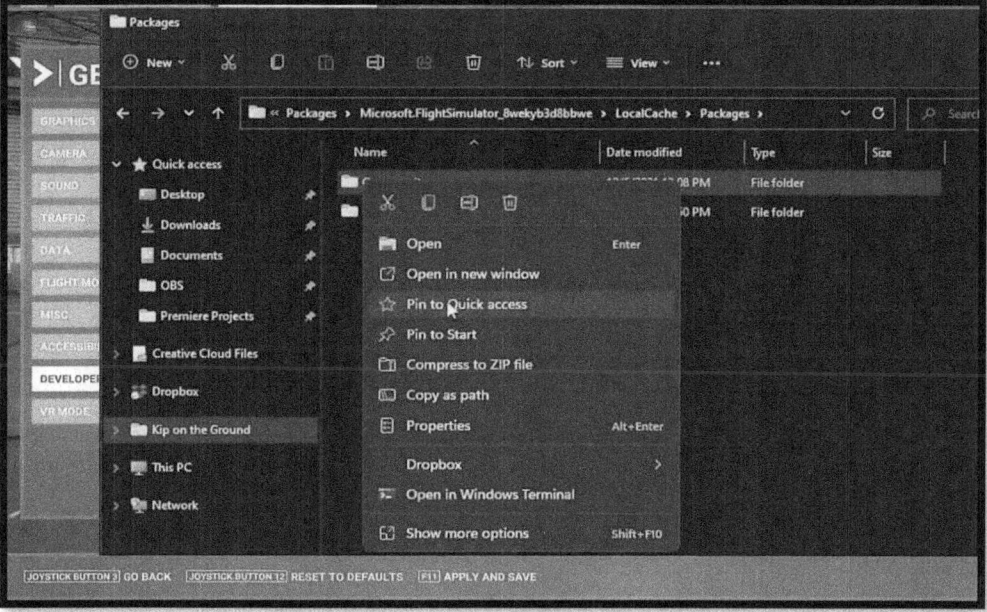

Downloading and installing mods

Next, if you haven't already, go and download the mods that you want to install. You can go to flightsim.to, for instance, and download the H135 helicopter. Once you've downloaded that you can find it in your downloads folder in Windows and what's very important is that you go into the zip file itself. Do not drag and drop the zip file into your community folder. Double-click the zip file to open it and then you can drag and drop the folder within it into your community folder here on the sidebar that you pinned earlier. Once you let go it should copy the files in and if you want to be safe you can go and click on Community just to verify that this new folder is there.

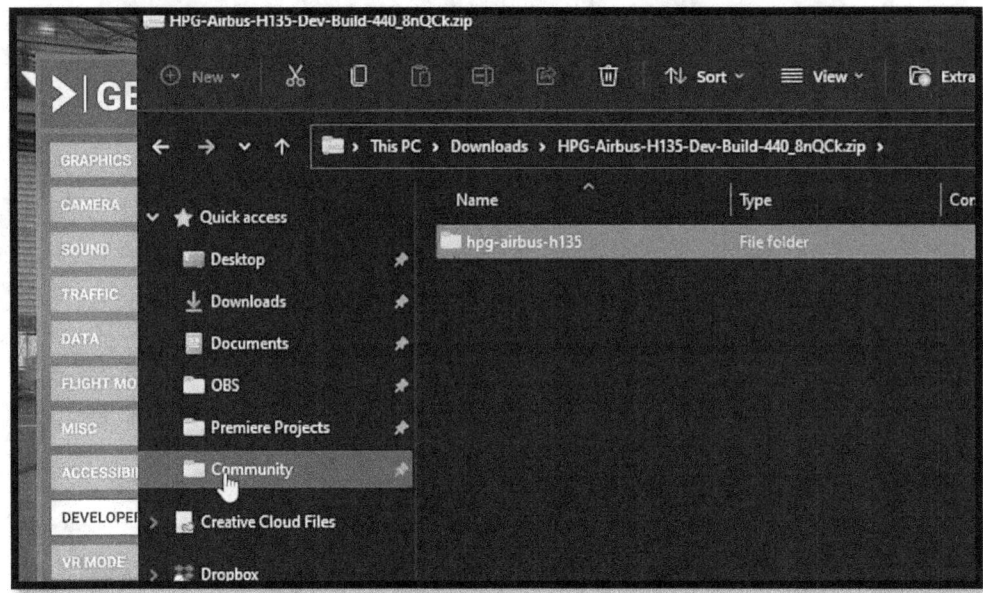

All you have to do next is close and reopen the sim and the mod will be installed. If you still have Dev mode turned on in the sim you can turn that off by going to the top left, clicking Dev mode, and then clicking Exit Dev Mode.

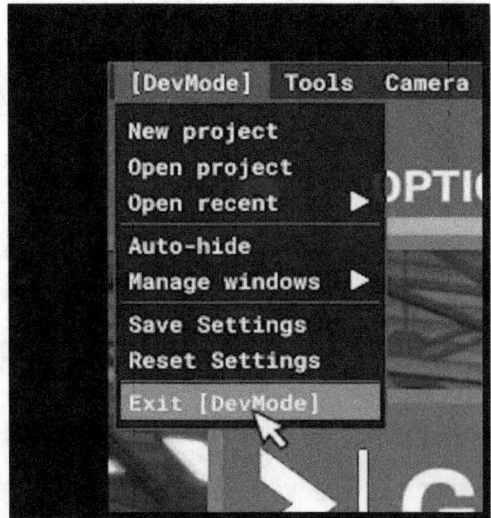

Note

Something to keep in mind is that whenever there's a big sim update there is a chance that the mods that you've installed will cause the sim to crash until they've been updated by their developers so in that case, you will need to go in and temporarily delete the mods until they've been updated.

Review Questions

1. Provide an overview of the multiplayer functionality in Microsoft Flight Simulator 2024, including the process of setting up and joining multiplayer sessions and servers.
2. Explain the various features and tools available for enhancing the multiplayer experience.
3. Describe the process of installing and using community-created mods in Microsoft Flight Simulator 2024.

CHAPTER 14

TROUBLESHOOTING YOUR MSFS

So you've downloaded and got yourself some nice freeware scenery or perhaps a payware aircraft loaded into Microsoft flight simulator but it's not there. If you've had this problem this chapter will be of great assistance.

If you want to successfully install anything into the Microsoft flight simulator there's one critical piece of information you need to know and that is the location of your community folder. What's important is not where you think it is but the path being used by Microsoft flight simulator and there's one sure way to check in SIM.

Checking Sim

After opening your community folder, you can take note of the drive path and directory being used in your community folder. You can do likewise for the official folder (this is where default add-ons such as aircraft, and scenery, are stored as well as anything installed from the marketplace normally, including third-party products subject to them being purchased again through the marketplace). Never delete or add items here. If you want to remove something, use the uninstall or install via the content manager. We mentioned this folder just for your info and we highly recommend you leave it alone.

Once you've confirmed the location of your community folder, turn Developer mode off, apply, and save and we can now move on.

Chances are that you've already installed Microsoft flight simulator and the path to your community folder is already defined. We do recommend however the best option is during the initial installation to define a location other than the default for your community folder. You aren't given that option but that way, you'll always know where it is. You can put it on your D drive if you've got lots of space plus it's an NVME Drive so it's very fast. This means less loading time.

Opening a file

After downloading the file you'll find the downloaded file in your downloads folder. You could extract the zip file directly here but it's always a good idea to save this file elsewhere on your computer for future reference and in case you ever need to rebuild your community folder. Remember, do not cut and paste this file directly into your community folder and then unzip it, the download will not be seen and the chances are you're extending load times and likely to crash your sim.

You can now copy and paste the downloaded zip file into the folder where you have already created a directory for the downloaded file. so you'll open that and paste the zip file there and now you can go ahead and unzip the file. To unzip it use the Windows default, it'll ask if you want it in this directory which you do, click OK and the file will unzip.

It is here where most of the errors take place because you inadvertently move the wrong directory to the community folder. There's a zip file and the unzip directory. Within the unzip directory is another folder that contains what you've downloaded and when you open that you see that this folder has the contents including content info and Sim objects.

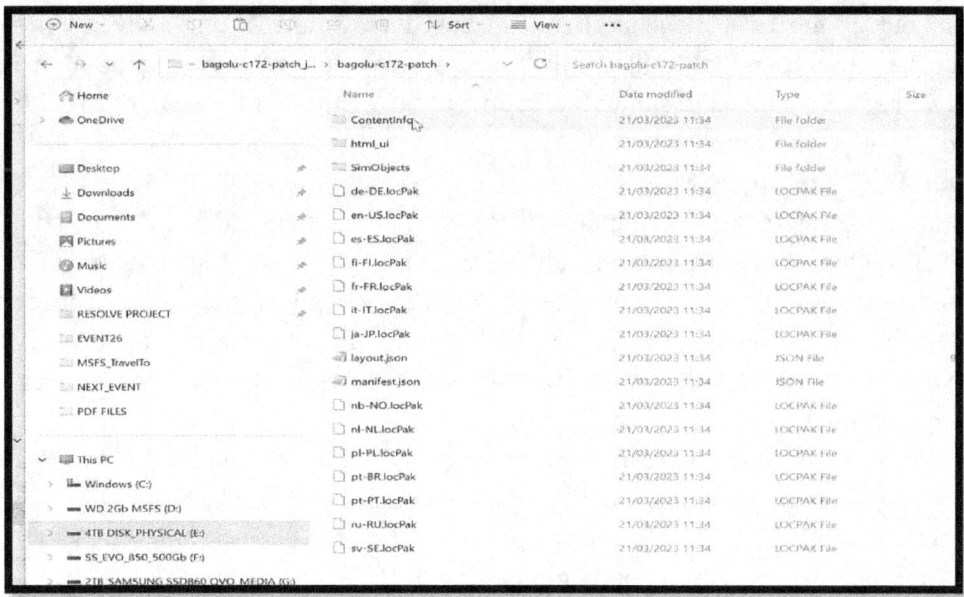

If you move this folder or directory into the community folder you won't see your installed file. The directory that you do move to your community folder should be the one directly above the one that contains the content info and Sim objects. If you'd previously installed the download, it is good practice to delete the one in the community folder first.

Version updates

One last important point to mention is to make sure you have the latest version that you're installing into the Sim, particularly with Sim Updates. This can have a big impact in terms of visibility as well as usability of the particular add-on. If it's scenery you've installed you'd need to go to that particular airport to check it out if it's an aircraft. So after installation go check out to see if it is recognized and if it is, you can assume at this point it's been a correct and full install. This particular install only affects one Livery and that's correct. You can now select that aircraft and go and enjoy your freeware download in-Sim.

If you've followed all these steps and it's still not visible then you need to contact the developer directly. You can be quite often tempted to take a shortcut here and there but if the wrong directory is in the wrong folder then your download simply will not be active in the

Microsoft flight simulator. There are a number of third-party applications which can manage add-ons for you so you can look into that.

Takeoff Emergency Procedures

In this section, we're going to be taking a look at a couple of different takeoff emergencies and how to approach them. First of all, takeoff is usually a moment when people don't think that we crash but about 10% of all accidents occur during takeoff and they're not always mechanical, sometimes people pull up too far or their seat comes loose or something like that so what we're going to do is to simulate a couple of the common times when we could fail as well as deal with it the simplest way.

When your aircraft engine fails

The first one is going to be what happens when your aircraft engine fails during your initial roll before you get in the air. The aircraft of our focus is a 55-knot speed which is not too much. Imagine this: our hands are on the controls, ready to go ahead and tug at that thing to get into the air and the engine fails. We'll go ahead and pull our controls towards us. We're going to pull our throttle to idle and we're just going to squeeze the brakes as well as we can while maintaining positive control of the aircraft.

Now you're probably sitting there asking why we pull the throttle out. The reason we pull the throttle out is because if we don't and the engine decides to come back we could be in this place where we can't control the plane and go rip right off the end of a much shorter runway.

What happens if the aircraft already gets in the air?

That gets a little more interesting. What we'll do is go ahead and hit our takeoff again running down and we're going to simulate a takeoff where we lose our engine as soon as we get up in the air. Now the big thing with that of course is you mustn't pull the nose back - you won't have enough speed to be able to maintain that landing attitude.

You have to let the nose come down a little tiny bit so if you get up in the air here and your engine goes up and fails, let the nose come down then Glide, NOSE up and we're going to let it settle back on the runway. Again, we're not looking for any awards here. One thing we want to keep in mind is if our engine does fail in that situation, we need to pull that throttle back. It'll be nice if it came back but that could also unsettle us and if we don't have a lot of runway to stop already that could be very problematic for us.

When we already have a little bit of altitude

Our third case is when we already have a little bit of altitude. Of course, there are variations on this thing here. If we have 100 feet is that enough to do with successful landing or do we have enough altitude that we can land on a parallel runway? That's going to depend on what happens but one of the important things is it always comes down to runway length so getting in the air now we could still pretty much safely land this plane directly at the end of the runway.

We're going to make things a little bit complicated for us by getting a little altitude and power out. We're going to let that nose come down and we're going to immediately get ourselves into our Landing configuration. In this case, we're going to slip a little bit and we're going to guide the plane down again, the plane has failed us but we don't care about the plane so much. We're going to settle down, it's not going to be an award-winning landing by any means but it will get us safe and you will not stop shaking for the next two and a half days after this happens to you by the way. If we take a look at our altimeter right now the altimeter indicates about five or six feet which is right.

These runways do flood a lot of times, especially during the fall so what happens if we are a little bit up but we're not necessarily properly up? The first thing we want to do is to get ourselves to a Glide. We want to look at our cell left and right and we want to identify a target that is within 20 degrees of us.

The important thing is because we are so low we can't turn the aircraft around. As a general rule, anything under 800 ft is considered a no-go. So what is the minimum altitude we would need to land back on the runway we took off from? The impossible turn is a classic thing to consider. The concept is that if you have about 1,000 ft of altitude underneath you should theoretically be able to turn around and fly back to the airport from which you just took off.

When you practice these different takeoff techniques, always be thinking about what's going to happen. One of the things that we like to do too in the real world is to have a plan before we take off.

Review Questions

1. Explain the process of opening and reviewing log files for troubleshooting purposes.
2. Explain the recommended procedures for handling various in-flight emergencies, such as engine failure.
3. Discuss the importance of staying up-to-date with the latest version of Microsoft Flight Simulator 2024.

CHAPTER 15

MAKING YOUR FLIGHT SIM REALISTIC

Microsoft Flight Simulator offers something most games or simulators cannot and that is a sense of limitless adventures but as with aviation in real life, it can be overwhelming and confusing. In this chapter, we'll be sharing some helpful information about Microsoft Flight Sim to help you get the most out of it so you can make it as realistic as possible so whether you're new to the Sim or a flight Sim veteran on PC or Xbox there is something for everyone.

Aircraft

Starting with the aircraft, this is the single biggest factor that will impact how realistic your sim feels flying around. With most default, Asobo aircraft leaves a lot to be desired. Many of these aircraft were visually nice, lacked system depth and once you've picked up the basics of flight you'll be crying for a lot more luckily there is plenty to choose from. From the freeware, A310 available on all Flight Sim platforms to the wonderful payware 737 and the BAE 146 with these two airliners being available on both PC and Xbox.

Now PC Pilots luck out with freeware airliner add-ons from the famous A320neo to the A330neo as well as the most realistic aircraft on the Sim at the moment, the Phoenix A320 which costs around 50 UK pounds. All of these aircraft we have listed are not the only ones you should look out for with plenty of superb general aviation and business aircraft available as well. If you can pick one of these aircraft and stick with it, learn the systems, and get a true feeling for flight, not only will you get immense satisfaction from it but your sim will feel exactly like a simulator and not like an arcade game although of course there's nothing wrong with that.

Updates

ASobo is currently overhauling many of its aircraft in collaboration with other developers with their aircraft avionics updates. For example, the 747 and the 787 are currently undergoing a makeover and with the beta, we have to say already they are brilliant. This beta is available on both PC and Xbox and it makes these aircraft (both the 787 and 747) incredibly fun to fly.

Scenery

Once you've picked your aircraft and you're satisfied that it provides a nice challenge, what about the world around you? Well, in fairness MSFS doesn't need that much help in terms of looking realistic because it already does a superb job at it but there are a few things you can do.

If you're on PC then without hesitation go ahead and download the free regions of WELOVEVFR by Puffinflight. This will go ahead and fill your world with more authentic local landmarks, from chimney stacks to power stations, oil refineries to antennas and so much more using real-world public data.

There is now worldwide coverage so wherever in the world you are there are no excuses. It is free and not too greedy for storage and it will instantly uplift your landscapes and be perfect for VFR flying.

World updates

Now regardless of whatever platform you're on, ensure you make full use of the freeware world updates that add points of interest, overhaul local airports, and sort out terrain in selected regions.

Keep in mind that some world updates are better than others and do watch out as they can be demanding in terms of file size but if you fly often in any area ASobo have covered with their world updates it really is a no-brainer and if there's an area that hasn't been covered by a server yet just wait because they are very frequent with these updates.

Ground Services X

If you fly any source of airliner you must try this out. It costs some money but for that money, every single major airport receives a jetway overhaul of some sort and of course a full replacement of ground services to better match real life adding everything from Catering trucks to Airline baggage carts, to passengers walking around towards your aircraft, hopefully nowhere near the entrance. It didn't have the best start but now all the bugs have been or most of the bugs have been ironed out and we'd say this is a must-have; it's not cheap but it is worth it.

Download Airports

Moving on, default airports are acceptable but more often than not they all look a bit cartoonish and seem to be in a lifelong stable manner with concrete so be sure you have a good look around for airport add-ons, both freeware or payware.

On flightsim.to which is the go-to add-on website they have an interactive map showing all of the website's add-ons in their location on the world map so if you fly on a PC, that is a very handy tool.

Weather engines

There's one thing that does not need to be improved by anything external in Microsoft Flight Sim and that is the weather engine. We would recommend you first set your clouds to the ultra setting if you can. Don't feel like you need to pay for an external weather injector; they made sense when the Sim was first released and live weather wasn't great but since then ASobo has done a pretty good job at updating live weather. We have to say that clouds are pretty much near to perfect, at times a bit pixely but that's never sorted out and a few of them are very expensive. Keep your money in your pocket. There is no need to do anything, just use the default here.

Sim settings

Now we will briefly touch on a few pointers to make your Sim look more realistic and hopefully help with performance as well.

First, prioritize your settings to allow for Ultra clouds. It is worth it. You can de-prioritize water waves or grass and bushes to allow for some wiggle room here because more often than not you're not flying right down near the waves nor are you flying right down near some grass unless, of course, you're a bush pilot.

In addition, while incredibly demanding on your system, prioritizing a higher quality of shadows will result in a noticeable uptick in how realistic your Microsoft flight sim world looks. Aircraft will look more shiny and the world will sort of feel like it's more blended into one as opposed to separate objects.

Now if you are suffering from severe blurry screens inside the cockpit, which is an immersion breaker you may want to change your anti-aliasing settings from DLSS to TAA (temporal anti-aliasing).

Nvidia Game Filter

While we're here talking about settings, let's briefly touch on Nvidia's game filter. You may find your flooring changes too much to find a filter that improves the Sim as a whole. We do understand that it is an incredibly powerful tool and can be used to boost the visual realism of your simulator if you use it correctly but then it's more hassle than it's worth and this one is PC only.

Air Traffic

Moving on to AI traffic, there is absolutely nothing like flying into an airport in Microsoft Flight Sim with some company airliners at the gate ready to pull up next to you or some aircraft to dodge in the sky upon departure. PC users: for freeware, we would recommend without a doubt FS LTL, and for payware, we would recommend just Flights FS Traffic at the moment. FS LTL is where they've recently added general aviation traffic making our skies feel more alive. You will experience a performance hit but all is worth it in moderation. Sadly, both of these add-ons are PC only but they are moving FS Traffic over to Xbox as well.

How about some live ATC?

Well, VatSim or IVAO have you covered. You need to do more of these because it is an absolute blast. Whether you're flying VFR (visual flight rules) or IFR (instrument flight rules), both of these online networks will mean you encounter professional air traffic control which can be quite daunting but the vast majority of this community is very helpful and before long you'll find yourself being vectored onto the ILS, into some of the Sim's busiest airports surrounded by fellow Pilots aiming for a high level of realism. At the moment, this is PC only and if you've done everything else well VatSim or IVAO is the final step to achieving a simulator that feels as close to real life apart from hopping in a Class D FAA-approved Sim as possible. They are good when it comes to boosting immersion.

Realistic Planning

If you want to fly in a manner that is realistic to real life you have to fly a flight plan which is realistic and NaviGraph is there for exactly that, providing the most up-to-date navigation data. Navigraph provides a holistic system for flight planning in Microsoft Flight Sim, from creating the route to giving you the vital charts you need for your SIDS and stars. While it is PC-orientated at the moment, Xbox developers can add Navigraph integration in their aircraft, meaning you can receive some airport charts right on your displays in the cockpit in some marketplace aircraft such as the Honda Jet.

Now this is payware and you do pay a subscription so again it's not for everyone but it is worth it if you want to fly realistic Airline routes following real-world procedures as closely as possible.

Anyway, if you want to fly VFR or aren't too bothered about paying then we would recommend the trusty little NavMap map. While it is not as glossy as Navigraf it allows you to plan a flight plan seamlessly with VFR landmarks if you prefer and the best thing is it's free.

Peripherals

Since Microsoft Flight Sim came out in 2020 there has been a fantastic explosion in the amount of flight Sim Hardware available and if you have the spare money, because let's be honest it is expensive, then this can be so far away from getting close to that sought after feeling of flight. We would recommend prioritizing boosting a computer first if that could do with an update but if not, Flight Sim Hardware is the way to go.

Review Questions

1. Discuss the various options and techniques available in Microsoft Flight Simulator 2024 for customizing and enhancing the realism of the aircraft models.
2. Explain the steps required to download and install these advanced sceneries.

3. Describe the role of air traffic in creating a more authentic and challenging flight simulation experience in Microsoft Flight Simulator 2024.

CHAPTER 16

MSFS TIPS AND TRICKS FOR BEGINNERS

The return of Microsoft Flight Simulator has been a triumphant one but at the same time given how much control it offers in its authentic simulation and the staggering level of detail it displays it's understandable that many, especially those not too familiar with the game might find the game a bit daunting, especially in the early stages but don't worry, we've compiled a list of basic tips and tricks that should make your early hours with the game much smoother.

Tutorials

This one should go without saying, especially given the sort of game that Microsoft Flight Simulator is but the tutorials here are not only very important, they're also very effective. Skipping tutorials is something that we often do reflexively but don't do that here. Collectively, they take about 30 to 40 minutes but they go over some of the most fundamental things you will need to take care of and do it well. By the time you're done with the tutorials, you'll have a solid grasp of how you should be playing the game.

Landmarks

Exploring an entire planet with no restrictions is one of the biggest allures of Microsoft Flight Simulator. If you're going to use the game to get your fix of virtual tourism as many probably will, you will of course want to fly over various landmarks across the world. Thankfully, they're very easy to find so rather than flying around and hoping you chance across one of them you can simply search for them in the search bar in free flight mode and chances are you'll find a hit traveling to landmarks.

When traveling to landmarks it's important that you set them as your destinations, not your departure points. Why? Well, if you set them as your departure points your aircraft will spawn in the air right by them and you'll fly past them within seconds which means you'll barely get the chance to take in the scenery.

Finding your house

Microsoft Flight Simulator recreates the entire planet impressively which means if you get the urge to fly over to where your house should be in the game's virtual version of the world you'll probably find it. Just head to the airport closest to your house's location and make your way to your destination. You'll have to find it manually, of course, and there's a chance that it won't be too faithfully recreated or detailed but there's a pretty good chance you'll find what you're looking for.

Larger planes

Microsoft Flight Simulator has a nice variety of aircraft that you can take control of and while it might be tempting to jump straight into the cockpit of one of the biggest planes you see, it might be a better idea to hold off on that in the first couple of hours for obvious reasons. The larger the plane, the harder it can be to control especially during takeoffs and landings as such, it's best to cut your teeth on the smaller aircraft in the game first and once you get the hang of them move on to the bigger one.

Long distance flights

Given the amount of real estate available in this game, you'll often be going on long journeys. Long flights, of course, can often be the best part of the game especially depending on things such as weather conditions or whether or not you take scenic routes but if you want to speed things along and get to your destination more quickly consider using jets or airliners. Those planes are the fastest of the bunch and great for long-distance flights.

Takeoffs

Taking off and landing can both be pretty daunting tasks, especially for newcomers in the very early hours of the game. With assists you can make things easier for yourself but there are other more direct ways to do so as well. For instance, taking off is much easier to handle when played in the third person since the UI is much easier to read and cleaner than the readouts. You have to keep an eye on the cockpit.

View assists

Microsoft Flight Simulator has an impressive level of detail in its simulation toolset and the level of fine control it can offer you is nothing short of staggering, however, if you're looking for a more relaxed experience the game's assists do a great job of making that happen for you. From fuel level to crash damage, to landings and takeoffs and so much more Microsoft flight simulator's assist options can ease the pressure on you in several ways so do yourself a favor and check them out to see which ones you want to fiddle with to tailor them to your needs and wants.

Challenges

Microsoft flight simulator has two dozen challenges that you can tackle and while you might be tempted just to ignore all prescribed content and simply fly off aimlessly into the sunset, we do recommend trying out these challenges. For starters, most of them are a lot of fun and test your skills in unique and interesting ways. They also let you get familiar and acclimated with various aircraft which of course is always a good thing.

Active pause

Owing to its very nature you'll be spending a lot of time in the Microsoft flight simulator just taking in and enjoying its beautiful vistas and landscapes or just taking a few seconds to catch your bearings to see where you need to be headed. The active pause function is great for both of these situations - it essentially freezes your game in time without taking you to an actual pause screen which means you can take your mind off flying your plane and just look around for as long as you want.

Your Avatar

Your character's avatar may not matter all that much or at all in a flight simulator given the fact that it is a flight simulator but the game does offer some customization options for it nonetheless. In the Miscellaneous tab under the General section of the Options menu, you can choose from a selection of two dozen different avatars for both your pilot and your copilot.

UI

Microsoft flight simulator's UI can get a little messy at times which is understandable. There's a lot that you need to keep an eye on and be aware of during flights which means there are always plenty of readouts and windows that you may want to keep on your screen at all times. If, however, you have a second monitor in your setup you can simply move all those windows to that and enjoy a UI-free view of your entire flight on your main screen.

CHAPTER 17

PRO TIPS TO GET THE MOST OF MSFS

In this chapter, we will be running through 10 beginner tips on Microsoft Flight Simulator. Although these are aimed at beginners, even if you're flying for a while there might be something here that you'll get out of this. Also, this is aimed at the PC users of Microsoft Flight Simulator. A couple of these tips do apply to the Xbox version but it's mainly for PC so keep that in mind.

Get a joystick

Some users out there can fly using their keyboard and mouse, and if you can do that good on you but it's becoming difficult. Conversely, you might want to use a gamepad or something like that which might be adequate but nothing gives you the sort of control that you need like having a proper joystick.

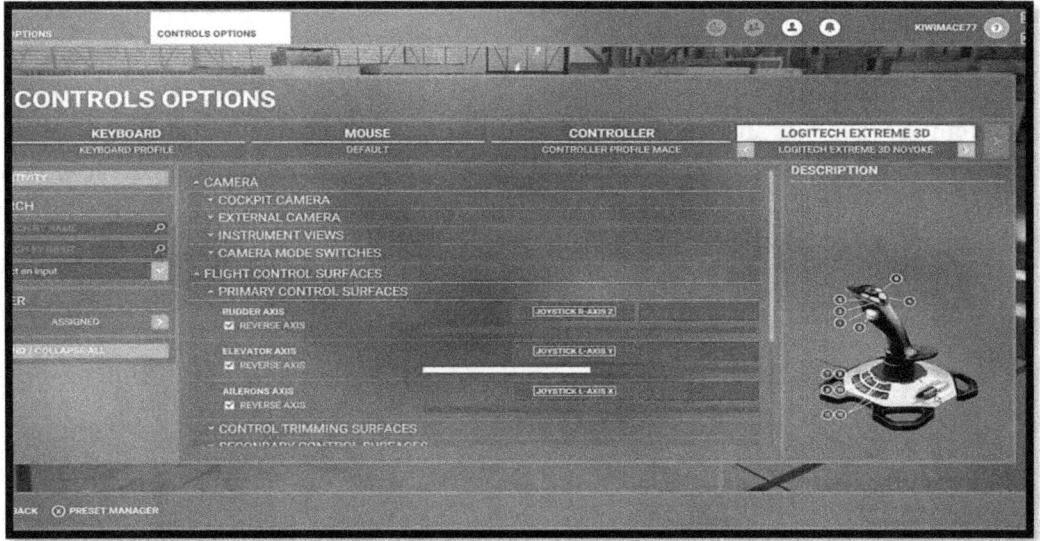

We highly recommend an entry-level joystick that's cost-effective but does everything you need it to do. Now when you're looking at a joystick, there are three things to look out for:
- The first thing is plenty of programmable buttons. This allows you to program things like the flaps or the landing gear, your comms, or changing views so having plenty of programmable buttons makes it a lot easier to be able to do things in the aircraft.
- The second thing that we recommend is an independent throttle and this is a swivel that allows you to control the throttle. Some joysticks come in a sort of setup where you've got a separate throttle and a separate flight stick, that's fine too but look for

one that is built into the joystick itself and that means you can have smooth engine control particularly for the **GA aircraft**.

- The third thing that we recommend that a joystick has is a twist handle. The twist handle is used to control your NOSE wheel on the ground and steers the aircraft while you're taxiing around on the ground. It allows you to put small inputs in and keep yourself nice and straight when you need to do that so having that twist joystick is going to help you out.

Complete the flight training

On the front page of Microsoft Flight Simulator go ahead and click on the Flight Training and it's going to bring up a number of different tutorials that you can run through. This includes everything from flying the small GA or general aviation aircraft right through to your bigger jets, the A320 in this case.

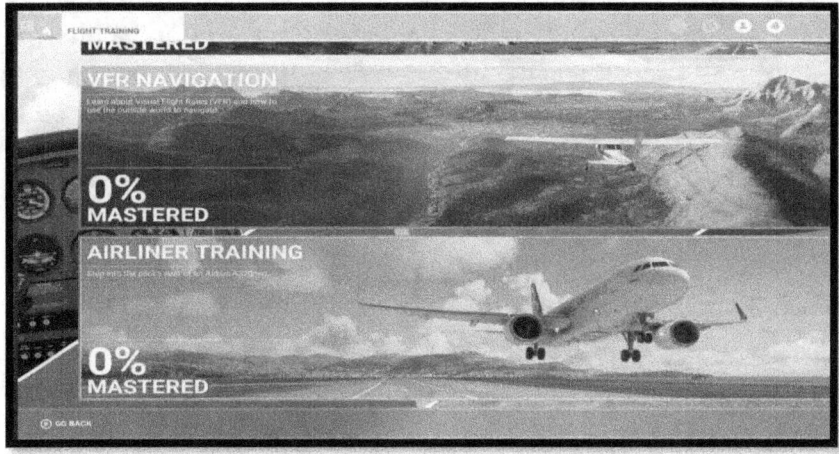

Now going and understanding the fundamentals of flights will ensure that you enjoy your flying much more. You're going to have a bit more confidence and you'll know all the different types of flying that you do, how to take off, how to land properly, how to run circuits and things like that, and if fly around like an absolute lunatic at least you know the kind of fundamentals that you're pretty much ignoring.

It's really good to at least get the basics under your belt so you can get in pretty much any type of aircraft, know how to how to get it going and how to get it from point A to point B so we highly recommend getting into the Flight training and learning the basics so you can enjoy your flying just a little bit more.

Install add-ons

One of the great things about Microsoft Flight Simulator is you can install a bunch of add-ons to make the Sim look even better than it already does. There are a bunch of different add-ons by the way but the two most popular ones are Aircraft Liveries and Scenery.

One of the things that you'll find yourself doing quite often is downloading some livery (that's the paint job on your plane) and there are heaps available.

For example, we are at Northshore Airport in Auckland, New Zealand. This is just the default scenery but then we might want to go and add a version that someone has handcrafted to make it look exactly like the real thing. There are a bunch of different add-ons available to enhance your scenery, some are paid but there are so many that are available for no cost at all due to the talented add-on community.

The first thing you need to do is find the add-on that you want to install and a good site to do that is flightsim.to. This is a fantastic site that has heaps and heaps of different add-ons. If you scroll through them you can see different little scenery, airports, and all that sort of thing. Sometimes it's airports, sometimes it's cities, there's heaps of different things that you can download. Going back to our example, if you want to fly around New Zealand, what you need to do is click on the file and download the file. You do need to register for the site and then extract that file.

So once you've got it downloaded, extract it onto your desktop and what you'll do is put it up on the screen. There are a couple of different locations where your community folder will be located and essentially, you want to just put your add-on folders directly into your community folder.

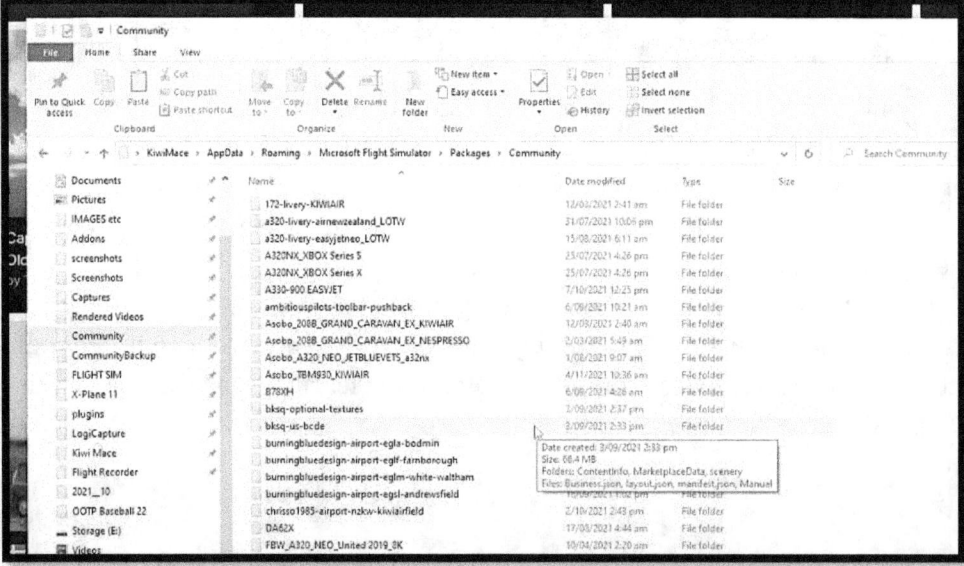

Now one little trick to think about and be aware of is that when you extract, say, an airport, usually there's a shell folder and then the actual folder you need to drag into. For example, you'll see straight away you've got ContentInfo, MarketplaceData, etc but sometimes you might click there and it's just another individual folder with this title in there. What we're saying is sometimes there's an extra folder you need to extract and all you'll do is just drag it in or cut and paste it into your community folder.

You can have a ton of different add-ons installed here on your flight simulator which just really adds to that immersion particularly when you're putting real-world airlines and real locations in the world to give that detail. So all you need to do for any sort of add-on that you download is that when it comes to deliveries and scenery just put it into your community folder. Make sure you've taken it out of its cover or shell folder and popped it into the community folder.

Get involved in multiplayer

Sim does a brilliant job and makes it nice and easy to hook up with your friends and go and do some flying together or join up a stream or whatever might be happening and join a group of people and go for a flight.

Now the first thing you want to do is make sure that you are online. At the top right-hand corner, there goes your online status which shows whether you are online or not. The next thing you want to do is particularly if you're flying with friends make sure that you're on the same server as them.

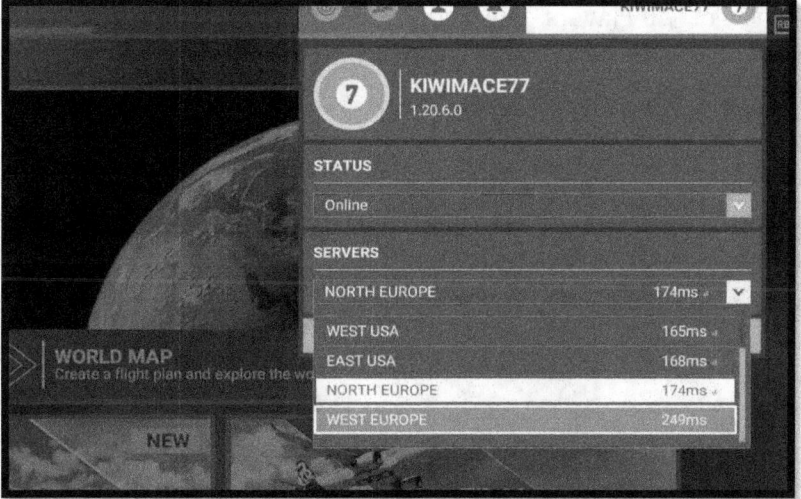

If we jump into the world map there's one quick way that you can join up and fly with your friends. If they've already loaded into the simmer, they're either at the airport or perhaps they might be in flight. If you wanted to join a mid-flight or if he was on the ground at an airport you can hover over him, left-click, go to "Set as departure" and spawn right on top of them. Then you can go ahead and fly the rest of the flight with him or if it's at an actual departure airport you can join up.

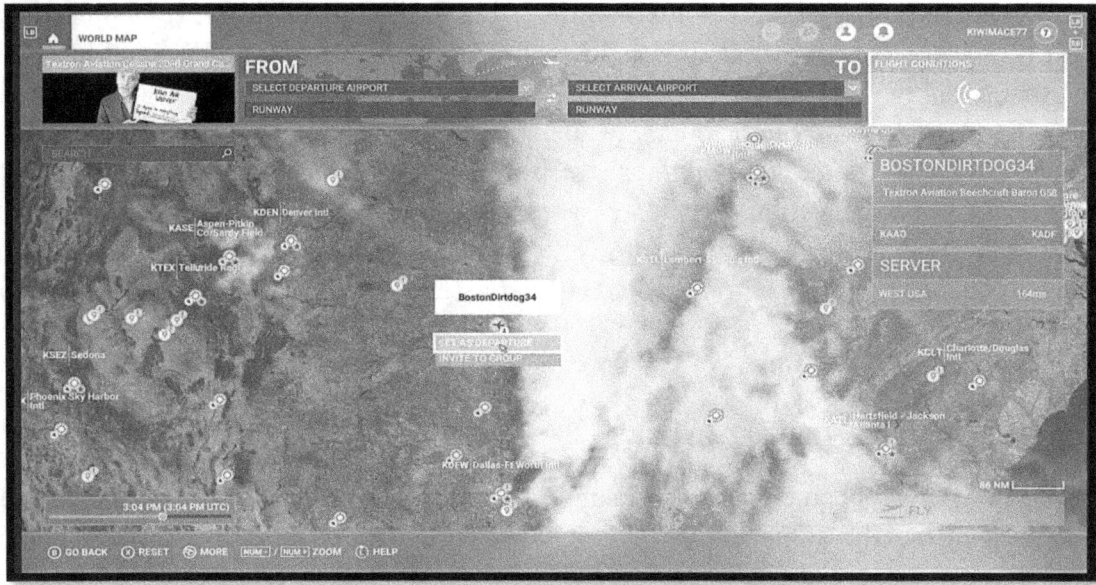

One thing you might find is when you load into the sim you might not be able to see your friends for some reason and this is a bit of a bug that does happen from time to time. Here are some key troubleshooting measures that you can go through:

- The first thing to do is go up to Flight conditions and make sure under multiplayer that you've got "All Players" checked.

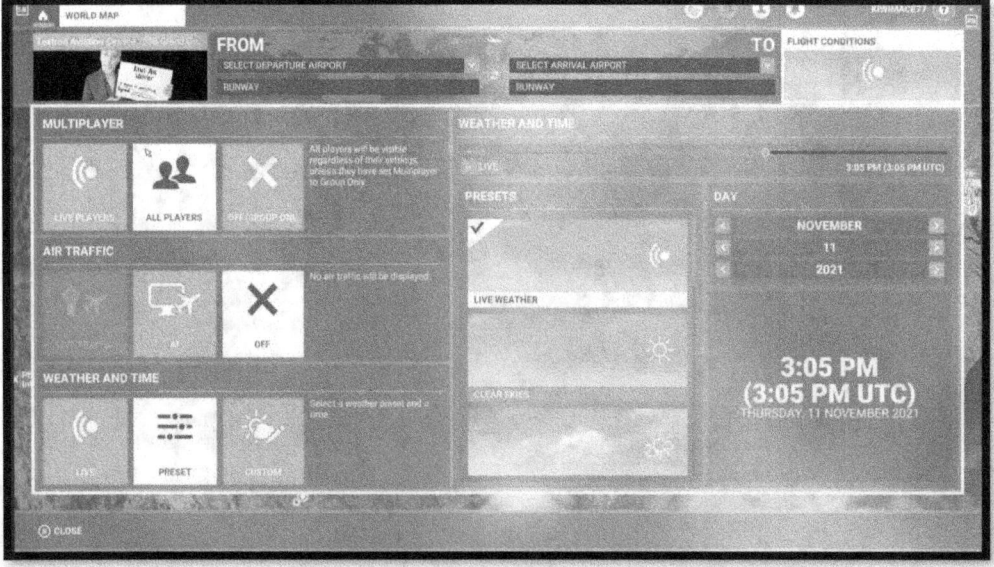

- Another thing you can do is go into your Settings, General options and if you go into your Data tab you can see Multiplayer right here. Make sure this is on and what this will do is ensure that you can see other players.

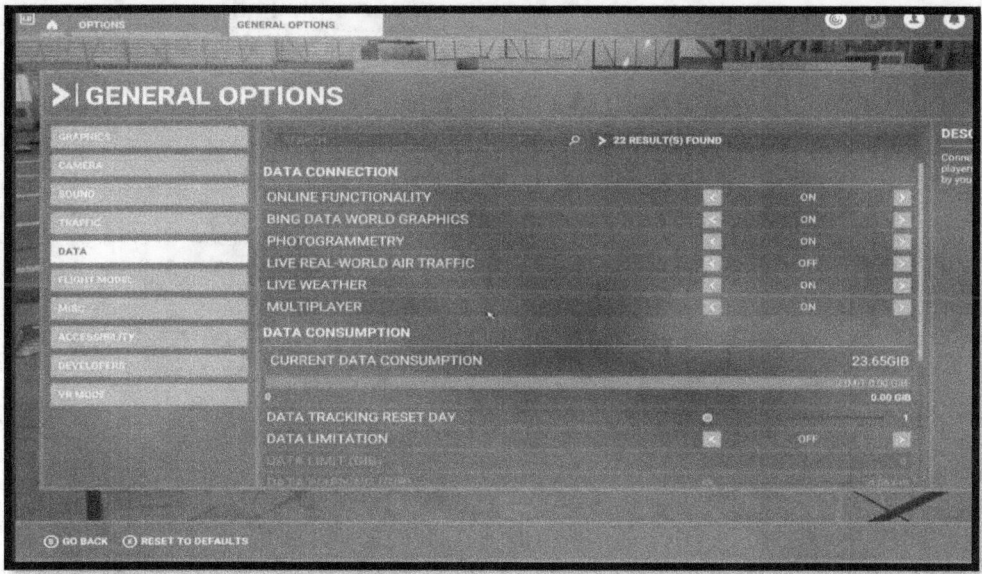

The other thing that you might want to see is the nameplates above the people that you're flying with or even general aviation traffic or just aviation traffic that's around. It's here under Aviation traffic. You can turn Traffic Nameplates on or off.

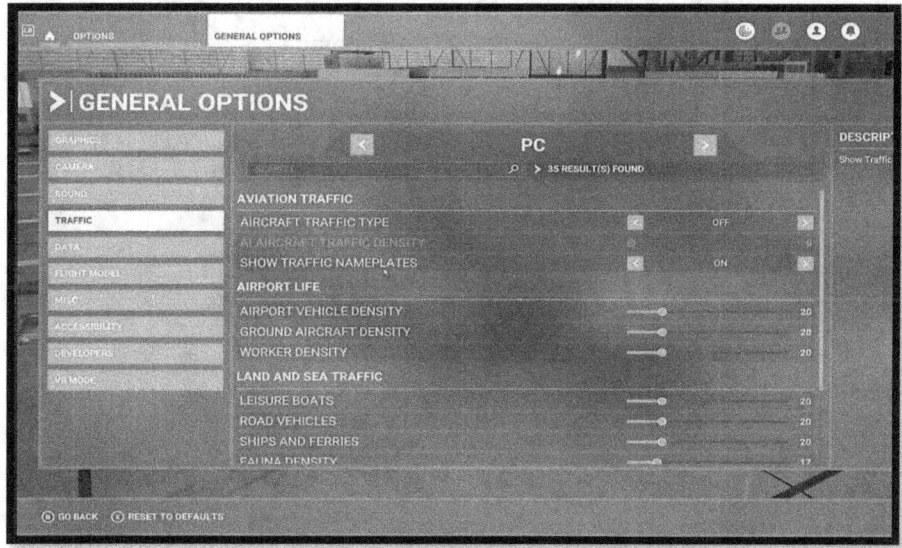

- One thing that we've found for some of the people who do fly and stream group flights is that if all that fails, log out of your Xbox account and log back in, and quite often that will reset things.

Set up custom views

While you're sitting in your aircraft, you can look around the aircraft and outside by right-clicking on your mouse and checking around. You can scroll in and out to adjust the zoom, you can also use your arrow keys to go left and right, or up and down. Press F and that will take you back to your central position. Press the spacebar and that also raises your eye line just a little bit.

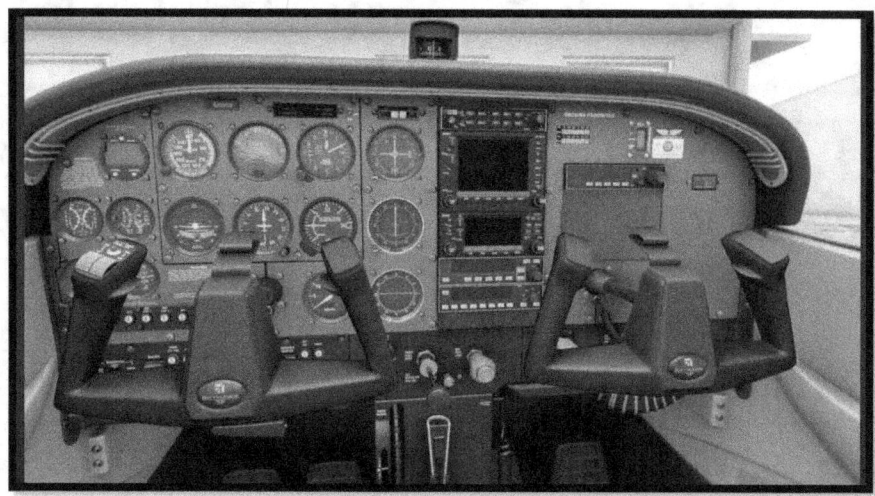

You might have a situation where you need to quickly adjust your GPS and rather than having to swivel around and zoom in and get the right sort of angle, you might want to set up a permanent view so that you can quickly flick to and it makes it nice and easy to view what you want to look at. Let's say it is the GPS that you want to adjust and you want a nice zoomed-in view, all you need to do is press CTRL and then a number on your number pad on the right-hand side of your keyboard. It's now going to bring you to a custom view.

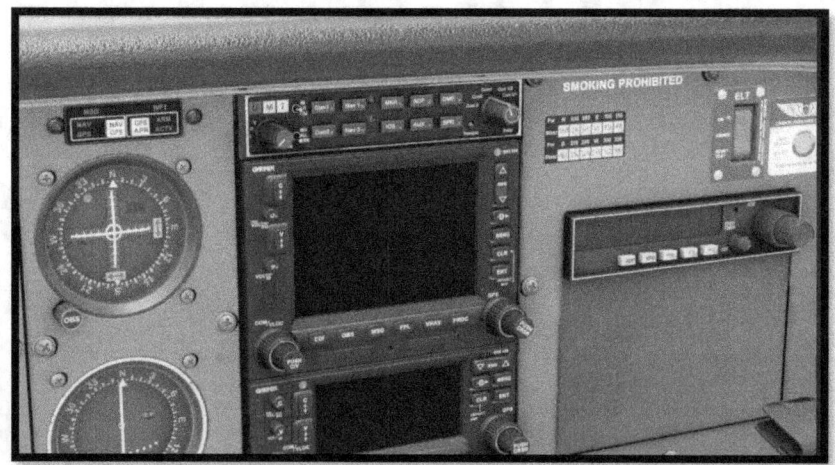

Press F to get back to your central view and now press the number you chose earlier, this takes you to a custom view setup and you can set that up for the rest of the number pad. You might have one to adjust your mixture and your throttle, you might want to look closely at your trim, or you might want one here to be able to easily turn on your master switches, your keys, and all your lights. There are a bunch of different views that you might want to set up: you might want to set up a view at the left-hand window, you can do whatever you want and it's nice and easy just press CTRL and the number pad number that you want to set that view to and that will then be set up within this aircraft.

Remember that this is individual to each aircraft so if you set this particular view up in the Cessna 172 then it's going to be different in the Cessna 152, for example, so you do have to set it up for each aircraft but it makes it nice and easy when you're flying along and you need to quickly look at something, you can do that just by pressing the keyboard.

Finding out your FPS

This next tip is for frames per second or FPS chases. If you are wondering how to find out what kind of frames you are currently pulling so you can do some tweaking in your system, well that's easy. Just press the Escape button, it brings you into the menu then go to General options > Developers and turn on Developer mode. Now if you apply and save that and then go back and resume into the sim, it goes right here under Rendering, you'll see the option to display frames per second.

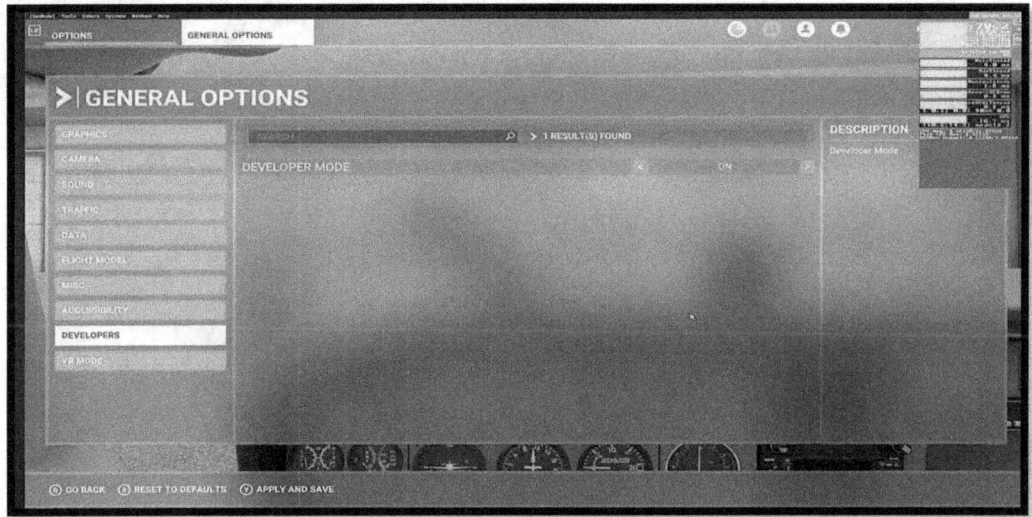

If you have a bit of a look through the Developers portal at the console, there are a bunch of different things you can do including changing your aircraft, but in this case, press "Display frames per second" and you get a counter up on the right-hand side showing you what kind of frames you're getting currently in your simulator. For example, it might cap out your frames and it might be because of your CPU, it might be because of your GPU, it's going to tell you all of that at the moment. That's how you go ahead and monitor your frames per second if that's something that you want to look at.

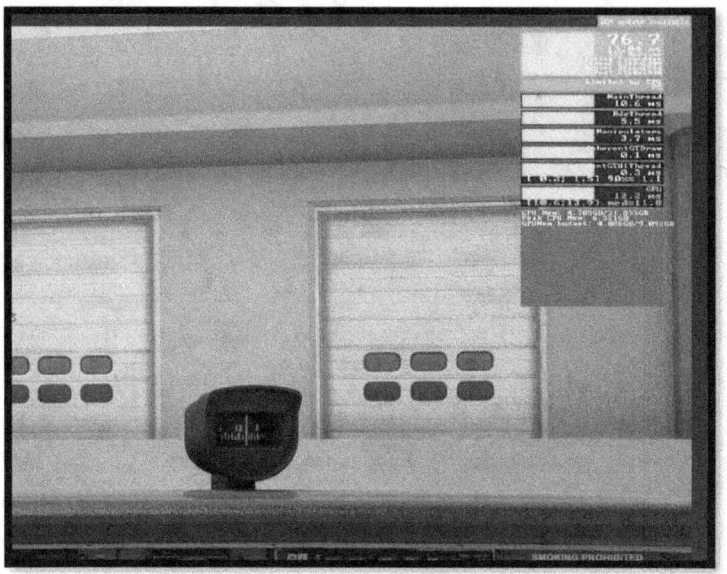

Using the drone mode

This is a great mode that you can use to have a look around the sim, particularly when you're flying you might want to check out some of the scenery. You can get drone mode set to one of the buttons on your joystick so when you press that even though you're outside the aircraft, you can go up and down and all around the place.

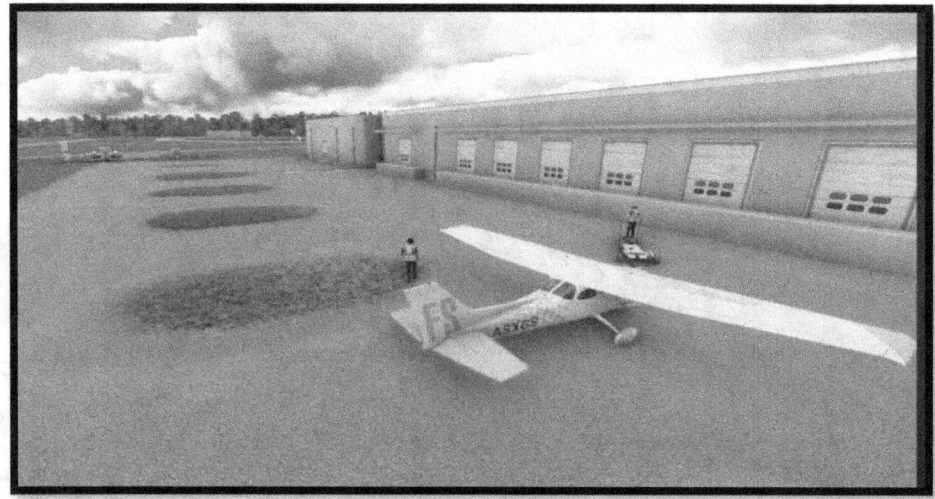

The way we recommend controlling this is using an Xbox controller. You can use the right trigger to go up and the left trigger to go down. You can use the sticks to have a look around and can also reset the view by pressing both the right-back and left-back buttons. You can also change the speed at which everything moves around by speeding it up or slowing it down. If you're outside the aircraft, particularly if you're flying with a group of friends you can jump outside the aircraft, take some cool-looking screenshots, and easily translate yourself around the scenery. Note that it's a little bit awkward when you first do it but once you get the hang of it it's easy.

One thing we want to show you in drone mode is if we go up the options at the top of the screen and open up our camera settings right here, we can see that under the Showcase tab, we've got all the drone options. We've got Drone Follow Mode means when your aircraft is flying the drone's going to sort of stay in line with your aircraft or follow your aircraft. You can disconnect that and your drone will stay exactly where it is and your aircraft will fly off into the distance. That's one thing you can do.

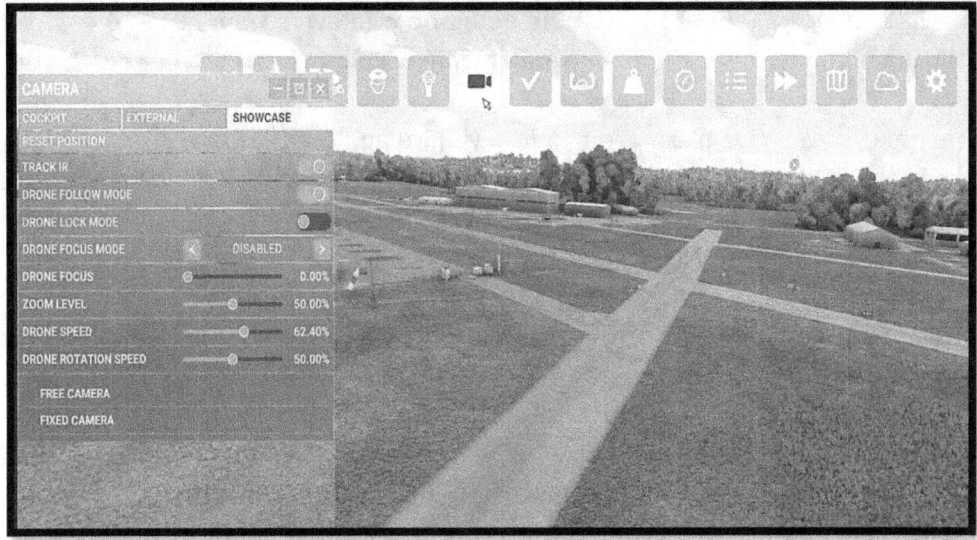

The other thing you can do right here is to go ahead and change the rotation speed if you don't want to do it on your own or if you haven't got an Xbox controller, for example. You can make a bunch of different changes like the way you focus in and out or the zoom level. You can control it manually if you want to but the drone is a great way to jump outside your aircraft and position the camera exactly where you want it in case you want to take a screenshot or in case you just want to check out the scenery. So get yourself involved with the drone mode.

Slew mode

If you just jump outside the aircraft and you press Y, what this allows you to do is move the actual aircraft anywhere you like. It might be in the sky or on the ground. We highly recommend finding out all the different default keys for Microsoft Flight Simulator or you can jump into your Options menu and Controls, look at your keyboard and it will tell you them all.

If you go ahead and press F3, you will see that your aircraft is moving up nicely and slowly. Press F4 and it goes up quickly and then with F1, it comes back down so this makes it nice and easy to change your altitude. The good news about this is if you crash your aircraft from time to time you can pull it out of the bush and reset it up in the sky. Press Y to go out of Slew mode and now you can continue your flight from here. This is a nice and handy way to move your aircraft around and position it wherever you might want to position it. Press Y to go into it and then check out the keys in your key bindings to find out how to move it around if you don't have an Xbox controller.

Time acceleration

You'd use this perhaps if you get up to cruise in altitude and it's going to be a long flight but you don't have time to sit there for all the hours or whatever it might be to complete the cruise. What you can do is speed up time and it will get your aircraft to your destination a lot faster.

To enable time acceleration press R on your keyboard and then press either CTRL+ on your number pad or CTRL- on your number pad to either speed up time or slow it down. It doesn't display the rate of simulation so remember that you've got to make sure you count the number of times you push it because to bring it back to normal time, you'll have to preset the same amount of time.

Let's say we press R on our keyboard, then press CTRL+ 1, 2, 3, 4, 5. Since we've got autopilot it's limited to that number. Now with the Sim rate enabled and we press CTRL- 1, 2, 3, 4, 5, we are back to our normal simulation rate.

One little hack is if it's got a digital clock counting down the seconds on your cockpit or instrument panel then you can look at the seconds to see if they're ticking normally. That's often a giveaway to see if you've got the right simulation rate set but time acceleration is very handy. If you haven't got time to hang around and cruise it can get you to your destination just a little bit quicker so you can get that landing completed.

Career Modes

A great way of doing that is engaging in one of the many career add-ons for the Sim. The good news is there are a ton of these available at the moment and some of them are free while some have a cost attached to them. So what you want to do is if you're looking to follow a virtual career path, you can go check out some of the free versions for a start. It's something that will bring a lot of purpose to your flying and give you some goals to aim for where you climb up through the rankings, buy and sell the aircraft, and work in a virtual economy. It's a lot of fun so we highly encourage you to go and check that out.

INDEX

www.ingramcontent.com/pod-product-compliance
Lightning Source LLC
Chambersburg PA
CBHW082233220526
45479CB00005B/1211